BRAND
child

Don't miss these other groundbreaking books on branding by Martin Lindstrom…

Clicks, Bricks & Brands
with Don Peppers & Martha Rogers PhD

'Martin Lindstrom understood the wisdom of the Net before most of us. Now he's sharing his best wisdom with you. Don't miss out.'

Seth Godin, author of *Permission Marketing*

This best-selling book explores the world's most controversial marriage that currently is taking place: the union between offline and online businesses. *Clicks, Bricks & Brands* is a bible for every business-to-consumer company that aims to gain strong market share in the century of clicks-and-mortar business.

ISBN 0 7494 3809 6

Visit MartinLindstrom.com or DualBook.com for more information.

Brand Building on the Internet
co-authored with Tim Frank Andersen

'Users rule the attention economy; if they don't click, you don't have a business. Lindstrom and Andersen know their click streams and tell you what users want. Listen or be doomed as your site suffers death by back-button.'

Dr Jakob Nielsen
Author and Web usability guru

Now in its 3rd edition, *Brand Building on the Internet* has been sold in more than ten countries since its first release. A corporate Web site on the Internet is no longer enough to survive in today's competitive online environment. This volume analyses a range of international companies to demonstrate how the Internet demands a strategic way of thinking about marketing interactive brands to consumers. It also gives readers concrete tools to create a brand strategy on the Internet.

ISBN 0 7494 3809 6

Visit MartinLindstrom.com or DualBook.com for more information.

Both the above titles are available from all good bookshops. To obtain further information, please contact the publisher at the address below:

Kogan Page Ltd
120 Pentonville Road
London N1 9JN
Tel: +44 (0) 20 7278 0433
Fax: +44 (0) 20 7837 6348
www.kogan-page.co.uk

And for more on *BRANDchild*…

BRANDchild workshops

The Martin Lindstrom workshop sessions allow participants to see theory in practice. Lindstrom's astonishing 85 per cent repeat-booking rate is testimony to his motivating energy, which fills participants with ideas and challenges their thinking on kids communication.

For more information and free workshop samples visit the 'Speaker section' at: MartinLindstrom.com.

BRANDchild e-Learning

Go online and learn how to understand and communicate to kids. The BRANDchild e-learning programs convert all knowledge captured from project BRANDchild into a step-by-step e-learning program package.

For more information visit the 'Consulting section' at MartinLindstrom.com.

MARTIN LINDSTROM

with Patricia B Seybold

BRAND child

Remarkable insights into the minds of today's global kids and their relationships with brands

 Millward Brown

squib

AFA

KOGAN PAGE

London and Sterling, VA

First published in Great Britain and the United States in 2003 by Kogan Page Limited
Reprinted in 2003

120 Pentonville Road
London N1 9JN
UK
www.kogan-page.co.uk

22883 Quicksilver Drive
Sterling VA 20166–2012
USA

ISBN 0 7494 3867 3

British Library Cataloguing in Publication Data

A CIP record for this book is available from the British Library.

Library of Congress Cataloging-in-Publication Data
Lindstrom, Martin, 1970-
    Brandchild : insights into the minds of today's global kids : understanding their relationship with brands / Martin Lindstrom with Patricia B. Seybold ; and contributions from Nigel Hollis and Yun Mi Antorini
        p. cm.
Includes bibliographical references and index.
    ISBN 0-7494-3867-3 (hardcover)
    1. Brand name products. 2. Child consumers. 3. Advertising and children. 4. Marketing research. I. Seybold, Patricia B. II. Title.
    HD69.B7 L55 2003
    658.8'34'083–dc21
                2002154220

Typeset by Saxon Graphics Ltd, Derby
Printed and bound in Great Britain by Thanet Press Ltd, Margate

DualBook and BRANDchild are Trademarks™ of MartinLindstrom.com.

MartinLindstrom.com publishes a weekly article about children, tween and teen branding. For permission to syndicate these articles apply to brand@lindstrom.com or visit MartinLindstrom.com.

Any further information about Martin Lindstrom's *Brand Building on the Internet, Clicks, Bricks & Brands* or *BRANDchild* can be found at MartinLindstrom.com or DualBook.com.

While every attempt has been made to incorporate correct information, errors are bound to occur. The author regrets any errors and invites readers of *BRANDchild* to contribute up-to-date or additional relevant information c/o Kogan Page.

Editor: Lynne Segal lsegal@optushome.com.au

Photography: Arunas Klupsas arunasphotography@bigpond.com

Cover photograph: Craig Cranko craig@craigcranko.com.au

Cover design and Web site: Squib Pty Limited www.squib.com.au

Praise for *BRANDchild*

"Bless this book. It is full of the kind of eye-popping statistics and pacy case-studies that make reading a business book actually enjoyable."

Rita Clifton, chief executive of Interbrand, writing in *Management Today*

"A real thought-provoker for marketing and business people. *BRANDchild* is a wonderful tool if you are marketing to kids and teens."

Stan Davis, author of *Blur* and *It's Alive*

"Fascinating insights into the world of tweens... *BRANDchild* looks at techniques and strategies that can help you reach and build relationships with this unique group."

Marketing Business

To my precious Allan & Vibeke and to my parents, who had the arduous task of raising such a challenging kid

Understanding what kids want isn't child's play.

But Millward Brown and its Kidspeak™ experts can help.
We have over 25 years' experience helping many of the world's leading global and local brands maximize their marketing ROI, as well as experience using Kidspeak™, our research approach specially developed for children. Let us put that expertise to work for you.

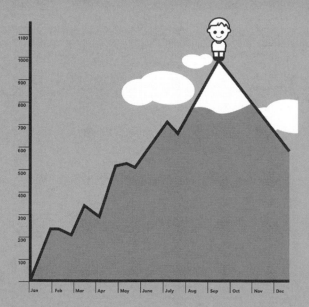

www.millwardbrown.com

Contents

About the study

PROJECT *BRANDchild:* THE WORLD'S MOST EXTENSIVE STUDY OF TWEEN ATTITUDES AND BRAND RELATIONSHIPS

Over almost a year a team of 500 people at Millward Brown, the leading global brands and communications research agency, spread across 11 countries, has worked on what has become the world's most extensive study ever conducted on tween attitudes and their relationship to brands (see Figure 0.1 overleaf) – a study exclusively conducted for this book. Many of the figures quoted in this book are based on the unique findings resulting from this study. Further information on how it was conducted is contained in Appendix 1.

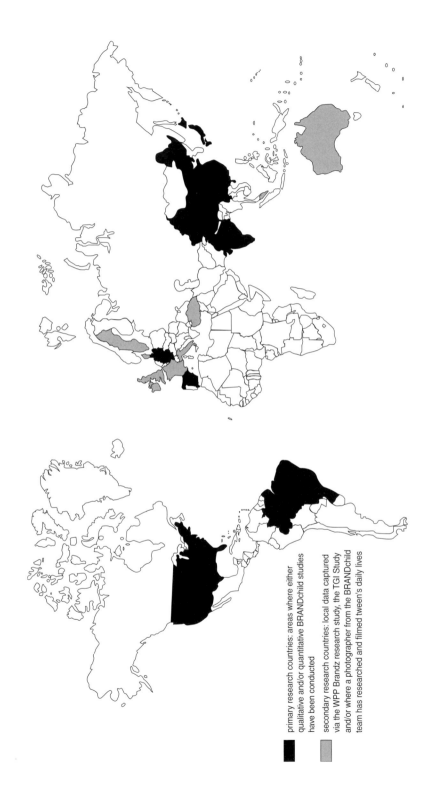

primary research countries: areas where either
qualitative and/or quantitative BRANDchild studies
have been conducted

secondary research countries: local data captured
via the WPP Brandz research study, the TGI Study
and/or where a photographer from the BRANDchild
team has researched and filmed tween's daily lives

Figure 0.1 *Project BRANDchild: areas of study*

About the authors and contributors

THE AUTHORS

Martin Lindstrom

Martin Lindstrom is recognized as one of the world's primary branding gurus. He is a leading thinker in the fields of offline, online and wireless branding, and has written several best-selling books on the subject of building strong international brands. These include *Clicks, Bricks & Brands* (with Don Peppers and Martha Rogers PhD), and *Brand Building on the Internet*.

Over the years Martin has advised several Fortune Top 500 brands, including Mars, Pepsi, LEGO, Cartoon Network, American Express, Mercedes-Benz, VISA, Ericsson, HSBC, Gillette, Yellow Pages and Microsoft.

He is the former COO of BTLookSmart, the international joint venture between British Telecom and LookSmart, and the founder and CEO of BBDO Interactive Asia, the region's largest Internet solution company. Lindstrom co-founded BBDO Interactive, Europe's largest Internet solution company. Lindstrom began his career as an advertising executive at BBDO.

He writes a regular column on branding that reaches a global audience of more than 4 million people in 30 countries. His acute insights have been featured in *The Times, Fortune, The Daily Telegraph* and *The Independent*, and on the BBC.

Patricia B Seybold

Patricia B Seybold has over 24 years' experience consulting to high-tech firms and to IT-aggressive businesses in a variety of industries, Patricia is a visionary thought leader with the unique ability to spot technology and business trends early on; she provides customer-centric executives within Fortune 1000 companies with strategic insights, technology guidance, and best practices.

Patricia is an internationally acclaimed best-selling author. Her book, *Customers.com,* provides insight into how 16 still-thriving companies designed their e-business strategies to improve revenues, increase profitability, and enhance customer loyalty. Patricia's latest book, *The Customer Revolution,* describes how 13 global businesses in a variety of industries manage to achieve customer value while they continuously improve the quality of the customer experience their deliver. Her books have been translated into over 10 languages.

In addition to writing business bestsellers, Patricia has published dozens of research reports each year since the late 1970s. Her work has also been recently published in the *Harvard Business Review* and *Business 2.0, CIO Magazine, Fast Company, Computerworld* and many other publications. She is frequently quoted in major publications such as *BusinessWeek, Wall Street Journal, Financial Times, New York Times,* and *Investor's Business Daily,* among others.

THE CONTRIBUTORS

Nigel Hollis

Nigel Hollis is the Group Strategic Planning and Development Director for the Millward Brown Group, and is based in the United States. He has extensive experience of market research, both from his 17-year career at Millward Brown and previously at Cadbury Schweppes in the United Kingdom.

Nigel's particular expertise is in the areas of brand equity research, online research and how marketing communications can build and maintain brands. His involvement with research on the Web dates back to 1996, when he directed the ground-breaking HotWired Ad Effectiveness Study. This proved that advertising on the Web has a strong effect on awareness and perceptions.

Since early 1997, he has led the development of Millward Brown's interactive research operations, which today supply a wide range of Web-based and Fortune 500 clients with online research and consultancy services. Nigel's papers have been published in a wide selection of journals and he has three times won WPP's Atticus Award for original published thinking in marketing services.

Yun Mi Antorini

Yun Mi Antorini was formerly the senior director at the LEGO Company. She was responsible for Global Brand Strategies including the development of the global LEGO brand. Prior to this, Yun Mi was the director for LEGOLAND and LEGO Group in Carlsbad in the United States.

BrandChild represents a culmination of the efforts of many individuals and organizations. Following the successful collaboration between Squib and Martin Lindstrom in the development of the DualBook concept for *Clicks Bricks and Brands*, Squib have again teamed up with Martin to add *BrandChild* to the DualBook™ library.

The main aim in the development of the online component of a DualBook™ is to provide a compelling relationship between the printed book and its associated web presence. The application of the DualBook concept to *BrandChild* has involved detailed research and involvement by key members of the Squib team who have been uncompromising in developing an interface that is useful, intuitive and most importantly adds strength to the DualBook™ brand. Squib's focus has been to develop a clear understanding of how people's online and offline encounters with DualBook™ could be intrinsically linked to create a truly valuable experience.

Squib is a digital communications agency fusing creativity and technology to develop effective marketing and communications solutions. Ideas lie at the core of Squib's success and these are supported by a sophisticated development and deployment process designed to ensure that all project and campaign objectives are met. To learn more about Squib, visit www.squib.com.au

BRANDchild updated at DualBook.com

I would have loved to claim that I got the idea for *BRANDchild*, but in all honesty I didn't. The inspiration came from thousands of readers of *Clicks, Bricks & Brands* who through the book's online component, DualBook, helped me decide to make kids my next focus.

In line with my last book, *BRANDchild* lives as a DualBook™ between the covers of this book and online at DualBook.com. It's a pioneering concept, the first of its kind in the world. It allows you to remain in touch with my latest views on the topic.

BRANDchild has no final page. It lives online fully able to accommodate its rapidly evolving subject of tweens and their relationship to brands. Every chapter in this book is open-ended, an invitation to go online and experience its interactive dimension.

Use the actual book as an entrée to the subject, then keep your involvement with it alive and relevant by visiting DualBook.com for all the updates every chapter promises.

How to activate your FREE membership

Visit www.DualBook.com and click on the Activate-your-membership icon. In the back of the copy you hold in your hand is a personal identification code enabling you to activate this personal membership. As soon as this happens, you not only have free access to all content related to *BRANDchild* but also to my last book, *Clicks, Bricks & Brands* (with Don Peppers and Martha Rogers PhD).

You can either visit each new *BRANDchild* article uploaded on DualBook in chronological order, **type in the individual Web address written on every page,** or secure access to the latest updated knowledge by typing in the Web addresses given on some pages, relating to the unique topics covered in this book.

BRANDchild is much more than this book. If you are passionate about the topic and want to dig even deeper, check out the executive *BRANDchild* workshops and the *BRANDchild* e-learning programs detailed at **DualBook.com/bc** and **MartinLindstrom.com.**

The next generation of kids have no borders between online, offline and wireless. To them it's all transparent. I hope you will feel the same about *BRANDchild*, and that it will help you understand tomorrow's generation. You will certainly be in a far better position to anticipate the world of branding.

Foreword

For the past 30 years, Millward Brown's mission has been to help marketers maximize their marketing and communications return on their investment. So, when Martin Lindstrom approached us and asked if we would be interested in providing the research findings to power his new book, *BRANDchild*, we readily accepted.

In today's world, many marketers are finding that their tried and tested 'rules' no longer always apply. Across all segments, social relationships are changing, media is fragmenting, and everything is happening at warp speed. But it is amongst tomorrow's consumers that the changes are having most impact.

By partnering in this groundbreaking project, our aim was to add to our understanding of the global consumer; particularly the one we will all face in the very different world of tomorrow. We believe this book and the associated research provide unique insights into the early origins of brand relationships and help us to understand what the future will hold with tomorrow's new and demanding consumer.

As input for the book, Millward Brown undertook research with 9–14-year-olds across seven countries representing a cross-section of economies, as well as western and non-western cultures. We also undertook qualitative work, reviewed learnings from our own kids research databases, and conducted desk research on perceived wisdom on tweens in the marketplace in general. The findings from all stages of the research are fascinating. Some we expected; many more were a surprise.

The fact that the research clearly demonstrates that young consumers don't just influence family purchases like breakfast cereals; but have an important say on big ticket items like cars and adult fashion has major marketing implications. Most importantly, the point to remember is that wherever you are based in the world, you should be thinking about whether your brand or service requires a 'tween' brand strategy.

However, if you do decide this is the route you want to go down, then prepare for the ride of a lifetime. You'll have to get to grips with new ways of thinking and new ways of communicating. You'll have to learn that when it comes to managing your brand or service, you have to be double jointed, not just flexible. You'll have to learn to work in tween time, ie 24 hours a day, seven days a week, and talk tweenspeak.

The book Martin has written is full of really practical tips to help you do this. Certainly, understanding kids today isn't child play. But we hope that this book will help you begin to get to grips with this increasingly influential consumer group.

Enjoy the read; I think Martin has written a stunningly interesting, entertaining and easy to read book and please feel free to contact Millward Brown with your thoughts and comments. We love feedback!

Robert D Meyers
Group CEO, Millward Brown
Mainboard Director Kantar – the information and consultancy arm of WPP

Acknowledgements

First of all thanks to the thousands of kids across the world who over the past year have answered endless questionnaires, patiently discussed brands in hundreds of group sessions, acted as models for our photographers and cinematographers, out-ranked professional artists with their imaginative drawings, and contributed with a level of fun no other generation could ever compete against.

It would be impossible to mention everyone who contributed to the ideas and knowledge I've drawn on for this book. So far close to 600 grown-ups spread across five continents have contributed knowledge, insights and hard work to make *BRANDchild* a truly global project.

Since my last book, I've met and worked with people in a variety of businesses from around the world, and good ideas have come from many different sources. Some who deserve special mention, however, include my editor Lynne Segal who's based in Sydney. She can, without a doubt, take a lot of credit for the final results.

Millward Brown Research have been fantastic to work with from the very first minute I approached them. It is true to say that this project would never have been the same without their global support. A special thank you to; Patricia B Seybold at Patricia Seybold Group in Boston for her insight into this topic; Lesley Brydon, CEO at Australian Federation of Advertising, and Betsy Horne from Millward Brown, Sydney, for their impressive support making parts of our global photo-tour a reality; Judith A Jewer for her inspiration; and creative director, Heath Rudduck, and executive director, Dean Joel, from Squib Advertising, Melbourne, for their distinctive work on the DualBook concept, the book jacket and a raft of elements making this project what it has become.

I would also like to thank my publisher Pauline Goodwin at Kogan Page, London, for her tireless patience towards all my crazy ideas, Nigel Hollis, the group director of strategic planning at Millward Brown, Connecticut, for his unique contribution to this book as well as group CEO of Millward Brown, Robert D Meyers, Naperville, CEO Asia Pacific, Andreas Sperling, Singapore, COO Asia Pacific, Adrian Gonzalez, Sydney, and group director of communication and marketing, Jean McDougall, Warwick, for their overwhelming support and contribution to this fascinating project.

Without an impressive team of psychologists, researchers and interviewers across the globe this project would never have been a reality. A sincere thanks to Rimmelle Freedman, Melbourne, Mark Zuker, Melbourne, Licia Allara, Milan, Lars Andersen, Copenhagen, Rob Batey, Connecticut, Pat Cahill, Connecticut, Joanni Geltman, Connecticut, Andrew Greenfield Connecticut and Anne McGrath, Connecticut.

Special thanks to Yun Mi Antorini Billund for her contribution; Dominique Lion, London; Henrik Kielland, Copenhagen; Margaret Manson, Melbourne; Andrea Scott, San Francisco; and Cosimo Turroturro, London, for their work on the creation of the *BRANDchild* world tour. Also thanks to Paul Smith, London; Craig Cranko, Sydney; Julie McNair, London Arunas, Sydney; and not to forget my favourite public relations genius Martha Fumagalli for all their work on the *BRANDchild* look and feel, merchandizing programs and public relations tour.

Children nowadays are tyrants. They contradict their parents, gobble their food, and tyrannize their teachers.

Attributed to Socrates in the year 425 BC

1

Tweens

Dream as if you'll live forever. Live as if you'll die today.

James Dean

When James Dean swaggered onto movie screens in the 1950s, his rebellious image encapsulated the daring and dreams of an entire generation. During his short career he managed to dramatize the questions that were on the lips of every young person in the mid-20th century.

James Dean was as much a product of his time and place as the youth of today are of theirs. His acts of rebellion are not, however, today's. And although his movies are as popular as ever, a rerun of a James Dean movie would barely raise a pierced eyebrow among a new generation weaned on special effects and digitized soundtracks.

Let's call this generation the tweens. Tweens span the pre-adolescent years through to the age of about fourteen.

MEET THE NEW KIDS

It is not surprising that this generation has been tagged the 'age of compression'. Almost every aspect of today's tween-ager is different from what we have seen among past generations. They've grown up faster, are more connected, more direct and more informed. They have more personal power, more money, influence and attention than any other generation before them.

No other generation has ever had as much disposable income as this one. So it's no coincidence that this emerging generation has become powerful enough to have a specific allotment in every marketing director's budget. They spend money and time with a casual and carefree attitude: they get what they want when they want it. And there is a reason for this.

This is the first generation that's been born and bred with an understanding of today's economic world. They play the stock market as if it's another version of a computer game. They talk about trading indices while they swap baseball or DragonBallZ cards, and they watch financial news as if it's an ongoing soap opera.

It's not surprising that 8 per cent of the teenagers in the United States have some or all of their money invested in stocks and futures. Twenty per cent have their own checking accounts, and 70 per cent would *love* a credit card if their parents (and the bank) would allow it. This is a generation that spends in excess of US $150 billion a year. And if this is not enough, then add another US $150 billion, because that's the amount that this generation actually controls when their parents are supposedly in the driver's seat, holding on to the family purse strings.

From a purely monetary perspective, it's no wonder that this generation has created such enormous attention and wielded so much influence among companies and their brands.

'Where's the cursor in my book?'

There can be no doubt that the steady diet of information, available 24 hours a day, 7 days a week, through a whole variety of channels, is playing a major role in shaping this new generation. Penetration through technology is a key factor in an unprecedented level of global integration.

This is the first generation born with a mouse in their hands and a computer screen as their window on the world. Tweens understood icons before they could read. They now surf the Net with an ease and speed that belongs only to those who are at home in cyberspace. They think in megabytes, pipeline sizes and screen resolutions, in the same way that previous generations thought about swapping stickers, memorizing football scores and perfecting wheelies on their bicycles.

Most of the barriers preventing older generations from fully embracing digital media do not apply to this new generation. In fact, electronic media is such an integral part of their life that it no longer holds any fascination in and of itself. In many ways, the heavy emphasis on technology we saw in the 1990s has shifted. The focus is now on content. The computer, with its awesome abilities, is now the vehicle for other activities. The emphasis is now on games, and how best to move through the levels, what mods (modifications) are available, and the release date of the next version. For the first time since computers entered our lives we're encountering a generation that is tuned into interactive media – and far less preoccupied with the infrastructure behind the screen that makes it all possible. Tweens have no notion of the fear that you and I experienced when we first turned our hard drive on and tentatively typed our first keystroke.

In other words, for this generation being online is as comfortable as being offline. According to our *BRANDchild* study, close to half the world's urban tween generation has access to the Internet, and about 20 per cent have their own mobile phone.

'Why doesn't this remote control work? I can't find the cursor!'

Living in an interactive world involves so much more than having access to the Internet. It means a whole new way of seeing. This dramatic change can be compared to the advent of colour television. Once colour came to the small screen, there was no going back.

In fact it's taken a mere four decades for *everything* that was once only available in black and white to be converted to colour. Brochures, newspapers, photocopiers, mobile phone displays. You name it. A black-and-white television set is a dinosaur. The only black-and-white movies you see are vintage reruns on late night television. And as for black-and-white computer monitors – well, they're now collectable antiques!

The introduction of interactivity is set to follow the same pattern, the only difference being that the period of market penetration will be shorter.

And this is where today's tweens have an advantage over previous generations. They *think* in an interactive dimension. The only mail they know is e-mail and they expect replies within hours. In fact, 13 per cent of wired urban tweens globally prefer to communicate via instant messaging or e-mails. A further 47.2 per cent of them enter chat rooms and engage in real-time conversations. They have long lists of contacts on their instant messenger service, which beeps them when a connected computer comes online. Of those who own mobile phones, 45.1 per cent will send several text messages a day, and expect replies within minutes. If they have to wait any longer, they give up and move onto something newer and more engaging.

'Is "snail mail" when you are slow at replying to your e-mails?'

Traditional information channels are seen by tweens as plain cumbersome, if not somewhat bizarre. Think about it. Books don't have clickable links offering further information. Music played on the radio is selected by someone other than themselves. Newspapers are far too general, and you have to wade through pages of print to find the odd snippet of information relevant to a tween's world.

This interactive generation is used to things happening instantly. And a generation that's only known instant gratification is a generation that's hugely demanding.

These two characteristics – interactive and instant – will affect the way we build and maintain future brands. And any company that ignores this core detail is doomed to join the black-and-white dinosaurs on the scrapheaps.

'People in Japan speak English, but they write it in a very funny way'

As a reflection of online interactivity there's a new twist for the emerging generation. Kids in the 1970s and 80s grew up independent of their counterparts in other countries. This is no longer the case, and it is one of the most dramatic changes that has taken place over the past decade.

Instant trends in the 1970s and 80s were created by the megastars of the time, the Madonnas, the Aquas and the Michael Jacksons. Like all bright stars, some faded while others are still burning. But because they were smash sensations on a global scale, they instantly influenced behaviour among their global audience.

Cast your mind back to the early 1980s when Madonna created her Material Girl. In no time at all we had girls wearing bras over their t-shirts. We had lots of lace and flesh and mussed-up hair. Ten years earlier, platform shoes kicked high on strobe-lit dance floors to the music of ABBA. And feluccas plied their trade to the sounds of Michael Jackson singing 'Beat It!'

These trends, like others, appeared instantly, spread globally and survived for months. From the instant they appeared they were picked up by a well-orchestrated team of media channels and millions of teenagers everywhere were exposed to them.

In today's world, this lofty power no longer belongs to a handful of celebrities. The instant communication across the globe between tweens has made it possible for the entire generation to adopt and develop certain trends and keep them alive for months. I call this phenomenon *fish streaming*. In theory, one tween can influence tens of others, and in almost no time at all millions of tweens are following.

This occurs with the globalization of brands, and also with the emergence of a truly global media. Instantly, a trend identified and adopted in one part of the world becomes commonplace over the rest of the planet.

MTV is one of the finest outlets for fish streaming. Its global message is channelled through 30 television stations sending the same message to its audience in more than 41 countries. Over the past few years, the Internet has played a major role in transforming local trends into global ones, within days. Of all urban tweens, 39 per cent have friends or relatives in other countries, and more of them use the Internet rather than snailmail to stay in touch. They do this several times a week. A gigantic tween network becomes a key driver in changing the direction of any given trend.

Of course, this phenomenon sets new challenges for the entertainment, fashion and computer industries, as well for most brands. Local product launches barely exist any more in the tweens' world.

'Is information overload when you load information?'

Do you remember the term 'information overload'? To some extent, we've all fallen victim to this over the past decade. Well, the term is dead. The so-called overload happened because at the time we hadn't yet developed the mechanisms required to handle the huge amount of information daily bombarding our senses.

Compare it to food shopping. Over the past 25 years, supermarkets have continued to develop. They started out as small kiosks, then small stores, then shopping markets. Then supermarkets became mega-markets became shopping centres. With each new growth spurt, they exposed an ever-increasing array of brands. And now this is what we expect.

Ultimately we've all managed to cope with the dramatic increase of brands – despite the fact that we've had no training in dealing with exposure to the explosion of items on the supermarket shelf. But the difference between our generation and the tweens is that they have grown up in a world of information overload. They know nothing else.

School-teachers of the 1970s and 80s spent a fair amount of energy teaching children to be critical of media messages, and how to be sensible consumers. These lessons are now irrelevant. The message-filter which most of us did not possess, but had to develop from scratch, is a integral part of the tweens' world. Superman's laser-beam eyes which were able to see through everything no longer belong to the realm of fantasy. Tweens have the ability to sift through the cornucopia of ads without appearing to so much as notice them. Whether it's a banner ad on the Internet, a jingle on the radio, or a commercial on television, they have the situation under control. They're aware of the intention of the communication, and more importantly they're aware of its down-sides.

Brands are part of their lives. They are exposed to more than 8,000 brands a day. Almost by force of circumstance they have developed an internal filter which absorbs, selects and adopts some of these in a way never seen before. Anyone with a young child will know that they only have to whiz past the Golden Arches, and they're guaranteed to hear 'McDonald's!' screamed from the back of the car. The tweens may even let you know why you 'deserve a break today'.

But it would be a mistake to think that children are merely regurgitating the myriad of messages they hear. This generation is also very skeptical. Tweens instantly question things that don't feel right to them. They seemingly have an inherent understanding of the value of the message or the intention behind it.

We're much less sophisticated. We still believe that James Bond actually chooses the bubbly he drinks in the movies. It doesn't occur to us that Mr Bond's choice of champagne is determined by a calculated product placement strategy. So just how many dollars did it take to get Luke Skywalker to take the Pepsi challenge in *Star Wars*?

Tweens are well aware of advertisers' intentions. They accept them as part of the landscape, providing they make sense. Later on, I'll discuss how the world of product placement is about to undergo some serious changes as a direct result of how tweens view communication. There was a time when children sat in the back seat of the car and played games like spot-how-many-blue-cars-you-can-see. Now kids play spot-the-brand. And more and more product placements are appearing in computer games, everything from Red Bull to Pepsi.

'What is God?'

Many tween values are the same as earlier generations'. They want to be loved. They want to be rich and famous. But the *BRANDchild* study has clearly demonstrated how the cataclysmic events of September 11 have had a dramatic affect on their priorities. They are suddenly preoccupied with a different set of issues. First and foremost is fear, followed by issues of trust. They've become preoccupied with what's permanent and what they can believe.

To be a solid citizen, someone who can be relied on and trusted, is becoming more important than being fashionable and trendy. September 11 contributed to this new set of values, but it's not solely responsible. The ongoing crisis in the Middle East, the failure of so many global corporations, the shaming of so many business leaders and the increasing impermanence in adult relationships are reflected in the tweens' critical perceptions of their world.

Brands also come under their critical microscope. Just how permanent a role can a product play in their lives? This will undoubtedly affect the way marketers will have to communicate to this super-critical generation.

'Visit me at my home page'

Tweens have global address books and they share information freely. They have evolved a whole new definition of what's private and what's public. They've set new parameters. To every other generation, it appears that very little remains private, despite the fact that privacy is a far greater issue for this generation than it's ever been before.

Media has had some effect on this, but in general the trend has been established more or less by the generation itself. Go to freeservers.com and you can see to what extent the privacy barrier has fallen. Here you can view thousands of personal Web sites representing tweens from all over the world. Our study shows that as many as 10 per cent of urban tweens across the globe currently have their own personal Web sites. And numbers are increasing.

The personal site phenomenon has evolved into several categories, including whole-family sites and personal diaries. The growth in personal Web sites offers a new venue for self-expression. Over one in five tweens who have one, share very personal information – including photographs and feelings – on their very public sites. They feel free to reveal their opinions, and there's a common desire to find a perfect person who will understand their soul. The interesting fact is that this behavior is not confined to a couple of countries. It's a truly worldwide phenomenon.

Personal Web sites are like detailed electronic business cards. URLs are exchanged in chat rooms, parties and on school playgrounds. Over time, the sites become more comprehensive, more detailed and more integrated with those of their network friends.

Members of older generations may find all this self-revelation exposes too much. But a Web site with personal details is a must-have for many tweens, as many as 42.7 per cent expressing the desire to have their own. It's part of their identity. And *not* to have one would be too embarrassing!

'Let's talk – send me an SMS'

 Visit DualBook.com/bc/ch1/mobile to learn more about the future of m-branding.

Global communication, instant messaging, and in-your-face sharing is altering the very nature of communication. It is fascinating to observe a new type of shift between written to verbal, and back to written communication.

For decades, if not centuries, letters have been the primary form of communication across any significant distance. Young girls also poured out their secrets in the pages of diaries that came equipped with a little lock and key. Then the MTV generation took over. Writing became unfashionable. And reading was just plain boring. Talk dominated. Lengthy phone chats and in-depth conversations at the local mall characterized an increasingly verbal generation. Teachers despaired over a loss of written-word capabilities, including grammar, and the almost complete absence of book-reading.

Interestingly enough, this trend is poised to take another turn. Verbal communication is still alive and well – but certainly not to the extent it was some years ago. The venues have broadened. Tweens now have the options of chat rooms, video games and mobile phones. All require the ability to read and write.

Chatting is the preferred way to meet and greet new people. As a result, over the past couple of years, a uniform language which is easy to understand has emerged. Only 30 per cent of urban tweens across the globe use standard language for chat. Already 19 per cent use a totally new vocabulary not found in any of the great dictionaries of the world. Not yet, anyway. But most importantly, our findings show, this abbreviated form of language is regarded as a cool, if not the coolest way to communicate. It is a language no-one learned in school, but in many respects it directly mirrors spontaneous and colloquial speech, with all its short-cuts and idiosyncrasies. And like everything adopted by tweens, it has immediacy stamped all over it.

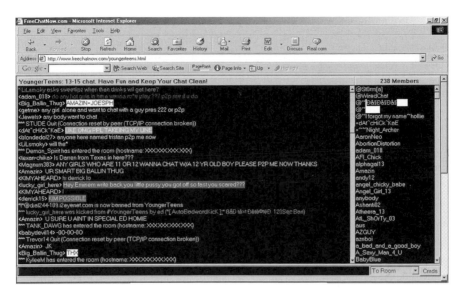

Figure 1.1 *A chat room. Of all tweens worldwide, 47.2 per cent chat on the Web several times a week. Brazilian tweens lead at 70 per cent versus Japanese kids at 19.1 per cent.*

On a recent visit to Japan I got talking to a group of young Japanese kids in a café. As tourists tend to do, I asked them what they recommended I do during my stay. I asked them where to go, what to see, and what to avoid. I expected them to think about this and to confer with one another before they replied. But without hesitation they pulled out their I-mode phones and typed in my question in Japanese. Within seconds they had a list of the 10 most popular attractions in Tokyo. There was a different list of the five events that would be most relevant to tourists that week, and the 10 places tourists should avoid. I asked for a pen to take down the details. No-one could help, but they asked for my e-mail address so they could send the information to my phone!

How this affects face-to-face communication is yet to be determined. Even at dance parties, tweens can be seen texting and talking on their phones. Perhaps it's the loud music, but not too many words seem to be exchanged verbally. It's all digital.

And this is where the personal Web pages come into play. A page in many ways acts as a brochure for the tween. It's their personal ad or online brand. So instead of repeating the same information about themselves again in the chat rooms, they can simply let their personal Web page do the work.

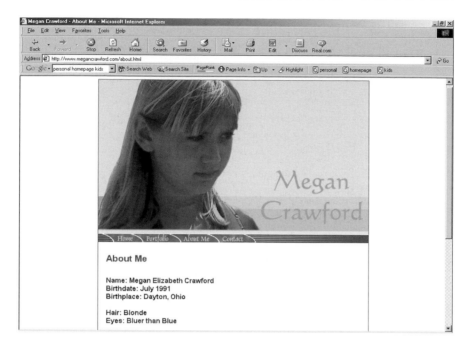

Figure 1.2 *A personal Web site. Brazilian (15 per cent) and American (13.5 per cent) kids have the most personal Web sites. However, globally, 42.7 per cent of all kids dream of having one.*

But it doesn't stop here. It wasn't so long ago that it was considered impolite to call anyone before 8.00am and after 9.00pm. Well, those days are long gone. This is a generation which you can reach 24 hours a day, 7 days a week, if not via the land-line phone, then via the mobile one or the chat room or an SMS message.

And almost without exception, one of these devices will be active – because 'what if something important comes up?'.

'When I have the remote in my hands – I am in control'

Tweens constitute a very different and very demanding consumer group. Apart from being born to the interactive digital age, there is a range of other factors that define them. It's to do with a trend that's been labelled KGOY – Kids Grow Up Young, and it relates to the fact that they've been exposed to much more at a very young age – younger than any other generation. It's all about more information, more entertainment, more communication and more brands.

Television has been instrumental in pushing these barriers. And soap operas have had a major hand in this. Think about it. All the soap families lurch from one crisis to the next. There's divorce and adultery. Even murder. Problems are solved in a short half-hour. Judge Judy can work her way through five court cases in a mere 25 minutes. And as for the complexities of war – well, that may take a little longer. But 120 minutes in the cinema should solve it.

Now add the Internet to the mix. Despite numerous attempts to keep tweens' eyes from certain Web sites, they still have access to content that neither you nor I would have seen by the age of 20, let alone 10. In fact, tweens have access to such a wide variety that, according to our study, 44.3 per cent find it acceptable that their access to the Internet is limited. But even if we could regulate children's viewing, 12-year-olds can pass themselves off as any age they wish in a chat room and engage in dialogue that would make their parents blush.

In so far as soap operas reflect real life, 50 per cent of this generation have lived through their parents' divorce. Divorce forces children to grow up faster. I don't think we should underestimate the effects of the fear, anxiety, lack of trust and impermanence to which this generation has been exposed more than any other.

Their awareness makes the tweens a NOW generation. They want things to happen here and now. They want to solve their problems now, not tomorrow. They must make their purchase now, win the game now or learn what they want to know now.

This is a generation with little, if any, patience. That's not surprising, given how few situations are available where they can learn it. The small screen presents a world where millionaires are made in half an hour, and pop stars are created in four weeks. Meals are whipped up in moments and babies only cry for a brief five seconds. In their world, the sky is the limit, as long as you can achieve it here and now.

'Everything is possible – I've seen it on television'

This is a generation without mental barriers. How can there be room for inhibitions in a world where everything happens in minutes and everything appears do-able? The lack of barriers is reflected in every channel of the media to which this generation has been exposed. When PepsiMax was first launched it presented the notion of extremity. Extreme sports presented the ultimate challenge to an older generation which identified with the idea that they themselves were extreme.

It worked for some months, but ultimately created a more difficult challenge for the marketers at Pepsi. The emerging generation, the tweens, were singularly uninspired by notions of the extreme. Quite the contrary. The ads had absolutely no effect on them, since they don't regard their sports as being at all extreme. It emerged that this generation is not easily provoked. Nor are tweens easily shocked. In fact, on the whole, they're far less motivated than other generations. And to further aggravate the folks at Pepsi, game manufacturers who are in tune with the tween generation's blasé attitude co-opted the term and gave it a deprecatory twist by applying 'extreme' to minor games. I mean, how big a whoop can you muster for the application of the Pepsi challenge to 'extreme' pinball?

'I *have* played outside today! I created a whole city in SimCity'

A disturbing trend is emerging alongside the proliferation of computer games. The tween generation seems to be losing its creativity. The toy manufacturer LEGO has been struggling with this trend for the past few years. LEGO is based on a combination of creativity, imagination and fun. Ten years ago, the standard box of LEGO blocks contained 500 to 1,000 bricks. They have recently come to believe that this is simply too complex for tweens to use. Not only do they not have the patience to collect a castle, a boat or a car, but they also lack the necessary imagination to create new forms and shapes.

As a response to this troubling trend, LEGO has decreased the number of pieces in each box. However, they've increased the size of each block, to justify the change. So where you once needed 100 blocks to build a house, today you'll need only 20.

The current lack of creativity and imagination can partly be blamed on the proliferation of computer games and the permeation of the media. Young people once spent hours outside playing in local parks and friends' backyards. They invented games, created rules, shot a few hoops, batted a few balls and rode bikes with cards pegged to the wheels. Kids were once creative directors in neighbourhood fantasies.

No more. These days, kids rarely leave their bedrooms. When friends come over they watch one another operating technology and give the odd instruction from the wings. Alternatively, they embark on multi-plays where individuals challenge an often faceless, nameless opponent from the comfort of their own bedroom.

Computer games most importantly require dextrous hand-eye co-ordination. Really challenging games that require flexible brain-power are few and far between. Computer games commonly provide all the creative solutions, and all that's required of tweens is to choose which solution they prefer. Too few games ask them to create the environment or the rules of play.

Sadly, the situation is not very different with television, movies or game shows. They all offer a choice of solution, but too rarely offer the viewer any opportunity to create their own stories with their own individual outcomes.

This lack of creativity will present another challenge to the marketers of the future.

'I trust brands as long as they have been on the telly'

So how is all of this going to affect the brand? So far, so good. A quick survey will reveal that brands are as hot as ever among today's tweens. The familiarity of brands adds security and offers a framework to their world. And in the best spirit of the marketers, brands have become symbols for an identity, offering the opportunity to be trendy, cool, rich, outrageous, rebellious or just plain stylish.

Brands have become an integral part of the way tweens define themselves. It's the way they express who they are at home, at school, at parties and even on the Net. Tweens are the most brand-conscious generation yet. Our numbers reveal that it is far more important to wear the right label than it is to wear the right clothes. It is largely through their choice of brands that tweens distinguish themselves from one another.

'I am very loyal to a brand as long as I am not the only one wearing it'

This devotion to brands should reflect a high brand loyalty. But this is no longer the case. In fact, the opposite holds true. Loyalty is first created among the group, which then identifies with a particular brand. This means that if one or several people in the group shifts brand (usually the result of observing other tweens, or fashion magazines or something on television) then the whole group will follow. Even though a tween might be a huge follower of a certain brand, this would not prevent an instant loyalty shift. There's no fear of the consequences of not shifting, either.

Quite simply, there is no similarity to the brand loyalty shown by 34 to 45-year-olds who rarely change their preferred brands, unless of course they yield to pressure from their tween!

Generally this lack of loyalty can be ascribed to the media which constantly define and redefine what's hot and what's not. It is a rare occurrence indeed to see a celebrity wearing the same outfit twice. They are constantly changing – clothes, cars, perfumes, homes and jewellery. Likewise the tweens want to change too.

'I can't stand Levi's'

The big ongoing question that marketers have to ask is: what's in it for us to appeal to an audience that constantly changes brands? Tactics have to be re-evaluated. Of course, not all businesses require a tween brand strategy. But many, perhaps up to 80 per cent of business-to-consumer brands do. You would be surprised to learn that most of these do not have a single tween product in their current portfolio!

Tween marketing is just as much about building a solid base for the future as it is about creating an ongoing dialogue with an audience that will, in a few years, become their major source of revenue. Many products aiming to create brand loyalty among the young might not have a huge market at the moment among tweens. But they should be laying the foundations of a relationship that could possibly last forever. Coke has succeeded in this area quite magnificently.

But this is not the whole story. Tweens are old enough to have formed clear brand preferences and young enough to be dependent on their parents. They form a perfect target group because of their ability to directly influence their parents' spending. In fact, our study has revealed that a substantial number of brands purchased by parents are so influenced by tweens that in some cases they can be characterized as the primary decision makers. This despite the fact that they may never use the product! Increasingly, companies are using tweens to communicate with their parents, thereby securing a positive place within the family. Remarkably, in more than 50 per cent of the product categories we tested, this actually works. Tweens *do* manage to persuade their parents to try something new.

But no matter what decision you take within your organization, it is all about staying committed. Once you are on the tween train, you can't get off. Tweens are so critical, so direct, so opinionated and so demanding, that at no point will they forgive you for establishing an image in the market merely to disappear shortly thereafter. It's a bit like yesterday's news. Once it has died in their consciousness, it's almost impossible to resurrect. Brands like Disney and LEGO are mindful of this death trap, and do whatever they can to avoid becoming merely a passing fashion or trend. Not that this isn't tempting. The instantly huge revenues are undoubtedly attractive. But the flipside is disastrous, because once a brand has peaked, it has nowhere else to go except down. With trend cycles lasting little more than four months, no established brand manufacturer can afford to drop.

So if you decide to go ahead with a marketing program aimed at appealing to tweens, ideally it should be fluid enough to prevent it from peaking and dying, and leave you with a point of return that will justify the investment.

PLANET KIDS

Tweens have just begun to be independent of the home. They live lives away from Mom and Dad or a carer for several hours each day. They're old enough to form their own clear opinions about brands, can affect household decisions regarding shopping and brands, and are distinct enough as a marketing group to form a workable profile that will be useful to any marketer's long-term plans. Generally tweens can be divided into four groups:

▌ Edges;
▌ Persuaders;
▌ Followers;
▌ Reflexives.

Edges

These are the independent rebellious tweens who don't necessarily see themselves as being on the cutting edge. In fact, they barely perceive themselves as members of the tween generation. They're anti-fashion, and supposedly anti-brand. However, they often identify with brands that reflect their rebellious behaviour.

They're the Wild Bunch. They tend to break the rules, slack off at school, are rarely home, partake in extreme sports, dismiss the norm and can in no way be classified as ordinary. But because they break the rules and run their own lives, they are perceived as independent trendsetters. They try products and brands long before everyone else – and they often combine old products in new ways, re-inventing them and making them cool.

Persuaders

Influencers are the most popular tweens. Their decisions are adopted by the group. This is the group that marketers vie to harness. Their influence is invaluable to any product.

Part of the reason they're so admired is because of their speedy adoption of new trends. They are cool and they are popular in a way that is far more accessible to most of the kids than the Edges.

Influencers are conscious of style. They spend a lot of time working on their appearance. They dress well and are especially conscious of their hair. This group is substantially more mainstream than the Edges.

Followers

This group represents the mainstream and forms the bulk of today's tweens. They listen to the Persuaders but also have an ear open to the Fringes. They're never the first to try anything. They're followers rather than leaders. Their self-esteem does not run terribly high and they don't consider themselves cool.

Reflexives

This group tries to increase popularity and acceptance among their peers, often without much success. Reflexives are an out-group. They rarely pick up fashion trends and almost never go out. Like Followers, Reflexives are distinctly followers who lack self-esteem, don't have many friends, but seek social acceptance.

'We are all different – almost'

Despite attempting to organize tweens into distinct categories, there is huge variation within the four groups. However, categorization helps us understand that tweens have differences and an internal hierarchy, which to a large extent determines their relationship to brands and their adoption rate.

There is a social pecking order which is not necessarily overt, but is understood and accepted by all tweens. Being familiar with the hierarchy is extremely valuable when you need to identify the best possible tween group for a specific brand. The wrong choice, the wrong message or the wrong image could easily ruin the effect of the campaign. It is therefore essential that not only should careful attention be given to the age definition of the tween group, but it also needs to be defined according to the social hierarchy.

'The world has five fashion kings who invent all fashion'

Each trend is set in the media. Peers learn about trends from lead-peers. Lead peers learn about trends from magazines. Many trends start their life on the street, but they're quickly co-opted by magazines and television, which expose them to a global audience. They then enter conversation at private parties where the latest fashions and trends are discussed, exchanged and examined in detail.

A study conducted by TRU in 1996–98 explores pastimes tweens have considered 'in' since 1996. Among the perennials are sport, movies, computers, the Internet, shopping, music videos and partying.

'My best friend lives a nine-hour flight from here – at least that's what my dad says'

Tweens are much more global than you think, not only because they spend so much time on the Internet but because of their substantial exposure to television and magazines. This is the most global generation the world has ever seen. They've been exposed to both local and international trends, literally since birth. They speak to as many people online as they do in their neighbourhood – if not more. Another aspect of their global disposition is the way they share similar brands with their friends who live on other continents, often thousands of kilometres away.

Of the 100 most well-known and respected brands in the United States, 92 per cent are represented in more than 10 countries. Should you have the misfortune to be without local representation, you're almost certainly able to access the brand on the Internet. E-commerce ensures that brands have wings even before the manufacturer has developed an international marketing strategy.

If you're in any doubt about how brand knowledge travels, you only need to spend a while in a chat room where tweens are discussing brands. You'll be privy to links to new sites, you'll hear opinions about music, movies and pop stars, and you'll soon find out the latest most desirable item to have in other countries. It's conversation that pushes brand talk far beyond national boundaries.

Some marketers have already tried to gain leverage from this oasis of advertising exposure by creating 'false' Web sites. They construct their site so it looks as if it's been created by a tween. It's essentially an ad, but it masquerades as a tween talking personally about life, friends and hobbies. As part of the conversation, brands are mentioned, specific links are targeted and there are even images that are designed to look unprofessional. The average viewer would believe the site belongs to a real live tween!

False personal sites appear on the Net via agents who carefully monitor chat rooms for hours on end, and craft programs that contain all the relevant key words and slanguage of the tweens. These agents go further. They participate in the chat and share their views. They exchange URLs and help drive traffic to their site which is masquerading as a 'personal' homepage, but in reality is all about product placement.

Figure 1.3 *A false Web site. Several thousand Web sites today are 'product placement' sites or 'false' Web sites claiming to be representing an individual's opinion but are in reality built by companies.*

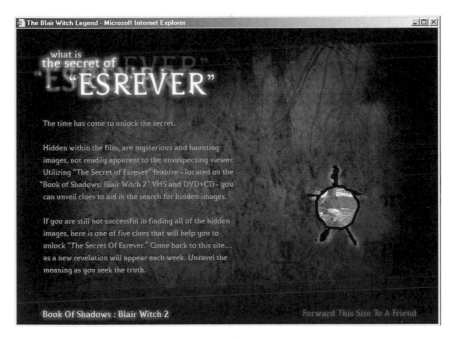

Figure 1.4 *A Blair Witch Web site. A $35,000 movie managed to generate US $100 million via viral marketing.*

There are quite a few variations on this theme. Another ploy has two agents entering the same chat room and creating a conversation about a product. The idea is for others in the room to take heed of what they're saying and follow their lead to the 'false' homepage.

Every day newer, more sophisticated marketing techniques emerge to spread the brand word. There was an amazing buzz surrounding the movie *The Blair Witch Project*. During the launch of the movie, A4 photocopied posters were strategically placed in major cities: London, New York, San Francisco, Sydney and Toronto. The style of the posters was similar to those used for missing persons. They created mystery.

The film was supposedly based on a true story of three student film-makers who disappeared in the woods near Burkittsville, Maryland in the United States in 1994. They were supposedly shooting a documentary about the legend (some say a true story) of the Blair Witch. A year later, their footage was found.

Each poster listed a Web address where people could find out more. Hundreds of thousands of people accessed the Web site during its online presence. So a movie that cost less than US $35,000 to make ended up one of the highest earners of 1999, grossing an astounding US $100 million at the box office. The marketing is rumoured to have cost less than US $100,000. In addition to the cost of the photocopied posters, the bulk of the expense involved paying students to put up the posters.

It is clear that creative branding campaigns have the capacity to push brands way beyond their national borders, often on a very limited budget. We've only just seen the beginnings of this trend. It is certain that the Internet will continue to contribute to the international growth of brands, as long as the marketers find the right buttons to push. On the other hand, the life-span of many an international brand will become shorter because of the reduced attention span of the tweens.

'People who love Abercrombie love Britney Spears – I hate Britney Spears'

Like many generations before them, music represents a united voice among tweens. In fact, our research shows that 45.4 per cent of the world's urban tweens prefer listening to music to watching television. But this is hugely paradoxical. On many levels music has become the province of the huge corporations. They put millions into individual-star packages. There's the mega-million costs of the video and the CD. You're blitzed with ads on the back of taxis, strategically placed billboards and posters in every bus stop.

But at the same time music is also more fragmented and offers more styles catering to more tastes and increasingly narrow segments. The online world offers downloads from others' hard drives, and sites where you can access almost any sound at any time, anywhere on earth. On offer is greater diversity than ever before.

It is fascinating to see how the segmentation of tweens takes place purely on the basis of their musical taste. The Edges and the Persuaders dance to a different beat. The Followers tend to listen to whatever the Persuaders were listening to a few months ago. The Reflexives don't seek anything out, but tend to pick up on the music that the commercial outlets play.

In the most general terms, the Edges like alternative music. They listen to trance, ska and metal. The Persuaders like rap, hip hop and rhythm and blues. The Followers tend to go with whatever everyone else is listening to.

Tweens' all-round preoccupation with music is reflected in the tremendous growth of music available on the Internet. Our *BRANDchild* study shows that 49.2 per cent of all wired urban tweens frequently download music from the Web.

But it doesn't stop there. From simply listening to music, many tweens have taken the next step and begun developing their own music online.

Often it is a remix of their favourite songs combined with tunes they have composed themselves. And this is where it becomes fascinating. Several sites have created a place to air these self-composed tunes. Their individual melodies can be shared with anyone who has a speaker and an online connection, in any country anywhere in the world.

The path from home-composed music to fame has never been shorter. Several hits, particularly in the United States, were first played on these sites and were later picked up by radio stations to make the successful transition to becoming a major hit. This trend to underground music and guerilla production has united groups across the globe who share common tastes in music.

This has created a totally oddball scenario. There is a huge proliferation of 'the same'. There's also more difference than ever before. MTV uniformly blasts music into millions of homes, but even that has become more refined. MTV is no longer a single television channel. It's now 30 different channels, each with its own content, style and brand images. Each one has the same critical mass to draw on, but has been individually programmed according to the culture for which its signal is destined.

However, MTV remains a recognizable world brand even if it does promulgate locally driven values that distinguish one station from another. It's like different flavours of the same brand ice-cream. In distinguishing local stations and giving them their own flavour, MTV has also become part of the deglobalization trend. In fact, if the world of tweens were as global as their communications imply, then MTV would not have 30 representative stations. They would need only one! Cultural differences around the globe are still enormous, even among the tween market.

Despite the fact that there are still significant differences between tweens across segments of the population and across countries, music is still one of the best possible ways to identify and categorize them. It both separates and unites various groups. It is certainly a clear indicator of their brand preferences, and offers useful clues as to how to approach them from a marketing point of view.

Often brand preferences correlate with musical taste. Even though this technique is not 100 per cent accurate, you can count on the music choice 90 per cent of the time reflecting brand clustering.

'I can write all my SMS messages without looking at the phone'

Music is merely one of the elements giving a good indication of tween behaviour around the world. Another area of great importance is how the use of icons and terminology has affected this generation. Icons were first used by England's Royal Navy during the Napoleonic wars. They didn't use smileys; they used flags. Each flag represented a letter, and each letter formed part of a code. The *BRANDchild* survey reveals that 13 per cent of all urban tweens prefer to use icons as their main language instead of more cumbersome words.

It is hard to believe that the 'PLAY' arrow and the 'STOP' square have only been around since the 1980s. Yet in two decades they have become a couple of the most highly recognized symbols in the world.

Apple was the first to develop computer icons. In 1984 their smiling-face screen icon greeted every proud new owner of the Apple Macintosh 128k. Icons were an instant hit. They crossed cultures with ease, they were easy to use and easy to understand. The little bin where you trashed irrelevant data and the little clock that told you to wait still form instantly recognizable icons on even the latest, most sophisticated Apple systems.

The icon trend continues to evolve. Almost all of today's technology-based hardware and software systems are based on globally recognizable icons. They have even travelled across media, and are seen everywhere from mobile phone screens to pocket computers, and from television remotes to microwave programming displays.

Tweens have grown up using them with an ease and understanding that appears to be instinctive.

'Italian food is from Minnesota'

One of the first signs of globalization emerged in our food consumption. Yesterday's choices involved chicken or beef. Today's decisions sound more like a global atlas. Chinese or Japanese? Vietnamese or Thai? It is not unusual to eat chow mein on Monday, pasta on Tuesday and couscous on Friday. We hardly give it a thought. We combine the global smorgasbord as if we were born with a sushi roll in one hand and a croissant in the other.

The proliferation of multicultural cuisines works both ways. Tweens around the world, from Bangkok to Beijing and Melbourne to Miami, like to tuck into a quick burger. Whatever we may think of it, the fast food culture has infiltrated every corner of the globe. We think in terms of meal packages. A burger is not just a burger. It comes with French fries, a drink and is served up in a colourfully branded cardboard box. After we've eaten, we wipe our hands on the branded serviette and dump the box and the branded cup in specially allocated garbage bins.

Food has become another way for tweens to understand and learn about other cultures. Fifteen years ago, I found Thai culture exotic, unusual and awe-inspiring in its difference. I was exposed to food, stores, clothes and a culture that I'd never encountered. A return visit a couple of years ago presented an entirely new picture. The cultural similarities were far greater. Most of what I saw already existed at home. Gap, Starbucks, Levis and McDonald's logos were prominent features of the street landscape. The food was the same as back home, and even the pirated sounds blasted out of Bang & Olufsen speakers at the Bangkok Night Market were the same sounds as the music that was played on local radio stations at home.

I visited a local Thai family and was taken aback to see that the family owned a DVD player and had more than a 1,000 DVDs in their library – all pirated copies, of course. I found we had an instant rapport. I could talk to the children about pop culture. We discussed movies and celebrities and food and clothing. The only difference between us was that they were Thai, and shared a home the size of my Danish living room with 12 people.

Pop culture is now global culture. The boundaries between 'them' and 'us' are becoming increasingly blurred. The distance between Thailand and Timbuktu is only a click. And no-one is more familiar with it than the tween generation who travel these distances every day.

SUMMARY

▮ This generation has been tagged as the 'age of compression' and has been called the KGOY (Kids Grow Up Young) generation. It's a 24/7-generation, and it expects 24/7 brands!

▮ Tweens have more personal power, more money, and more attention focused on them than any other generation before them, influencing spending of up to US $600 billion a year, and affecting close to 60 per cent of all brand decisions taken by their parents. Not surprisingly, they are exposed to some 40,000 commercials a year.

▮ Brands are as hot as ever among today's tweens. They have become an integral part of the way tweens define themselves. It's the way they express who they are at home, at school, at parties and even on the Net.

▌ This is the first generation born with a mouse in their hands, and a computer screen as their window on the world. For this generation, being online is as comfortable as being offline. It is a truly interactive generation, and one that's only known instant gratification. The term 'information overload' is irrelevant to them.

▌ Verbal communication is no longer the premium form of communication. Written communication is making a come-back.

▌ The two main features of this generation is that they require their lives to be interactive and instant. More than anything else, it is these two characteristics that will affect the way we build and maintain future brands.

ACTION POINTS

▶ Determine to what degree you believe your brand is dependent on the tween generation, either directly or indirectly. If possible, attempt to establish to what extent there's a direct or indirect tween influence. Place a dollar figure on your estimate.

▶ How would you evaluate the future of your brand? Does its current profile, image and product offerings match the aspirations of this generation?

▶ How much influence do tweens currently wield in your category? And at what ages to they wield it?

▶ If the current degree of tween influence is limited, can you change it?

▶ Develop a list of the five points you believe are the major strengths of your brand. Also list the five weaknesses.

▶ Identify your two main competitors, and estimate their position regarding their five strengths and five weaknesses.

▶ Now decide how you're going to beat them. First read Chapter 2, then make up your mind.

2

Tween dreams for sale

'I don't wanna leave without my teddy'

Traditional lore tells us that little girls are made of sugar and spice and all things nice, and boys are made of frogs and snails and puppy dog tails. But there are no guidelines to getting inside the dreaming hearts of today's tweens. We can only look back on recent marketing successes to see if we can find the formula that made the Ninja Turtles and Pokèmon the winners that they were.

Probably without even knowing it at the time, their inventors got the combination right and somehow pressed all the right buttons. Popularity and fame score high on tweens' dream list. If they aren't after it for themselves at this stage, they're deeply in love with those who have it. Our *BRANDchild* study shows that more than half the tweens we interviewed worldwide – 52.7 per cent – want to be famous. Interestingly enough, Indian (90.3 per cent) and American tweens (60.9 per cent) topped the list with this desire. In sharp contrast, only 27.7 per cent of Japanese tweens and 47 per cent of Danish tweens share this ambition.

Along with fame, there's the desire for fortune. After all, money guarantees dreams of the good life, and 64.2 per cent of urban tweens globally share this dream. Again, it was the Indian and American kids who topped the list, with 75 per cent wanting to be wealthy, whereas only 53.3 per cent of the Chinese tween population expressed the desire for riches.

A careful study will reveal that there are six distinct characteristics that go to make up the most successful brands and toys, worldwide. What we find is a recipe incorporating the right measures of fear, fantasy, mastery, humour, love and stability.

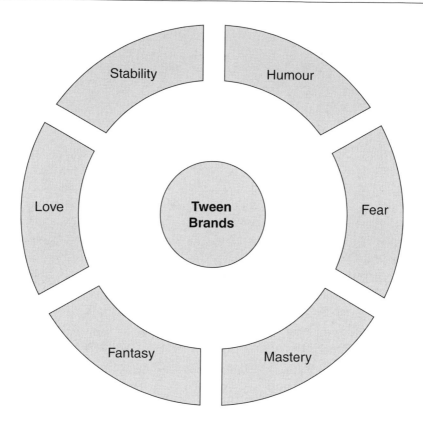

Figure 2.1 *The six core values driving all successful marketing to tweens.*

FEAR

'Can monsters see in the dark?'

The fear factor encompasses terror, horror, panic and war. Although many of the great marketing successes have appealed to both boys and girls, in their tween years, it's the boys who are largely consumed by ideas of the fear that goes with horror, panic and war. And while their male counterparts are out on imaginary battlefields, the little girls are pledging their loyalty in friendship and love.

Boys also team up with their buddies. As many as 80 per cent of all boys want to be part of a group, not only when they're playing at war but in almost all game situations. But according to our survey, the need for connection and relationship remains just as intense in girls.

Boys are more drawn to mastery than girls. They aspire to have the same control that they witness in their heroes and warriors. But this does not mean boys want to be leaders. Less than half the boys and girls surveyed liked to make the decision in their group. German tweens are the least comfortable about taking control, with only 20.5 per cent of them expressing a desire to do so. You may ask if this result draws on their historical heritage, or if it's just coincidental.

There are no firm and fast rules in the wider game of growing up. The boundaries between the dreams and inclinations of boys and girls are often blurred. And the successful brand concepts embrace a variety of combinations of the elements that make a war hero and the love sought by their female counterparts. Humour easily reaches across the gender divide to find itself a winner in both camps, as does fantasy, providing the fantasy is not too unrealistic.

The Concise Oxford Dictionary defines fear as an unpleasant emotion caused by the belief that someone or something is dangerous, likely to cause pain, or a threat.

Fear is a primal reaction; it lies in wait for as long as it takes for the lights to go out, and appears just after children have been tucked into bed. That's when the monsters that lurk behind closet doors take over. So being safe is important to 91.9 per cent of all urban tweens. It's one of the most important values in their lives. So it comes as no surprise that successful marketers of tween toys have so far been smart enough to incorporate 'fun fear' and 'scary fear' in concepts aimed at boys.

Fear is also an essential part of the learning process. As tweens begin to understand how little influence they have in the big bad world, fear comes into play. Think about the various aspects of fear incorporated in toys, advertising, books, movies, and even the branding of candy.

The film, *Monsters, Inc.* produced by Disney Pixar, exemplifies fear building. The story is based on Monsters, Inc., the largest scream-processing factory in the monster world. It has a single mission: to scare children. Its enormous success is born not only of its incorporation of fear. It also provides space for the conquest of fear, showing children and tweens a way to overcome their bedtime nightmares.

Fear is invidious; it lies deep within the experience of all tweens and it is an emotion with which they obviously identify. A fight between Mom and Dad can be just as frightening as a confrontation with a monster or an unwelcome visit from a space invader. The idea of being kidnapped or being left entirely alone in the world without parents can be equally scary.

Teenage Mutant Ninja Turtles, invented in 1984 by Kevin Eastman and Peter Laird, is a brilliant example of a group of characters incorporating responses of fear and humour. The team of four heroes is named after four great classical artists. There's Raphael, Donatello, Leonardo and Michelangelo, and they all have a mission to conquer evil.

In a style that is wonderfully reminiscent of stories such as Hans Christian Andersen's, these creatures, dressed like turtles, behave like human beings. This infallible human-animal combination has universal appeal for children. The concept taps into the tweens' deepest emotions and ideals. The Teenage Mutant Ninja Turtles are fun and intelligent, they have a strong friendship, they are in control, and they show all the characteristics of real heroes. Cleverly, the story is open-ended, leaving as much room for Teenage Mutant Ninja Turtles movies and comics as the market will allow.

Spider-Man is another hero who wrestles with fearful situations and presents children with tangible ways to conquer their worst nightmares. The merchandise offers something for each age and stage. There's everything from a Sky Rider play set to Spider-Man electronic gloves which optimize touch and equip them with special powers. The Spider-Man concept travels seamlessly between the cartoon, creating its own life on the movie screen, energizing the play on the floor, and sparking the competitive element on the computer screen. The common link is to conquer the enemy.

The *BRANDchild* global survey determined that 37.7 per cent of the tweens interviewed considered the movie *Spider-Man* the hit of 2002. A further 24.3 per cent stated that they believed Spider-Man would stay popular forever. There's an interesting twist here. *Spider-Man* was substantially more popular outside its home turf, the United States, where only 30.4 per cent considered it the best of the year, in contrast with Germany, where 57.5 per cent of tweens rated it Number One.

The similarity between the Spider-Man and Teenage Mutant Ninja Turtles concepts is clear. The only difference, probably explaining why the Ninja Turtles instantly rocked the box office, is that those feisty Turtles represented a whole variety of human characteristics with which children can easily identify.

The incorporation of fear to create thrills and chills is hardly confined to the tween segment of the market. James Bond movies, which first came to the big screen in the 1960s, are based on an almost identical set of emotions and experiences as Teenage Mutant Ninja Turtles and Spider-Man. The Martini-drinking, girl-chasing Bond uses highly-developed technological equipment in his fight against evil and terrorism. His transformable cigars and his secret weapons appeal to a sense of humour and require an active imagination. Many generations have been introduced to Secret Agent 007. To date there have been 20 Bond movies made.

Over the last 50 years there have, however, been vast changes in the fear-producing technology that outdo even Bond's secret weapons. Turn-of-the-millennium technology has introduced multimedia and interactivity. Where toys of the past decades had only limited 'feedback', today's tween products will bring new challenges.

Skannerz, a game concept based on a barcode scanner, allows any kid to scan UPC barcodes and, as the commercials say, unleash the world of monsters, magic and mayhem that has been trapped on earth from a distant planet. The idea behind Skannerz is once again the conquest of fear, made all the more intense by technological wizardry.

Coca-Cola has never been slow on the uptake, and they are right up there as far as interactivity goes. Coke's advertising campaigns targeted at tweens in Europe and Asia all incorporate interactivity. Each Coke bottle contains a secret phone number and code. SMS the phone number with the secret code and you instantly become part of an online Coke competition. Winners receive notification immediately. For those who don't win, there's always the opportunity to enter the next round. The game also incorporates an element of chance: it's the gamble one takes each time one takes part in the competition.

FANTASY

'Is the moon made of cheese?'

Fantasy is liberating because it is unlimited. It expands the imagination. The younger the child, the greater the capacity for fantasy. This is because children are not yet affected by the restrictive boundaries of traditional thinking. Imagination is a key word. Tweens spend a lot of time pre-occupied with daydreams which often star themselves as a hero of one sort or another living in a boundary-free world. This happens habitually and increasingly, often when they experience their real worlds as boring or trivial.

The life of most urban tweens is one of routine. They rise early, eat an obligatory breakfast and walk or ride to school, where they're holed up in a compulsory classroom for hours. Then they return home to do their homework. By this stage of the day, escape is their deepest desire. How do they do this? The best way to find out is to go online! One thing is common to tweens across the globe, regardless of nationality or even gender, and this is that the Internet is an overwhelming presence in their after-school lives.

A substantial 45.7 per cent of all urban tweens worldwide use the Internet regularly. The United States leads the way, with Internet penetration of 72.8 per cent. This is followed by 56 per cent in Japan and 52.5 per cent in Germany. The lowest penetration, although it can hardly can be characterized as low, is found in India. There, 23 per cent use the Internet regularly. In China, 31 per cent are on the Net.

Goodbye creativity

Despite the amazing change of media use that's occurred among this generation over the past seven years, games still dominate as the major source of online appeal. Electronic games have clearly become the global factory of fantasy material, independent of any national borders. Our survey shows an astounding 68.3 per cent of tweens who are online buy or download games from the Internet. Indian tweens lead the way with 77.6 per cent, followed closely by the United States with 75.7 per cent. Surprisingly, 74 per cent of Chinese tweens who are online play right alongside their global contemporaries.

Critics have commented that tweens are increasingly absorbed with online entertainment, with the Internet merely a device for escapism. And they may be right. In fact, this may well provide a worthwhile clue to marketing success for this group. Capture the tween fantasy; provide the tools that will enable them to create the world of their escapist dreams, and *voila*, you've got it made in the proverbial shade.

However, as I discussed in Chapter 1, it would appear that with the development of new technological toys, the *active* fantasy life of tweens has decreased over the past decades and this has been a blow to more classic toy concepts now struggling to justify their existence.

The first time I noticed the decline of the tween imagination was eight years ago, when I was conducting field research designed to learn about the attitudes of children to their toys. Most importantly, I wanted to know what type of concepts continued to sustain their interest. It was depressing to learn that LEGO models tended to remain on the shelf, like trophies. Once built, they were never taken apart.

It seemed that once the tweens I visited had built the pirate ship, the castle or the LEGOland city, they lacked the motivation to start again. Why should they do so? What was the point of playing with LEGO if it offered no opportunity to score points or compete with friends?

At the time I did my research, the really popular games were all computerized. The question was whether to buy a GameBoy or a Nintendo, both hand-held and easily accessible. A box of LEGO was no longer enough. In reality, what was required was a box containing pre-programmed fantasy. LEGO became aware of this and in 1994 the company teamed up with MIT Laboratory to incorporate technology-driven interactivity in their toy products.

Since then LEGO has formed alliances with the marketers of some of the world's most established tween fantasy concepts. Dreams that have already been established and recognized by tweens such as *Winnie the Pooh, Star Trek*, and *Harry Potter* can today be found in most boxes of LEGO. By understanding that this group of youngsters is no longer fantasy-driven but fantasy-receiving, LEGO secured its future success.

It is debatable whether or not this is the right kind of fantasy to push these days, since imagination is becoming increasingly restricted. It is no longer in the possession of creative toy manufacturers like LEGO, Fisher-Price or in the minds of tweens. Rather, dreams are held in the domain of media creators such as Disney Studios, *Star Wars* creator George Lucas, the *Harry Potter* license owner, AOL Time Warner or Steven Spielberg.

Goodnight Harry

The upside of not owning blockbuster concepts is that the company doesn't have to weather the bust after the boom. In fact, our study reveals that a steady global decline of the Harry Potter brand has begun. Today only 27.4 per cent believe that Harry Potter is a happening trend, while 38.5 per cent consider him a fading phenomenon. It's important to note that the tweens who consider Harry Potter still viable are mostly from countries where English is not the first language, so that the trend came later than in the English-speaking world. If brands like LEGO or Fisher-Price had been based on a Harry Potter platform, the future of their company would be in serious jeopardy.

Ownership of dreams is not, however, the sole issue. It is essential that every toy, every tween campaign, and whatever is communicated to this audience all appeal to the imagination in some way. This is precisely what JR Rowlings's *Harry Potter* series succeeded in doing, for a while. The plot lines advance the principles of good fighting against evil, just as the classic Grimm and Hans Christian Andersen fairy tales did. In these

Figure 2.2 *A LEGO–Harry Potter co-promotion. The licence deal between Harry Potter and LEGO managed to turn around LEGO's constant loss of market share.*

stories, someone always receives powers or achieves wealth and success. The creation of Harry Potter's new universe allows tweens to dream themselves out of their workaday routines. The strength of the concept is remarkable; and its power outshines the multifaceted brand merchandising. Quite simply, it unambiguously reinforces the dreams that tweens have about wanting to run the world.

MASTERY

'I want to run the world'

Tired of lavishing attention on your little one? Just wait until their childish needs are replaced by control needs when the tween years come round. And be warned: the desire is just as intense. It's all about testing boundaries. The question becomes inverted: 'How far can I go *before* I attract Mom and Dad's attention?' 'What will Grandma do if I place my spider monster in the hall?' 'Will my teacher freak out if I throw an egg bomb into the classroom before the lesson begins?'

From a statistical point of view this becomes even clearer, with 59.3 per cent of all urban tweens across the globe preferring to 'do things their own way'. Japanese (82 per cent), Danish (81 per cent) and German (71 per cent) lead this trend, with a surprisingly low 35.9 per cent of tweens in the United States declaring their desire for independent behaviour.

For our imprudent tweens, the idea of pushing the limits without taking the rap is not the only reason for their actions. They need to know who's in charge. If you want to understand the concepts of mastery and control, then listen to tween talk. 'I bet you wouldn't dare scream "idiot" at that man.' 'This is my room! Touch anything and you're dead.' If you want to connect with those who have recently untied their mothers' apron strings you will need to make sure that they feel they are in charge.

Battlebot, a tournament game fought by real remote-controlled models, has swept the global game world with resounding success. The concept is based on a range of television shows where tweens take up cudgels against each other's Battlebot. More often than not, the winner has the most innovative construction, the smartest navigation and the best strategy. But Battlebots come in the wake of a raft of merchandising providing tweens with a chance to fight and take control of their own game. *Battlebots* is currently the US's third highest-rated sports program on basic cable. It is rated behind *World Wrestling Federation* and ESPN's *NFL Sunday Night Football*. Every week more than 3.5 million people watch the Battlebots in combat.

The LEGO Company's Vision Command, ideal for control freaks and secret hunters, gives tweens a chance to hold the reins. Vision Command comes in a box along with a LEGO cam. With this device it is possible to program a gamut of controlling tools, from motion-sensitive spy cameras to control-freak robots. The spy theme, a hot favourite on the entertainment circuit for almost a century, is still hot and looks set to remain that way. Now 12-year-old boys with a new home spy tool have the facility to check out their sister and her boyfriend catching up on a quick snog, right there on their own sofa.

Every tween knows that winning is about being in control. But the old idea of 'winner takes all' is no longer all that it's about. The journey is just as important as the destination. Tweens still have all their senses sharp and keen, unpolluted by adult life. Cool graphics get tweens going, so they are fully tuned in to detail as they ascend each new giddy level of success in games designed for victory. Winning in a decent tween game should not be too difficult to achieve. But nor should it be too easy.

Take computer games, for instance. Surely it is not by chance that they have succeeded in capturing the imaginations of millions of tweens around the globe. Each new level of challenge is adjusted to match the player's level. It's hardly fun to win every game every time. But nobody wants to lose all the time either, especially when this is undeserved. Computer games for the Sony PlayStation and X-Box adjust their level of challenge according to a range of different factors, ensuring that the game is always a bit more challenging.

Tweens are captivated by the score list, which is publicized on the Net as well as at the PlayStation. It separates the masters from the losers, and makes winning a serious affair. Topping the score list is an honour beyond dreams. Whoever sees your name up there on the score list has the right to challenge you for your title. Ask any 11-year-old player what they dream of at night and they will answer: to be the master of the universe.

HUMOUR

'Fun is when my dad forgets that everything he puts in my magic cup turns red'

Is humour important? What a question! Having fun was rated by 86.2 per cent as the most important element in tweens' lives.

Tweens have their own special humour, intrinsically related to their own unique concept of fun. And what is this fun? Fun is when the legs of the chair on which Uncle Sol sits on give way beneath him. Want a good laugh? Hide an unwrapped hunk of cheese behind the toilet and let it ripen until Dad blows his top.

'Fun is when Mom realizes all her credit cards in her wallet are gone!'

Tween humour develops from the naïve to the sophisticated. The idea of someone else losing control while they're holding the reins is guaranteed to bring on a laugh, as the producers of *Shrek, Toy Story* and *The Simpsons* well know. Making your friends laugh also generates acceptance and loyalty.

You may recall that some years ago toy stores could not get enough stock of a nasty slimy green substance called Slimuck. It was amazing. Slimuck held together beautifully. You could slap it around and let it spread all over without the fear that this little green bit of goo would absorb anything. It was perfectly safe.

Heard the one about the writer, the floppy disk and the Slimuck? Well, the writer came home one day to discover a green slimy mass spread all over the floppy disks which stored the chapters of his first book. And over his papers and computer keyboard – more Slimuck! The writer turned green, and his nephews, who had plastered the strangely-textured stuff on the tools of his trade thought they were about to die of laughter. To gain control over the vulnerable adult, even for a few moments, was a peak experience for these youngsters.

The fundamentals of tween humour lie at the heart of cartoons like *Tom and Jerry, Roger Rabbit* and *Road Runner*. They involve pushing the limits, making fun of adults and doing crazy things that no one has done before. For over 50 years, *Road Runner* has been hunted down, and often been close to meeting his end. Yet he still survives. *Shrek*, a movie from DreamWorks, is also built on a combination of humour and fear, and closely resembles most of the movies that take place in a world parallel to ours.

LOVE

'Love is a wedding with millions of roses'

When you scratch the surface of any thrill-seeking, fear-loving tween you will find the universal need for love. Children know there's nothing quite like mother love. Many little boys start off life wanting to marry their mothers. In the natural course of events, this love is projected onto their teddy, who takes over the role as full-time, all-weather guardian. Some dads say it's a losing battle competing with the teddy for attention from their little darlings.

Are girls really so different from boys? If love is what it's all about for everyone, how different can they be? Are girls more able to express their love because they have communicated with their dolls? Or do the games they play with dolls simply make them *appear* more loving? Do boys lag behind in the love game because of something innate in their behaviour? In any event, the fact remains that girls express love more directly than boys.

Girl tweens began with Barbie. Barbie, the trusty blonde with down-home family values, has been the recipient of young-girl love for the past 40 years. Barbie is versatile. She comes with options. She can travel solo, or she can team up with her perfect husband, Ken, who of course comes with the perfect wedding. They have the perfect home and a permanently starry future. You can pick up the story at any stage of the game. Not unlike teddy, Barbie carries within her the dreams that guide little girls on life's pathway. She is very reliable.

As we mature most of us feel the need to nurture those we love, particularly when the object of our affection comes in the shape of something small and cute, like a baby. This is one of the reasons the Cabbage Patch dolls are successful. Take the Cabbage Patch Kids, probably the most successful doll concept created after the Barbie doll. Each Cabbage Patch doll has been individually created. The dolls looked different, and not quite human. They had flat puffy faces but their behaviour was as close to human as dammit. But most intriguingly, Cabbage Patch Kids are not sold. They're adopted. Each doll comes with its own name and adoption papers.

The success of this concept brings us back to basics: dolls fulfil a clear need to give love and nurture, and in turn to be loved and nurtured. Cabbage Patch Kids need children, and everyone wants to be needed. The Cabbage Patch Kids concept may sound simple, but it's not everyone who has been able to crack a game that's such a hit with little girls who are looking for love.

A more profound version of this need to nurture emerged in the Tamagochi craze, which first surfaced in Japan in the late 1990s. Tamagochi, which means cute small egg, is essentially a pocket-sized video screen with three buttons encased in a shell. When you put in the battery, the egg hatches and out comes a chick. From this moment on, you're the chick's official carer. It beeps when it is hungry, tired or needs to be cleaned up. If your response time is not up to par, there are consequences. It will stop playing and refuse to eat, and if neglected for too long, the chick will die. The battery has to be re-installed, a new chick is born and a whole new caring cycle begins. Needless to say, the shops were unable to keep up with demand. Interestingly, this was a game of love and nurture that not only appealed to girls. Boys were right in there changing diapers with the rest of them!

Since 1935, LEGO has dedicated huge resources to bringing the girls to a market that has been sustained by boys. But they fell short when they went all girly and pink with their Scala Necklace system. They simply did not think hard enough about their concept. The Scala Necklace system lasted only three years. It was clumsy and masculine, and its appeal for girls was zero. In 1999 LEGO cracked Belleville, a winning concept, by breaking the rules. Belleville compromised the LEGO guidelines. Pastel colours prevailed. For the first time there were pinks and light greens. Cotton materials were added to the Belleville sets, and girls loved them.

In contrast to all the other LEGO products, Belleville contained real items. And this was shown on the boxes. Carpets were made of real cotton, rather than stickers. There were thoroughly realistic plates and cups, curtains and pillows, ironing boards and stoves. So with the introduction of Belleville, LEGO moved from a geometric angular world to a more organic realistic one. It was a place where a girl could make a home.

STABILITY

 Visit DualBook.com/bc/ch2/stability to learn more about how tweens of the future will be affected by the value: stability.

'Harmony is when Mom and Dad love each other'

The events of September 11 put an end to the stability the Western world took for granted. Before the Twin Towers attack, the search for stability had more to do with the equilibrium most families strive for, against a backdrop of challenges. Widespread financial instability came with the aftermath of September 11, as the job market suffered. Given the massive global coverage, the attack on the Twin Towers proved to have implications for tweens around the world.

A year later, 52.5 per cent of all urban tweens state that terrorism still worries them. Only 11.6 per cent are less worried about it now, while at the same time another 11.7 per cent have more important worries. A small 5.2 per cent claim to have never been worried by terrorism. Japanese tweens are the most worried, and a full 70 per cent expressed their concern.

In the world of tweens, stability usually means a safe and functional home, food on the table, clothes on your back and paid-up school fees. It means continuity; no moves away from friends to new schools, no divorce to break up homes. It means support when things don't go your way, and a deep sense of faith that things will eventually correct themselves, even if Mom and Dad fly off the handle at each other.

But as things stand, the divorce rate among couples in the United States and Europe is currently as high as 50 per cent. In addition, 10 per cent of all people in the Western world are unemployed. Twenty per cent are struggling to make ends meet and run a household and 30 per cent are in credit card debt. No wonder tweens find stability a desirable state. For tween product manufacturers this is not as dramatic a concept to work on as fear, but stability is of growing importance, nonetheless.

As things stand, tweens tend to project their love and need for stability onto boy and girl pop bands. Band members promise some kind of larger-than-life reality of glory and fame. When the boy band Take That broke up in February 1996, 10 girls attempted suicide. They had put their trust in their favourite band members, and taken all the song lyrics of dreams and hopes very seriously. They had invested their pocket money in all the Take That merchandise.

Merchandise was a more than substantial source of income for Take That. On average, 20 per cent of the revenue at a typical boy or girl band concert would come from ticket sales. The remaining 80 per cent comes from merchandising products. This concert-product ratio is the norm.

Tweens spend thousands of dollars on posters, t-shirts, cups, badges, hats and their favourite band's latest CD – since it buys them a piece of their hero, idol or star!

Beyond the six fundamental motivations that contribute to the success of tween products are three 'drivers' that are key to success in the tween market. These differ from the motivations that drive tweens subconsciously. They provide added appeal and attraction and have been around for as long as the tween market has existed. Concepts that incorporate the *mirror effect, collection value* and *gaming ability* individually or in any combination have enormous appeal for tweens.

THE MIRROR EFFECT

'I love being Mom when playing grown-ups with my best friend'

Imitating the grown-up's world has always been a tween occupation. Almost every aspect of parental life has been mirrored in various tween toys and entertainment concepts. Tweens acquire an understanding of what it would be like to be a real parent through observation and play that involves imitation. Imitation is the bedrock of the Fisher-Price range, which offers a total kitchen selection, plastic food, small appliances such as hair-dryers, living-room furniture and more.

The mirror effect works in two ways. It places tweens firmly in the centre of a world they admire and to which they aspire. The concept is bound to succeed if it ensures that the tween is firmly positioned in the

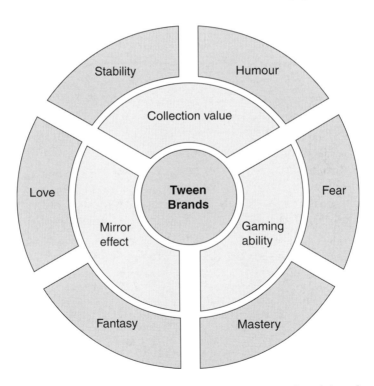

Figure 2.3 *The mirror effect. There are three tactics that drive almost all successful tween concepts. Combining these with the six core values of successful tween marketing (Figure 2.1) will result in the basis of tween marketing.*

centre of the dream, whether this involves becoming a super-cool pop star, a movie celebrity or a burly old Mr Plod.

COLLECTION VALUE

'I have the biggest Yo-Gi-Ho! collection in the universe'

From way back, collection cards have been a hit among kids. The first sets of soccer cards came in a cereal box. The trend took off. There have been bubblegum cards, chocolate cards, newspaper collection cards, and later came *Star Wars*, Pokèmon, Ninja Turtle, *Lord of the Rings* and *Harry Potter* cards.

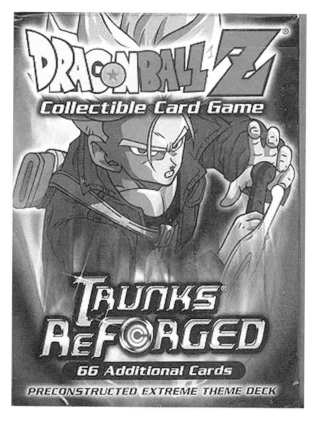

Figure 2.4 *Collectible card game. Trading cards are highly successful among tweens and are likely to continue to be so for the foreseeable future.*

Collection requires perseverance, and to own the best card collection may help place the tween among a group of admiring classmates. The formula is simple: the more cards you collect the greater control you have, and the more attention you receive.

Let's take a look at how far this trend has shifted. Up until the beginning of the 1990s, only celebrities ever appeared on cards. This has since changed, and your average everyday tween now occupies the spotlight. A team of talent scouts from Boy Crazy created a huge success in the late 1990s when looking for boys with appeal. With free Happy Meals at McDonald's, the boys are persuaded to let themselves be included in the Boy Crazy concept. They answer a few questions about their lives and have their pictures taken. The result: collection cards which girls could purchase and exchange with each other. This has become an extension of the 'swaps' that they had been doing with pretty pictures and cartoon characters since the 1950s.

Based on the boys' looks and their often less-than-modest self-descriptions, the girls started their own card collections. As the popularity of these cards grew, another dimension was introduced. This was the possibility of writing to, and later actually conversing with the boys featured on the cards.

Each card-boy was issued with a card e-mail address, which obliged them to answer questions from girls in the afternoon hours. To prevent this becoming a dating service, no personal contact details were to be exchanged, and certain topics were considered out of bounds. Cindy Thornbury, the inventor of the Boy Crazy concept today runs one of the worlds largest collection cards company, Decipher, the company behind successes such as the Star Wars collection cards.

So card collection is alive and well and equally popular with boys and girls. Small and large fortunes have been made by the card collection industry, and whoever may be entering it, as long as they offer the right formula.

GAMING ABILITY

'I'm number 1, 3, 8, 13 on the high-score list in Circus Maximus: Chariot Wars'

Over the past 10 years, the world of games has grown exponentially. Board games have always had appeal, but their attraction paled into insignificance when we saw the passion for electronic games when they were first introduced in the 1980s.

The fundamental concept of a game is to challenge players and to create a winner and a loser. If the toy doesn't initially build on high-score lists, level versions and points, you will still find that most tweens will create game rules around it. They will transform it into a game including at least one of these three evaluation criteria. If the competition is not to build a tower fastest, or to create the biggest collection, act fastest or create the most goals, it is unlikely that tweens will go mad to join in.

Almost all computer applications include a gaming component. However, some, if not most, are 100 per cent based on gaming, resulting in a winner, a loser and some sort of points system. There is no doubt that gaming is here to stay, and every indication is that it will become even bigger. As computer technology creates ever-more astounding graphics, faster reactions and cooler interaction with its players, games are set to move into the future.

Although incorporating any of these characteristics – fear, fantasy, mastery, humour, love and stability – is no guarantee of winning a prime spot in the tween market, without doubt each of the world's most success-ful brands is built on one or several of them, and have at least one of the three key drivers. Barbie is based on love and the dolls mirror a dream world in which the girls see themselves taking part. Star Wars is based on fear and mastery, and players have to compete with the enemy in order to survive. All these successful brands have one thing in common: the play value of the brands becomes increasingly valuable as your collection grows. What more can you ask for?

SUMMARY

▌ The life of most tweens is one of routine. The role of your brand is to break this routine.

▌ For a brand to be successful among tweens, it needs to be based on fear, fantasy, mastery, humour, love or stability. But most impor-tantly, the brand needs to ensure that the tween is placed in the centre of a world they admire and to which they aspire.

▌ Popularity and fame score high on tweens' dream list. If they aren't after it for themselves at this stage, they're deeply in love with those who have it. Along with fame, there's the desire for fortune.

▌ Boys are more drawn to mastery than girls. Not surprisingly, boys are mostly driven by the fear that goes with horror, panic and war. The winner-takes-all competitive model is no longer what it's all about. The journey has become as important as the destination.

▌ Banal as it may sound, girls are still drawn to love. The success of this value brings us back to basics: dolls fulfil the young girl's need to give love and nurture. Humour travels easily across the gender divide, and finds itself a winner in both camps. Fantasy travels as well as humour, providing it's not too unrealistic. It involves pushing the limits, making fun of adults and doing crazy things that no-one has done before.

ACTION POINTS

▶ Outline all the different values your brand appeals to among kids. Use both the positive and the negative.

▶ Rank the values of your brand and compare these with the values described in this chapter. To what degree do you see a match?

▶ Would any tween be a proud owner of your brand? If so, it will generate sales among their peers. If not, work out what elements are missing in order to elevate your brand to such a level, and because of this generate sales among peers. What elements are missing to elevate your brand to this level?

▶ To what degree is your concept and communication open-ended? Does it leave room for fantasy and imagination? Is there room for another version?

▶ Is your concept suitable for an online, offline and radio presence? If so, what should the split be?

▶ Before you race ahead with your concept and communication strategy, read Chapter 3. It will help add new dimensions to your brand, particularly in regard to how it will affect the parents of tweens.

Bonded to brands: the transition years

Nigel Hollis

CEO'S HEADS EXPLODE!

Jeremy Bullmore once stated that, 'Brands are fiendishly complicated, elusive, slippery, half-real/half-virtual things. When CEOs try to think about brands, their brains hurt'. We might add, when CEOs try thinking about brands in the same way that tweens do, their brains explode! How many of us understand our own kids, never mind ones that live half a world away? And yet, in today's world of global marketing, we are required to do just that.

Three basic factors conspire to make the task of understanding global tweens a monumentally difficult task:

Complex

The international marketer is faced with a complex Rubik's Cube of variables. These include the brand's competitive standing in a particular country, the influence of local culture and consumer life stage. These all combine to determine the success of a particular brand proposition or marketing strategy. In order to be successful on the global stage, the marketer must understand the differences between countries and cultures, while leveraging the *underlying* commonalities that will make their brand successful.

Dynamic

Kid's markets are by their very nature dynamic. Kids grow up fast. One minute they are playing with LEGO or Barbie, and seemingly the next second they are immersed in SimCity or listening to Eminem. This is particularly true of tweens, who undergo a physiological as well as psychological transition, all in the space of a few years.

Cluttered

One other aspect of the tweens' market further exacerbates these issues. Over the last 10 years we have observed an increase in the number of marketers competing for kids' attention. In particular, car companies, airlines, hotels and financial services are competing with traditional kid marketers to establish a relationship with young consumers. Initially targeted at teens, research and marketing programs are now seeking to understand and develop a relationship with younger consumers in the hope that their predisposition toward their brand will sway their purchasing decisions in the years to come. The result has been a dramatic increase in the number of advertising messages targeted at tweens, making it increasingly difficult to get an individual brand message across.

Why it's worth the pain

Ask any parent, and they will tell you in detail just how much of their disposable income goes towards satisfying their children's needs, wants and desires. But tweens are more than just end-consumers. Tweens command a substantial disposable income of their own. In the United Kingdom, 8 to 14-year-olds are estimated to command a disposable income of US $2.7 billion a year, from pocket money, gifts and odd jobs.

Table 3.1 *Purchasing power: claimed weekly disposable income from pocket money, gifts and odd jobs (in US $)*

Age	Male	Female
8–10	$ 7.00	$ 6.60
11–14	$12.95	$13.46

Source: BMRB's UK Youth TGI, 2001

The amount of money spent by tweens in the United States is estimated to be over US $20 billion, reflecting the larger population and a higher average disposable income. For marketers of toys, candy, soft drinks, games and movies, this represents a massive opportunity, well worth the pain of understanding the potential customer.

But these numbers underestimate the total scope of the tween market. It is not just a matter of how much they spend directly. Tweens command a massive influence on brands, well beyond the ones they buy themselves.

Brand advocates

Tweens are active lobbyists when it comes to brands. A survey commissioned by the Center for a New American Dream suggests that even when their parents say 'no', nearly 6 out of 10 kids keep asking for brands they want – an average of nine times. Annoying though this may be to their parents, it results in kids having tremendous say over what gets bought by the household. Don't think this is limited to brands bought in the supermarket or the toy store. Tweens have a strong influence over major household purchases too. Witness Josephine, the 12-year-old daughter of some friends of mine, who persuaded her parents that their choice of minivan was the wrong one for their needs and lifestyle. And she's not alone, as we shall see later. In the United States, Dr James U McNeal estimates the direct value of pester power to be US $188 billion, with a further US $300 billion coming from indirect influence, where the parent makes a purchase taking the kids' needs and desires into account. Examples are cable television, calling plans and restaurants.

Brand loyalists

There is good evidence that brand relationships formed in childhood do last into later years, even though the relationship is initiated when the brand is not one that is actively consumed or purchased. As long ago as the 1960s, longitudinal studies by Lester Guest (*Journal of Applied Psychology,* April 1964) demonstrated at least 23 per cent of brand preferences persisted from childhood to adulthood. Nostalgia and childhood associations can have a powerful influence on adult brand allegiance. There would not be so many middle-aged executives riding Harley Davidson motorcycles on weekends in the United States if this were not the case. Brands that can create bonds with tweens, and then hold true over time, will maintain a powerful advantage over competitors as their 'loyalists' enter later life.

So how do you tap into these markets to benefit your brand? In both cases, either current brand advocacy or future loyalty, the key is to establish a strong and enduring relationship with tweens.

FORMING THE BOND BETWEEN TWEENS AND BRANDS

Do tweens have the same type of relationship with brands as adults do? Does the relationship that a kid has with M&M's, McDonald's or MTV obey the same 'rules' as the relationship that an adult has with Mastercard, Marriott or Mercedes?

Real brand loyalty needs strong foundations

Brand relationships don't form in a vacuum. You need to create strong attitudinal foundations before people become truly loyal to your brand. We can visualize these foundations as a pyramid. The people who make it to the top of the pyramid hold a strong attitudinal allegiance to the brand – they are 'bonded' to it – and are highly likely to buy it and remain loyal to it over time.

The construct of the pyramid in Figure 3.1 can be applied across different brands, product categories and countries. The levels break down as follows:

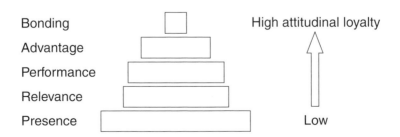

Figure 3.1 *The BrandDynamics™ pyramid.*

Presence

More than just brand awareness, presence implies that the consumer knows something about the brand promise, enough for them to accept or reject it.

Relevance

To offer an acceptable choice, a brand must avoid the negatives. People need to think the brand will meet their basic needs of the category: that it is in the right price range and that it 'fits' with their self-image and values. If it fails to meet any one of these criteria for an individual, then they remain at presence and do not advance up to relevance.

Performance

To climb to the next level, people need to experience the brand – to eat it, drive it or use it. People will move up to this level if they confirm to themselves that the brand delivers on its basic promise.

Advantage

In this age of aggressive marketing and product development, a good product does not necessarily provide a brand with a competitive advantage. To be successful in the long run, a brand must find a dimension that will give it an edge over the competition, be it rational or emotional. Many kids' brands seek advantage through accompanying peripherals, rather than the product itself. For instance, toy manufacturers are launching state-of-the-art, customizable battling tops in the United States, riding on their success in Japan. Hasbro's Beyblades, has its own animated television show, while Bandai's robotic-shaped Cyclonian tops come with comic books detailing each top's characteristics.

The problem with this type of advantage is that it is relatively short-lived and commits the manufacturer to a continuing cycle of add-ons and news. Establishing advantage by tapping into real emotional needs can create a far stronger bond.

Bonding

So how do people reach the top of the pyramid? They reach a degree of attachment to it that excludes other brands from their frame of reference. In some way their brand is unmatched by the other brands against which it competes. The underlying causes of this attachment will be unique to a brand, but all successful brands achieve it in some way. On average, people who are bonded to a brand are nearly 10 times more likely to buy it than those who do not make it to presence.

THE POWER OF BRANDS TRANSCENDS GENERATIONS

The brand pyramid allows us to classify brand relationships in the same way across kids and adults. Research into the consumer equity of over 20,000 brands worldwide, for both kid and adult brands, confirms that the underlying foundations of brand relationships are the same, across age group, category and country.

The fascinating finding is that brand allegiance changes very little across the generations.

In two out of three categories, adults and kids are bonded to the same brands. This finding is not just unique to the United Kingdom. Many brands around the world manage to tap into needs and desires that transcend the age of the consumer.

In many cases, product segmentation is the key to creating strong brand relationships across age groups. Kellogg's dominates its market by offer-

Table 3.2 *Brand allegiance by generation*

Category	7–10 years old	11–14 years old	Adults
Fast food	McDonald's	McDonald's	McDonald's
Sports clothing	Adidas	Adidas	Adidas
Television media	Cartoon Network	Nickelodeon	BBC
Soft drinks	Coca-Cola	Coca-Cola	Coca-Cola
Chocolate bars	Mars	Mars	Mars
Cereals	Kellogg's Frosties	Kellogg's Cocoa Pops	Kellogg's Cornflakes

Source: BRANDZ study conducted for WPP, United Kingdom, 1999

ing different products for different tastes. Not only is the product different, but the presentation differs too, from Frosties' Tony the Tiger, a
friendly, jovial, cartoon character that younger kids like, to cheeky Coco
Monkey speaking for Cocoa Pops. Each of these brands is carefully
tailored to meet the needs of its target audience in terms of product and
promotion.

The same type of pattern can be seen in data from the United States,
India and elsewhere. Tweens and adults are often bonded to the same
brands, even though culture and competitive context differ.

Tweens bond with brands in the same way that adults do, but the allegiance *is* weaker than for adults. On a like-for-like comparison across
scores of brands, kids were 40 per cent less likely to be bonded on
average than adults asked about the same brands. This is in spite of the
fact that all the other levels of the pyramid were very similar. So tweens
are just as aware of a brand's promise, and just as likely to think that one
brand has an advantage over another. They just do not display the same
degree of emotional allegiance as adults do, although as Figure 3.2
demonstrates the degree to which people bond to brands increases
strongly through the teen years.

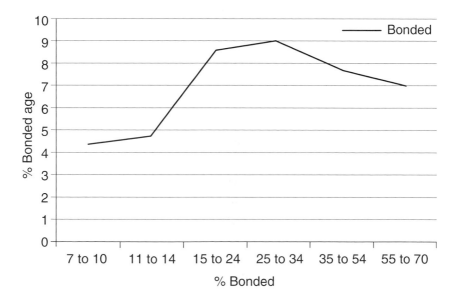

Figure 3.2 *Bonding patterns according to age.*

It is definitely true that marketers have inundated kids with a barrage of news, new products and promotions in the battle to build or maintain sales. This does not always work as intended. In Italy, for instance, Millward Brown's Kidspeak researchers report cases of brands being bought for the promotion item more than the product. Mothers who bought certain snack brands for their kids were disgruntled when their kids kept the promotional item but threw the product away! This is not the sort of action that guarantees repeat purchase! So, is the lack of tween brand loyalty solely the result of the barrage of marketing activity aimed at them, or does it reflect something more fundamental?

Peer pressure helps undermine tween loyalty

A fundamental factor of tween life is peer pressure. They are more subject to the pressure from their peers than adults or even teens, and tend to follow the herd rather than their own instincts. This makes them less likely to develop a strong relationship with a single brand, unless it also appeals to their friends.

Peer pressure diminishes as kids move from tween to teen, as Table 3.3 demonstrates.

The drop in peer pressure reflects the kids' rational and emotional development. In younger tweens, there is a strong emotional need to fit in. This is partly an inherent desire to feel one of the group and a need to feel secure. This drive towards conformity carries over from childhood into the tween years. As the child grows older, they develop an increased sense of individuality and autonomy, which results in a desire for freedom from rules and a lessening reliance on peers for a frame of reference. We can see this from the *BRANDchild* research, where we observed a marked shift from Conformity to Autonomy from ages 9 to 14 as Figure 3.3 shows.

The developing understanding of themselves as individuals and the world around them as they age is reflected in what tweens buy. Table 3.4 documents the rapid changes in what tweens spend their money on.

Table 3.3 *Do you sometimes feel pressure to buy certain products, such as clothes, shoes, CDs, or anything else, because your friends have them?*

	12–13 years old	14–15 years old	16–18 years old
Yes	54%	30%	17%

Source: The Center for a New American Dream, 2002 Youth Survey

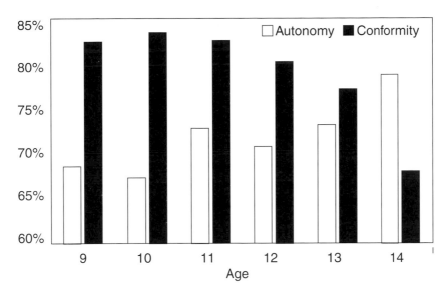

Figure 3.3 *Changing emotional needs.*

Table 3.4 *How tweens spend their money*

	Males	Females
Going out		
8–10 years old	16%	22%
11–14 years old	57%	71%
Tapes and CDs		
8–10 years old	53%	49%
11–14 years old	45%	60%
Computer and video games		
8–10 years old	53%	15%
11–14 years old	40%	26%
Clothes		
8–10 years old	14%	44%
11–14 years old	33%	57%
Toys and games		
8–10 years old	67%	50%
11–14 years old	29%	26%
Toiletries and cosmetics		
8–10 years old	2%	14%
11–14 years old	23%	53%

Source: BMRB's UK Youth TGI

As tweens become more conscious of their image, so the basic function of a brand changes. What was once a simple icon becomes a more personal statement, one that reflects who they are as an individual. Brands begin to be desired for their functional benefits around the age of four, as children take a more active role in choosing brands in the supermarket, or demanding a Happy Meal because of the play value of the toys. By the tween years, requests for products peak, as kids begin to distinguish between a knee jerk 'I've got to have that!' and a more deeply felt 'I want that because...' Even when they reach 12 to 14 years, however, some tweens may still not appreciate brands as a means of expressing a specific individual identity. Rather, this age group often prefers one brand over another *only* because of their acceptance or popularity with more aspirational members of a peer group (mainly girls), or due to their linkage to activities of interest, such as basketball, soccer or skateboarding (mainly boys).

So there are three basic reason why tweens are less likely to bond with a brand than adults:

1. They may appear more fickle than adults because they are subject to extreme peer pressure.
2. They 'grow through' brands very quickly. Their basic interest in toys, magazines and entertainment changes year by year, and so does their allegiance to different brands.
3. They are subject to a host of marketing tactics designed to promote change from one brand to another.

All of these factors combine to undermine the continued loyalty to brands targeted at tweens, but it does not mean that they are incapable of forming deep attachments. In fact, our research implies that many brands do not do a good job of tapping into kids' real needs and emotions to create lasting relationships.

The glass is not 40 per cent empty, it's 60 per cent full

Knowing that tweens are 40 per cent less loyal than adults might tempt one to conclude that money spent on building relationships with tweens is wasted. But our research suggests the opposite. The glass is not 40 per cent empty, but 60 per cent full. All our evidence suggests that tweens have a good understanding of brands. From LEGO and Nike to Gucci and the Ford Focus they know their names, remember what they see and hear about them, and form opinions. The potential is there, so what's the missing ingredient that would help turn this knowledge into a lasting relationship?

The answer must be experience and involvement. An adult has many more years of exposure to brands than a tween, and many more years in which to develop a relationship with them. At the age of nine or even 14, the world is still a place to be explored and experienced, and this is just as true of brands as it is of any other facet of life. This is why it is so important for brands to establish a relationship at this age rather than later on in life, when views are more established and inertia takes hold.

To build a deeper relationship, interaction is the key. An engaging and involving experience in which the brand plays a lead role is the key to building a successful relationship with tweens. Interaction helps accelerate the development of brand relationships that would otherwise take years to develop.

Brands like McDonald's, Adidas and Mars survive from generation to generation by staying true to their origins, satisfying the same basic need over time, but continuing to surprise and be innovative in the way that they communicate to keep the brand fresh in kids' minds. All too often less savvy marketers take the superficial fickleness of kids at face value and play to that rather than their fundamentals needs. This creates a cycle of news for news sake. This is all too easily broken or bettered by competition.

While tween loyalty appears low, the potential to build strong, lasting relationships is there. The degree to which people bond with a brand increases rapidly from 10 years of age. So if you can lay the groundwork of the brand relationship in the tween years it creates the potential to really form a strong bond in later years.

TAPPING INTO THE POWER OF TWEEN ADVOCACY

Tweens have a powerful influence on purchases directly consumed by them, but what of brands bought and used by their parents? Earlier I mentioned Josephine's power of persuasion. Right or wrong, she helped to determine which minivan her parents should buy. Was she in the minority to tackle her parents on the subject and win? Not according to the kids we talked to.

In the context of the *BRANDchild* research, we asked kids about their influence on three types of adult purchase: cars, designer fashions and mobile phones. Over half the kids claimed that they would voice an opinion if their parents were making such a purchase. A further 15 per cent said that they would have an opinion, but that they would not discuss it.

What is particularly intriguing is that so many kids said that their parents ask for their opinion. We had expected this phenomenon to be stronger in developing markets, and more apparent for technology products like mobile phones, where adults might feel alienated from the product category. However, the responses show a remarkable consistency across countries and categories, and there is no a particular educational or socio-economic bias. In almost one in three households, parents ask for their kids' advice when buying a new car.

Differences in response between the product categories are partly driven by the kid's interest in that category. On average the child was 50 per cent more likely to claim that they had a say if they also claimed to be interested in the product category itself. This interest in turn appears to reflect the local culture. Kids in India, the United States and Japan are more likely to express interest in cars rather than fashion, and to voice an opinion about their parents' purchase of that category. Brazilians and Europeans are more likely to be interested in fashions, and were more likely to voice an opinion about what clothes their parents might buy.

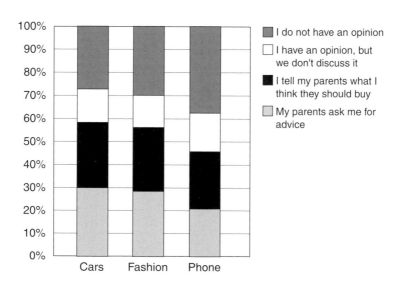

Figure 3.4 *Tween influence on household purchases.*

The other major determinant of whether or not the kids voice an opinion is, of course, age. The older the kid gets, the more likely they are to have their say. Overall, the likelihood that the child will express an opinion increases from 36 per cent at age nine, to 60 per cent at age 14.

TAPPING INTO FUTURE LOYALTY

Exploring tweens' relationship with adult brands

Many companies, particularly automotive manufacturers, have studied the brand preferences of teenagers. But kids are exposed to adult brands every day, so perhaps they develop fixed ideas about what they want even earlier than the teen years. Our *BRANDchild* research provides a unique insight into how tweens bond with grown-up brands.

We chose two categories for exploration: cars and fashion. In part, we were working to a gender stereotype in making these choices, but we felt that these were both categories where kids were likely to receive a considerable amount of indirect marketing exposure. Cars are clearly not bought by tweens, although The Center for a New American Dream did report that when asked what they most wanted, but had not been able to persuade their parents to buy, 4 per cent of 12 to13-year-olds said a car! (The proportion rose to 38 per cent among 16 to 18-year-olds.)

'I like Toyota', Huang Li Min, aged 9, China

Tweens are clearly more interested in fashion, but while a minority of them claim to buy their own clothes, most rely on their parents to pay for them.

When asked who chooses the specific brand, however, just over half the UK tweens said that they did. The lack of control over the actual purchase can lead to frustration for some. The Center for a New American Dream study reports that fashions that were seen to be inappropriate were mentioned by one in 10 tweens as something that they could not persuade their parents to buy, second only to video consoles, and ahead of inappropriate video games, CD-ROMs and body piercing.

As we saw when it came to advocacy, whether a tween has an opinion about a brand depends on how interested they are in the category. And yes, gender stereotypes are still alive and well, whether we like it or not, as Table 3.5 demonstrates.

These interests are well established at nine years old, the youngest age in our sample. Interest in cars remains relatively constant for both boys and girls as they age. Interest in fashionable clothes develops more as the kids grow older, but starts pretty high for girls. So in the majority of cases, kids claim to be interested in both these categories.

Table 3.5 *Interest in cars and fashion by gender*

	Boys	**Girls**
Cars	71%	41%
Fashionable clothes	44%	70%

Tweens do bond with grown-up brands

Earlier I reviewed how adults and kids developed relationships with brands in similar ways. While this is true of tweens in relation to their own brands, do the principles hold good when kids think about more adult brands like cars or fashions? The answer must be yes. They still form opinions and attitudes about adult brands, although their perceptions of performance and advantage may differ from an adult's. For instance, the acceptability of a minivan may be determined by the amount of room in the back for friends, or the presence of a television screen, rather than more fundamental issues like fuel economy and good brakes.

Using the *BRANDchild* research results we created brand pyramids for each of the fashion and car brands that we asked kids to talk about. In terms of cars, we deliberately limited the list to a variety of mid-priced

Table 3.6 *Tween's relationships with adult brands*

	Fashion	Cars
Bonded	33%	41%
Advantage	44%	56%
Relevance	53%	65%
Presence	58%	69%

Note: We have excluded the performance level of the pyramid, since this was not covered in the research

vehicles. With fashion we went for a broader, more eclectic spread, from brands we knew would appeal to kids to some that we thought would be distinctly more adult, like Chanel, Burberry and Armani. Table 3.6 shows the percentage of kids who had bonded to *any* brand in the two categories.

One-third of our global tweens were bonded to a fashion brand. They wanted to wear the brand and had a strong, positive attitude towards it. Older tweens were more likely to be bonded to a brand, with the proportion increasing from 29 per cent among 9 to 11-year-olds, to 38 per cent among 12 to 14-year-olds. Given that we had presented a rather diverse list to our respondents and, moreover, one that could not hope to be representative of the fashion market in each country, it is amazing to see so many tweens demonstrate such a clear predisposition toward these brands.

More tweens were bonded to one of the cars on our list than one of the fashion brands. Over 40 per cent of tweens were bonded to a car brand. Again, the proportion of kids that are bonded again increases with age, from 37 to 45 per cent.

Presence creates potential

Desire is prompted first and foremost by exposure to the brand. Whether exposure is seeing a friend wearing Diesel jeans, or a PT Cruiser drive down the street, it triggers interest in the brand. Using the example of the brand pyramid, it creates presence.

What is apparent from our research is that presence has an over-riding effect on perceptions of brand acceptability. We asked the kids whether they had an opinion about the different brands included in the research, and which ones they would most like to own or wear. There is a strong relationship between the two. Seventy per cent of the variance in which car tweens would most like to own can be explained on the basis of whether they have formed an opinion about it or not. The proportion is over 80 per cent for fashion brands. Similar relationships exist in all adult categories, but not normally to this degree.

So just making tweens aware of the brand promise is a big part of determining what they think of it. Of course, it isn't as simple as that. Presence is not an end in itself, but a means to an end. It implies that a person knows something about your brand, but doesn't really say what it is that they know.

BRAND ATTRACTION MATTERS

The relationship between opinion and desire to own tells us quite a bit about the basic attractiveness of the different brands.

Take as an example two of the best-known fashion brands, Calvin Klein and Tommy Hilfiger. Both have a similar level of presence, with 27 per cent claiming to have an opinion about Calvin Klein and 22 per cent about Tommy Hilfiger. But more kids claimed to want to wear Tommy Hilfiger than Calvin Klein. This clearly implies that on a like-for-like basis Tommy Hilfiger is much more attractive to these kids than Calvin Klein.

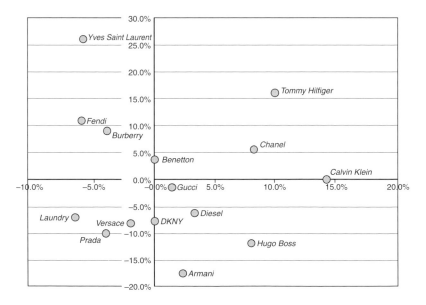

Figure 3.5 *Fashion brand map.*

Using the degree of presence relative to the average for the brands in the category, and the relative attractiveness, we can now plot out a simple brand map of presence versus attraction.

In Figure 3.6, brands on the right are better known than those on the left. Brands at the top are more attractive than those at the bottom. Brands in the top left quadrant would be expected to grow, provided they improve their presence. Brands in the bottom right are better known, but are less attractive than might be expected. They need to figure out what is putting kids off and address the problem. Brands in the top right are well-known and highly attractive.

In the context of our research, the overall picture reflects some strong regional differences. It confirms the strong position of Tommy Hilfiger, mainly driven by kids in the United States, and to a lesser extent Germany and India. Hugo Boss looks weak on this overall map, in part because its strength lies more in Europe. Chanel was the most recognized name among the brands included on our list, and it is relatively attractive to tweens, but mainly in Japan and China. Chinese tweens were the least likely to have an opinion about any brand, and tended to know only the classics. Chanel has a strong presence there, probably bolstered by the cheap copies sold everywhere in the major urban areas. Attraction to Yves Saint Laurent was also particularly noticeable among Chinese tweens, and this appears to be driving its Little Tiger positioning at the top right of the map.

Looking at the right-hand top quadrant of the list that we presented to the kids, there is no car that stands out with the same strength of presence and appeal that Tommy Hilfiger does. As with the fashion map, the overall picture hides some strong regional strengths and weaknesses due to distribution. Overall, the car with the most appeal, given its presence, would appear to be the smaller, sportier SUV, the Toyota RAV4, with the new Mini and Hyundai Elantra just moving into the frame. The new Beetle and the Honda Civic are better known, but do not appear to have quite the same degree of attraction. Cars with significant 'pulling power' among tweens but low presence are the Mazda Miata and the Jeep Wrangler.

Avoid the negatives

In order for someone to have the potential to bond with a brand, the brand needs to avoid the three negatives. If a brand is not thought to meet a person's needs, is thought to be too expensive or unappealing, then it is unlikely they will bond with it. There is no difference for grown-up brands and tweens, except that needs and expense take a back seat to appeal.

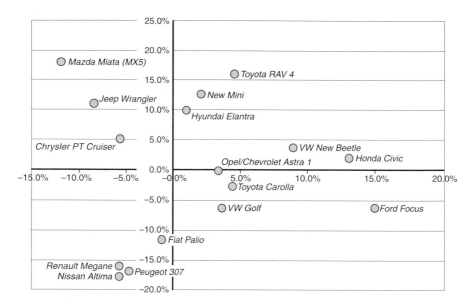

Figure 3.6 *Car brand map.*

Broadly speaking, any brand is potentially attractive to kids, provided it meets the key criteria of being cool and fun. Additional benefits are perceptions of broad acceptance – that most people will like it – or that it will be popular forever. In a minority of cases 'rarity' – the perception that not many people owned a brand – was a positive influence. These basic guidelines applied to both fashion and cars.

Tweens, especially girls, tend to divide the world into acceptable and not acceptable brands, and it is the negatives that really define whether a brand is attractive or not. In our research if the tween chose any of the following words in relation to a brand, then they were unlikely to want it:

- normal (as opposed to cool);
- too many people have (as opposed to most people like);
- weird or too silly;
- past it (strongly associated with being boring and not cool).

Brands that stood out were considered 'happening', meaning that the brand was trendy or the current fad. The word was used to describe brands in a way that was opposite to 'most people don't like', but was not strongly associated with the four positives: cool, fun, most people like and popular forever. This suggests that kids do make a distinction between true popularity and a passing fad. This is borne out by other qualitative research results. Tweens will jump on the bandwagon when a craze starts up. They want to be in on it, but have a good understanding of what has lasting value rather than just the latest fad.

A brand that is seen to be fun and cool today is likely to be the one that will still be desirable in 10 years' time. Needs change and the sports car you wanted as a tween may no longer be affordable or sensible when you have two kids of your own. Later in life, however, nostalgia may draw you back to your childhood dream. More subtle, but just as potent, is the potential transference of appeal, particularly for categories like automotive, where the model may be unattainable, but the make may not. So maybe the Dodge Viper is way out of your league, but the Dodge name can still bring a cachet that it would not do otherwise.

Television is still the focus of attention

Where do tweens get their information on brands like the ones we have been looking at? We asked tweens about three categories: cars, fashion and cell or mobile phones. Figure 3.7 summarizes the results for the global sample.

Again, our data highlight the commanding influence that television has over tweens' view of the world. In our research, virtually every tween had access to at least one television, and 36 per cent had their own. No other medium comes close to having the same reach among tweens, for now. Obviously, the strong role of television will reflect news and special interest programs as well as advertising. The same is true of magazines, newspapers and the Internet.

Which channel will offer the best opportunity for communication varies by country. Tweens in the United States and India were most likely to mention multiple sources of information, over four on average. There is a strong emphasis on newspapers as a traditional source of information in India (where there are over 350 national and regional newspaper titles). As a result, 64 per cent of Indian tweens mentioned newspapers as a source of information, versus only 22 per cent in the United States. Indian tweens also mentioned their parents as a source of information, more than others and reflecting the far closer family relationships that exist there. New media, like the Internet and cell phones, also demonstrate strong regional variation in penetration. The Internet was strongest in the United States where 73 per cent claimed to use it. In India, 23 per cent of tweens used the Internet, although many more visited a cyber café to do so than

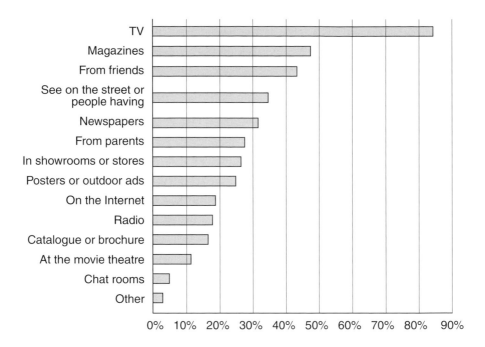

Figure 3.7 *Sources of brand information.*

elsewhere. In Germany, over 50 per cent of tweens had a mobile phone, far higher than even Spain or Japan, indicating both the independence of tweens in that country and the strength of SMS messaging in Europe.

Why television advertising is still so important

With the same level of exposure, kids are three times more likely to remember that they have seen a brand advertised on TV than adults. There are a number of reasons why TV advertising is so powerful, some inherent to kids and some to TV as a medium. Kids relate to television in the following ways:

▍ television is a central part of their lives – the benchmark against which other media are judged. Across our sample of urban tweens, 85 per cent agreed that they loved watching television;

▍ kids actively pay attention to what they see on television and absorb more details than adults – even from ads not directed at them;

- kids genuinely enjoy advertising. They are twice as likely to say that they enjoyed an ad as adults;
- life is less cluttered than for adults. Shopping and choosing brands is an enjoyable experience, not a chore! 'Let's get a piece of paper and a pen each, and we can spend Saturday morning watching the adverts so we know what to put onto our list for Father Christmas.'

The medium itself has certain advantages too:

- television delivers messages in a way that combines the visual elements so important to a kid's world, with fun sounds and music;
- television is a stimulating, shared experience. Kids can sit with their friends and comment on what is shown;
- as a broadcast medium, television makes it relatively easy to reach both parents and kids with the same communication channel.

A key point to note, is that all our research worldwide suggests that kids react to advertising in ways similar to adults. The principles of what makes an ad successful for adults hold good for kids. To be successful, what is involving in the ad, the truly creative and compelling aspects, must be inextricably linked to the brand and the message.

Television plays a major role in creating awareness and desire for a brand, but it can rarely stand alone, and it would be wrong to write off media other than television and print on the basis of results like these. Earlier we touched on the critical role of other media to leverage the presence created by television to develop stronger brand relationships through more interactive media, promotion and PR. Their impact is set to greatly increase in future.

Times are changing fast. A large 46 per cent of our tweens had access to the Internet, and 19 per cent had their own mobile phone. This could not have been the case just 10 years ago, and while penetration levels differ widely by country, the numbers are increasing everywhere.

There is little doubt that these media will be the dominant means of communication in years to come.

TWEENS ARE JUST LIKE US, ONLY MORE SO

Building brand relationships that will last over time is an investment. It is an investment that needs to be made with a good understanding of the market and target audience's needs and desires. As Charlotte Beers stated, 'Any CEO who cannot clearly articulate the intangible assets of his brand

and understand its connection to customers, is in trouble'. Gaining that understanding can be tough when your target audience is a 12-year-old. However, the foundations of what makes a lasting brand relationship are the same for adults and tweens. And if you think about it, the desire for that holiday home, the BMW Z3 and the African safari don't really seem SO different from the 12-year-old's desire for a Game Cube, a Tommy Hilfiger jacket or the Screenblast Creation Suite. It's just that with tweens the desire for the brand they want is much stronger, the requests for it much more vocal, and they want it NOW!

SUMMARY

▌ The foundations of strong brand relationships are the same for tweens and adults, but the depth of the relationship differs.

▌ Tweens are less likely to be bonded to a brand. In fact they are 40 per cent less likely than adults to have a strong emotional loyalty to just one brand.

▌ Experience is the key driver of the difference in brand allegiance between tweens and adults. Tweens have not had the same amount of time to develop strong bonds with many brands.

▌ The potential for a brand to develop a strong relationship with tweens does exist, and some brands build such strong relationships with their consumers that people across all age groups remain loyal to the brand.

▌ The degree to which people bond with brands increases rapidly from the tween years to the late twenties. This means that barriers to changes in brand allegiance increase during these years. Tweens are open to the initiation of new relationships.

▌ Tweens are strong brand advocates, for both tween and grown-up brands. They have a strong influence on brands bought for them and brands bought for the household.

▌ In our *BRANDchild* research, one in two tweens claimed to express an opinion about grown-up purchases made in the household (cars, fashion and mobile phones). 20 per cent suggested that their parents asked for their opinion.

- Over one in three tweens in our research were bonded to one of the car brands or grown-up fashion brands included.

- Presence, or knowledge of a brand's promise, plays a large part in determining the desirability of a grown-up brand for the tween audience. Just knowing about the brand creates the potential for a deeper bond to form.

- Differences in brand attraction are driven by perceptions that the brand is cool, fun and generally popular. Critical to the desire to own the brand is the avoidance of negatives, including the perception that the brand is normal, too many people own it, or that it is weird, silly or past it.

- Television still plays a central role in tweens' lives. It is still the prime means of communicating with tweens today, particularly in creating presence and seeding interest in a brand. However, other media, PR and promotions are critical to creating the interaction that leads to strong brand loyalty.

ACTION POINTS

Ascertain whether or not tweens have an influence over purchases of your brand. It may be bought by grown-ups, but as we have seen, tweens influence the purchase of all sorts of household purchases, not just the ones that are bought for them.

How might a stronger relationship with tweens benefit your brand? In addition to direct tween purchasing, which of the following might apply?

1. Tweens actively desire your brand and persuade their parents to buy it for them, for example, food, toys and games.
2. Tweens are attracted to your brand and influence their parents' purchasing decisions, for example, cars, premium cable channels and travel.
3. Tweens act as references for adults who are less savvy about product categories or service, for example, technology products and services.
4. Tweens aspire to your brand as a status symbol, for example, Gucci or Yves Saint Laurent, and actively lobby parents to buy on their behalf.

5. Image is transferred from premium or aspirational brands to entry-level purchases bought by teens or young adults.
6. Parents-to-be choose your brand because it is the one they grew up with, for example Chex, Marmite or Vegemite.
7. Adults purchase specific brands for themselves because of nostalgia.

Assess current situation

There's every indication that tweens have a strong influence over the purchasing patterns of their parents. Thus strengthening your relationship with them might benefit your brand. It is therefore important for you to work out what your brand's status is amongst tweens. You will need to know:

1. How many tweens know your brand exists?
2. What do they think of your brand today?
3. How attractive is it to them relative to its presence?
4. How does it vary by gender, age and country?

Going forward

If Presence is low, how are you going to reach tweens? What media or channels will you need to use?

▌ If you choose television, how are you going to leverage its reach to create stronger interaction through other media, promotion or PR? The latest marketing trend embraces what is called 360-degree marketing. But when it comes to tweens, where their needs and desires are so driven by perceptions of popularity, television becomes the major means of inferring ubiquity and popularity.

▌ In-store presence is also critical for many brands, whether bought by kids or by their parents. If kids see a brand they want, they will ask for it. Ensure that your brand has prominent display, making the most of aspects featured in the advertising – in other words, the visual triggers that will catch the tween eye in-store. Use broadcast advertising to feature promotions and, again, make sure the visual trigger is there.

▌ What is the aspect of your brand that will strike a chord with tweens and create strong brand attraction?

▌ What is there that is cool, fun or classic? Beyond the basics of gender and age, what are the core emotional needs of the tweens to whom you are talking? Is the best strategy to reassure, inspire curiosity or tap into that rebellious streak?

▌ If you are to successfully leverage the potential in the long-term, it needs to be part of the brand's essence, not a superficial or transient element. It must also avoid the negatives. What do you need to downplay or avoid?

Every brand is unique. The specific nature of its relationship with tweens will vary accordingly. Following these Action Points should help you work out the value of tweens to your brand and strengthen the relationship with them – hopefully without your head exploding!

4

Exit fairyland

'My dream is to build a house like Hansel and Gretel'

The more uncertain things become around us, the greater our need for belief. Beliefs come in various shapes and sizes. We have the ability to dream, to aspire; we are gifted with the ability to have ideals. Each aspect of our belief system ensures that we have certainties to wake up to each morning, no matter how abysmal things seem.

BELIEFS VERSUS DREAMS VERSUS ASPIRATIONS

Dreams and aspirations are more easily explained than beliefs. They are tangible thoughts for which concrete descriptions can be provided. Describing beliefs is more difficult. Perhaps this is because beliefs are often based in emotion, which makes them more difficult to articulate.

Beliefs in the Western world can be compared to trends in the fashion industry. If you stick around, every 10 years or thereabouts, you will recognize the same fashion trend reappearing on the catwalks of Paris, Milan and New York. There will be slight adjustments to the original form, but the trend will usually be close enough to be recognized as the same.

Cycles of belief are not so different. Some decades are dedicated to spiritual renewal, while others are driven by money or even greed. These cycles are often a reaction to the one before. An example of this is the flower-power generation of the 1960s. The message preached by the youth culture was non-materialism; it was anti-war and embraced equality. Then came the Me generation of the 1970s, where the only spiritual focus was on the self as the idea of neighbourly sharing and caring fell by the wayside. The 1980s saw the emergence of a power-seeking, money-focused generation. This was the generation of young upwardly mobile professionals – who became known as yuppies – and the only institution they worshipped was the stock market. The freewheeling 1990s saw more wealth among the young as the Net spawned the most youthful entrepreneurs and unprecedented investment. Never in history had more money been placed in the hands of such a young group.

With the advent of the new millennium it became clear that the Internet start-ups were increasingly becoming Internet shut-downs. The dominoes began to fall. Life was becoming more financially unstable. So by the time the World Trade Centre was attacked, every certainty that once existed lay buried in the rubble of uptown Manhattan.

GOD INC.

 Visit DualBook.com/bc/ch4/religion to learn more about brands and religion.

'Mom – does God have a clothing store?'

Since September 11, the Bible has been on the Lycos list as the fiftieth most searched-for term. The movement towards religion not only offline but also online cannot be ignored. The Internet is a major purveyor of spiritual expression at a time when spiritual hunger is growing in the West.

One of the newest crazes sweeping the Net doesn't involve video games, music downloads, geek jokes, dancing babies or cracker codes. It involves God. Millions are flocking to reata.org, a homespun site run by Reata Strickland, a Tuscaloosa, Alabama, Sunday school teacher who took a short, anonymously written 'Interview with God', and set it to Shockwave animation. The inspirational prayer asks God what's most surprising about humankind. God answers: 'That they get bored with childhood. They rush to grow up and then long to be children again. That they lose their health to make money and then lose their money to restore their health.'

Figure 4.1 *Reata Strickland's Interview with God site attracts several million people every month.*

According to Jupiter Media Metrix, 2.4 million people visit the site each month. Interviewing Reata, she claims claims there are now more than 12 million visitors since she posted her 'Interview with God' on the Web site of her local United Methodist Church district. And all of this attention is happening by word of mouth. There has not been a single advertisement for the site, it's barely rated a mention in the media and all the while Reata is trying to figure out how she can pay for the cost of 40 gigabytes of bandwidth a day. The t-shirt, mouse pad and screensaver sales are only just managing to keep Reata afloat.

The site's popularity comes at a time when Christian-themed entertainment is playing an increasingly central role in mainstream culture. The apocalyptic Left Behind products have sold more than 40 million copies and continue to be a national phenomena. Parents have so far bought over 22 million copies of the Christian-based children's videos, Veggie Tales. And according to a *Newsweek* cover story, 'Jesus Rocks', contemporary Christian albums sold more in 2002 than jazz, classical and New Age genres combined.

Beliefnet is signing on average 35,000 subscribers per day to its e-mail newsletters, and claims to receive about 3.2 millions visits to their site a month.

The *BRANDchild* study shows that more than a year after September 11, 56.1 per cent of all urban tweens across the globe found the word 'religion' important, with US (76.6 per cent) and Brazilian tweens (78.8 per cent) expressing the most reverence for the word. Given the widespread anti-God message that has existed in recent history in China, it's not surprising that only 20.7 per cent of all Chinese tweens considered religion important.

The Nordic Youth Research Organization released the results of a study on Civic Participation among Young People in Europe in 2000. It reveals that over the past nine years, active church membership was the fastest growing trend among tweens. It goes on to state that there's been a five-fold increase in church memberships in Central-Western Europe and North-Western Europe. In South-Western Europe, this has increased ten-fold.

Since September 11, religion has been on the rise. Beliefs were shaken to the core, changing the way we all perceive our destiny. Beliefs that flourished at the turn of the twentieth century are under review. The effects of the Twin Towers falling have been questioned, explained, explored and analyzed in every which way and on every media channel.

Perhaps more tellingly, people are examining what they believed they stood for and how it relates to their changed world. What they once thought right for them in the world that existed before the cataclysmic events, no longer necessarily applies. There is a need to go back to basics, and a search for classic values and beliefs that may provide guidance to a more meaningful future.

This dramatic quest for spiritual sustenance has had a very strong effect on today's tweens, making the search as much their own as their parents'.

'Why do all religious people fight?'

Up until the early 1970s most people's belief systems in the Western world were firmly rooted in traditional religions. And then they lost their foothold, particularly among younger generations. Since the fight against non-religious Communists in Vietnam, many wars and skirmishes are based on religion. Even the death of 3,000 people on September 11 was based on religion. People around the world continue to be tortured, bombed, maimed and killed in the name of religion. So it's not surprising that tweens' perception of religion is quite different from that of past generations.

Tweens are not quite sure what to believe. They may say they believe in some sort of religion, but on further examination you realize that their responses to any questions of belief are riddled with clichés designed to blend in with current thinking in their community. In most cases, they don't believe in anything at all.

THE DEATH OF BELIEF

'I believe in nothing'

When Elizabeth Taylor ended her eighth marriage it was partly a reflection of her personal inability to sustain a married relationship, but it was just as much a reflection of a more general trend in a society that has steadily developed a more relaxed attitude to marital vows over the past 40 years.

So even if God can't be defined, marriage with all its flaws still can. Tweens continue to place their hopes in this institution, despite the fact that there's a divorce rate in the Western world that is edging close to 50 per cent.

Beliefs are not only created, however, by formal religions or romantic notions of marriage. Essentially, they are passed on by parents. Ideally, parents remain the major role models for tweens. However, this is also a fairly problematic situation. Parents rarely follow the beliefs and values that they're attempting to impart to their tweens.

The new-found openness that exists in tween households tends to expose the daily moralistic lessons about lying and cheating as fraudulent. An astounding 83.3 per cent of all urban tweens worldwide regards 'Obeying rules' as one of the most important phrases in their life. Likewise 'Not cheating others' is similarly endorsed by 82.6 per cent. However, only 69 per cent of German kids thought 'Obeying rules' was important.

These *BRANDchild* figures stand in stark contrast to the practices at home, where an astonishing 40 per cent of all households are believed to cheat on their tax forms and artificially inflate insurance claims. So on the one hand, tweens are taught to follow society's rules, while on the other they witness the way their parents openly break the law: by speeding, running red lights, driving without seat-belts. And don't forget how even corporations, highly respected industry icons and media gurus are caught with their hands in the till or failing to pay workers in foreign countries a living wage. Tweens' lack of respect towards the grown-up generation is a reflection of their disappointment in the way their parents live their lives and so often compromise their own beliefs.

Ultimately, it is not hard to understand why today's tweens have difficulty seeing their parents as idealistic icons for the perfect family life. This is a generation that holds their parents accountable, and the 'Do-as-I-say-and-not-as-I-do' approach no longer works.

THE NEW ICONS

'I want to be a real grown up!'

The younger you are, the older you want to be. The older you are, the younger you want to be. And so it's always been. Nine-year-olds want to be 14, so they can be categorized as *real* teenagers. But 14-year-olds think teenagers suck. They are waiting to become *real* adults. Australian tween Nikki Webster became an overnight sensation with her impressive performance at the Sydney Olympic opening ceremony in 2000. She launched her first CD and merchandizing program in 2002, but her make-up range proved to be a commercial failure. The problem? She appeared young. And even though she was actually 15 years old, she looked about 12, and tween girls rarely make peers their heroes.

It's part of growing. Everything older, bigger and smarter commands their admiration and their desire. There's a whole crop of children's movies based on this premise. In *Big*, Tom Hanks is a wild and crazy kid in a grown-up's body. At the tender age of eight, Harry Potter is given unlimited power to conquer the world. So products that allow tweens to act as players in an adult world are bound to succeed.

Take a look at the last few success stories. For a start, tweens respond positively to what is real. In three short years, mobile phones have achieved a market penetration of 25 per cent in Australia and Europe. Reality television is also walking off with the rating awards. Millions are tuning in to *A Real World, Big Brother* and *The Osbournes*.

'I want to be an octillionnaire!'

Alongside tweens' aspirations to adulthood is their aspiration to wealth. They want to know that when they walk into a shop they can afford to buy whatever they want. And they have big shopping lists. They want the most up-to-date technology, the hottest clothes, the smartest bikes, the fastest rollerblades and the most recent DVDs. To *have* the best is much the same as *being* the best. Theirs is an absolutely material reality where they *become* their possessions.

Close to half the world's urban tween population states that the clothes and brands they wear describe who they are and define their social status. Although American tweens lead this trend, they're adequately supported by their Danish (51 per cent) Spanish (59 per cent), Indian (61 per cent) and Brazilian (64 per cent) contemporaries. In stark contrast, only 10 per cent of Japanese tweens believe they're defined by the clothes they wear and the brands they own.

In general, tweens who wear fashionable clothes with admired brands are likely to be the most popular. Unsurprisingly, a whole raft of manufacturers has begun tapping into this behaviour, offering newer versions of older products.

'Is Mom and Dad Version 1.2 on sale yet?'

Just think about this. Less than 10 years ago this statement would have no meaning. Version 1.2? As software continues to upgrade with newer features, we're becoming increasingly used to versionized products. This leaves the door open to manufacturers to produce better, faster, more streamlined versions – and tweens tap right into the buzz for new versions before they even enter the marketplace. For those who have the skills to download the pre-released version off the Internet, well, the kudos knows no bounds.

Take the radio. A radio is a radio – right? Once you buy one, you're not likely to get another until the old one burns out. You're even more unlikely to buy another simply because it comes with a new feature or a more contemporary design. Well, this type of reasoning is lost on tweens.

The Sony PlayStation is an excellent example of how the having-more-having-better-having-faster generation has taken over. So eBay recently offered to *give* PlayStation 1 away for the price of the shipment. This is pretty astounding in light of the fact that PlayStation has only been on the market for five years. Essentially PlayStation 1 has absolutely no value today, even though it still works and you can still buy the games for it.

PlayStation capitalizes on tweens' fear of being perceived as old-fashioned. But perhaps even more importantly, it taps into the fact that those who have the latest version of PlayStation will sit at the top of the social hierarchy. They will invite friends over to play. And in this climate, there is nothing more humiliating for a tween than to be seen playing with a PlayStation 1.

The same trend can be seen in all the software being sold today. Whereas you or I are quite happy with our Microsoft Word Version 98, nothing but XP will do for our tweens. We need to see a clear functional reason to do an upgrade – but clear and functional reasons are not part of the tween ethos. Some games such as Final Fantasy are now out in the *tenth* version, using the same name, but different plots, different characters, new battle systems and an increasingly diverse range of weaponry. Final Fantasy is an interactive 'book' with a whole lot of in-depth stories. It has been ascribed a first-play value of 56 hours!

This trend is unlikely to be confined to the software industry in the near future, but will to spread across every well-known manufactured item. Product life cycles will need to adapt to follow this new direction. Computers, films and books already follow this trend, but in less than five years' time, car models, food, toys, hardware and sound equipment will change as well.

TWEENS ARE INSPIRED BY TWEENS, WHO ARE INSPIRED BY TWEENS...

'Why is the day only 24 hours long and not 50?'

Being a tween also means that you are still growing and learning. This is the age when a great deal of behavioural development is based on what is observed in the outside world.

Testosterone levels enter the picture anywhere from age nine, although it is usually more likely around 11, to peak at 14, when the young boy's testosterone level is about 800 per cent higher than it was when he was a toddler. The hormones don't usually settle down until the mid-20s. Obviously each individual matures, but the hormone's chemical effect on physique, behaviour, mood and self-understanding was summarized by the controversial columnist Andrew Sullivan, in an article he wrote for the *New York Times* in 2000. Sullivan who was being treated for HIV, was receiving fortnightly injections of synthetic testosterone. The long-term side-effects he noticed were that his appetite, in every sense of that word, expanded beyond measure. His body bulked up, he had strength and energy to spare, and his depression lifted. 'I feel better able to recover from life's curved balls, more persistent, more alive.' The short-term effects were even more striking. 'Within hours, and at most a day, I feel a deep surge of energy,' he wrote. 'It is less edgy than a double espresso but just as powerful. My attention span shortens. In the two or three days after my shot, I find it harder to concentrate on writing, and feel the need to exercise more. My wit is quicker, my mind faster, but my judgement is more impulsive. In a word, I feel braced. For what? It scarcely seems to matter.'

Tweens, like so many other peer groups, are the main source of inspiration for other tweens. And as they do in every other generation, they form groups and cliques with shared values and similar beliefs. The exchange of identities that takes place between friends of this age means that they not only inspire each other, they also contribute to the formation of each other's personalities. So it's not surprising that 80 per cent of all urban tweens state it is important for them to feel part of a group.

It is clear that tween groups always have always existed, although perhaps not quite to the same extent as our *BRANDchild* figures show. But this new generation is emerging with fading parental role models from more dysfunctional families in a world where beliefs are less certain than ever. This means that the tween peer group often becomes the replacement for the role traditionally occupied by the family.

A challenging community

Many peer groups choose to give their 'shell' or the group a name they feel best expresses their attitude. A group of Arabic-speaking tweens named their group *Shi Be Fas'I* which means 'Something that terrifies'.

Although many aspects of the camaraderie are positive, in some cases it also creates a whole new set of problems. Denmark has a frightening 20 per cent attempted suicide rate among their tween population. In fact, our study shows that 67 per cent of all Danish urban tweens look forward to being adults. This unacceptably high rate may be partially attributed to the large proportion of tweens who stake their lives and reputations on belonging to the right group. Everything that is at stake in a young person's life is vested in their group. Each group has a sophisticated hierarchy with unofficial rules. When the rules are transgressed, the feedback is harsh and direct. The take-'em-out mentality of the computer game prevails on the playground, and the peer pressure is immense.

Tweens not only have to prove their worth in this important arena, but are also under pressure to perform both at school and at home. Parents work long hours and their contact with their children is eroded. This leaves tweens to spend most of their time with their peers.

'It's all about being heard'

When you break through the strong barriers created by tweens' posture and attitude, it becomes clear in almost every case what they want. They want to be listened to. They want to be understood.

Their parents' response to financial strain by working even longer hours means that there's more time for media consumption and even less time for tweens to express themselves and be heard.

This further reinforces the notion that it takes a tween to understand a tween. One tween sums this up succinctly: 'The only time my parents listen to me is when I need to remember something for them.' And then computer games come along and allow the tween to become a hero. The games place the tween firmly in charge, giving them a chance to express themselves and be heard. No wonder their attraction is universally magnetic to the tween generation.

'No-one listen to me but my friends in ICQ'

Some of today's most successful marketing campaigns work because they understand that tweens need to be heard. Tweens become central to the campaign. Since its launch, this is the criterion on which the PepsiMax campaign has been based. Pepsi's major problem was that their Diet Pepsi was perceived as very feminine. This put the guys off what they considered to be a drink for girls. Obviously this has nothing to do with the fact that boys are more conscious of their physical condition than ever before. In fact, all market research has indicated that boys were ripe for 'lite' products, particularly among the tweens and teens.

PepsiMax was developed to cater specifically to this audience. Blind tests showed that the taste of PepsiMax and Diet Pepsi were virtually indistinguishable. However, their images remain poles apart. PepsiMax is all about breaking boundaries, being cool and being in the centre. PepsiMax drinkers are tough guys. The commercials leave no doubt that PepsiMax drinkers belong to a cool group of people. PepsiMax is all about the gang.

THE SEARCH FOR THE TRUE TWEEN ASPIRATION

So what do tweens believe in? Well, tweens often believe in other tweens – their peers. If a popular member of the group leans heavily towards a certain brand, the rest of the group is likely to follow. If one of the leaders is an outspoken fan of a certain band, the group is likely to adopt it. In short, tapping into the leaders of the pack is the first important step to achieving brand acceptance among the whole group.

Abercrombie & Fitch is an impressive example of how a strategic marketing campaign managed to reach millions of tween groups across the United States. Right across the country, Abercrombie & Fitch's marketing division visited schools and hand-picked the most handsome, the most admired and the most respected group of tweens to represent the Abercrombie & Fitch brand. Essentially they became the models for the Abercrombie & Fitch catalogue. This catalogue proved so popular that customers paid US $10 to receive it.

The Abercrombie & Fitch strategy was extended to in-store marketing. Teams of Abercrombie & Fitch tweens were carefully selected and employed to work in the retail outlets, attracting peers and encouraging them to be just like them. It worked. Abercrombie & Fitch zoomed right into the tweens' desire for fame, placed them firmly in the centre of the action, and managed to retain the most fickle audience in today's market. By 1999, Abercrombie & Fitch had become the largest tween retailer.

Abercrombie & Fitch started the trend which set out to create tween stars, who in turn became tween icons. Not to be outdone, Hollywood has refined the star-making machinery and has everything in place to offer the chosen icon a shortcut to global popularity. Everyone buys into this dream. *Popstars*, a television program based on manufacturing the icon, which then becomes the tween icon, now runs in four versions in more than 15 countries. Their pitch is firmly in the corner of every tweens' desire to be rich, famous and popular. When the talent hunt for *Popstars* was launched in Australia, there were more than 120,000 entries. Becoming rich, famous and popular is the goal for a substantial number of today's tweens who want to be discovered and thus saved from a world of boredom.

What were once unreachable dreams have now shifted to actionable definable desires, supported by heavy media campaigns. Television, the Internet and tween magazines all trumpet the same song, keeping dreams of fame and fortune tangibly alive.

Boy bands such as the Backstreet Boys,*NSync and Westlife receive 10,000 fan messages a day. Anyone can visit Jennifer Lopez at her site and chat with her online. Today's stars and icons communicate directly with their fans on their Web sites, often directly e-mailing their most important notices. Mariah Carey bypassed the press and her record company when she spoke directly to her fans on her site about her depression. Madonna calls for feedback on her last concert by e-mail. She's even gone as far as to arrange exclusive Internet-only concerts for her devoted followers.

The long distance between the average tween and stardom has become shorter. The possibility of discovery becomes ever closer.

TRIBES

'I believe in brands'

Being famous *and* surrounding yourself with the right brands go hand-in-hand in the life and aspirations of tweens. Brands have almost acquired a religious feel and exist right up there on the ladder of priorities for today's tweens. Functionality of a product was the main attraction to the tweens of the 1980s, but since the 1990s brand has taken over and is ultimately more important than function.

What has become clear is that more and more tweens define their worth, their role in the social hierarchy, their popularity, and their success by the brands they wear, eat and live with. It is therefore logical that increasing numbers of tweens endeavour to surround themselves with the best possible brands as this helps them gain the recognition and social status to which they aspire. The role of brands has therefore changed – functionality takes a back seat to the belief that along with ownership of a brand comes success and admiration.

The admiration of the group is very important, but despite everyone being aware of the 'officially' popular items, personal taste and individuality also play a role.

Tweens choose their friends by the clothes they wear, the music they listen to and the electronic games they play. It's all part of the package that creates an identity and a sense of belonging. It could be said that those that share brands belong to the same tribe. Members of a tribe share more than brands. They share a taste in music and will likely identify with the same sporting teams – if they identify with sport at all. The ties that bind members are not necessarily dependent on the more traditional definitions of identity – ethnicity and gender, age and location. These are ties based on shared passions. And what's unique about tween tribes is that they have become active advocates for the brand. The members share a sense of ownership of 'their' brands, which helps market the product and drive the sales.

The dramatic change in the role of brands has been part of the advertising agencies' long-term goals. It was initially the advertisers who envisioned turning brand into a form of religion, to increase their sales. And it has worked.

What makes them believe?

If you can help tweens dream you are well placed to capture their imagination. In 1962 during the early days of space exploration, JF Kennedy promised that within the decade man would step on the moon. He managed to appeal to the collective imagination of the Western world. Everyone who looked up at the night-time sky and saw the moon couldn't help but think that soon someone was going to be walking up there.

Capturing the imagination of tweens is about creating enough space for dreams. *Star Wars* and *Spider-Man* succeeded because both movies successfully combined fantasy and reality.

The dream factory

Almost all tween films that have been box-office successes have blurred the divisions between fantasy and reality. This formula has made Steven Spielberg one of the most successful movie-makers in Hollywood history. It was nearly two decades ago that he created the adorable character, ET. *ET – the Extra Terrestrial* was embraced in a decidedly human way. Despite his baggy skin and odd-shaped head, 34 million tweens came to own a replica of him in one form or another.

AI Artificial Intelligence, a more recent Spielberg movie, attempted to appeal to the tween audience by again mixing dreams and reality. The creation of an artificial human being, almost as human as a real human, was introduced into a real family. The boundary between the real and the artificial was seamless, often making it difficult for the viewer to detect the difference.

In *Jurassic Park*, a zoo of dinosaurs was re-created using genetic material and cloning technology. The movie used a persuasive argument for how Jurassic Park could become a reality. Many tweens almost believed that the story was true.

One thing that these fantasy-reality movies have in common is that they all have a character that differs from the others. ET, David in *AI*, Harry Potter and Shrek all stand apart as unusual or odd. They are different from all the others in their world. They have either special skills or problems with being accepted, and they take risks that no-one else dares to take. Characteristics of perfection appeal to most of today's tween audience.

Facing daily challenges to be good at school, fighting and often failing to be the best player on the team, and struggling to win acceptance among the opposite sex are all problems that they feel they alone are suffering. Tweens all experience problems of connection to a greater or lesser extent. They all long for acceptance; nobody wants to be left out of the crowd.

The common denominator for these successful movie concepts is that as well as mixing fantasy and reality, they leave the story open-ended so that tweens can pick up and continue where it left off. This way tweens have *carte blanche* to dream away without ever losing credibility in the eyes of their friends. And that is exactly what the fabrication of dreams is about: finding common denominators between the audience and the movie, the toy, the clothes – in other words, the brand. The dream weavers create an opening for the audience to let their imaginations run freely. They can be different without being laughed at.

Building trust among a skeptical audience

Creating space for the imagination is easier said than done. No amount of audience research can secure a film box-office success. No amount of product testing can assure a winning toy or clothing item. They can only, maybe, prevent a market disaster. However, it is possible for extensive testing to prevent innovation.

There are always stories about the one that got away. No publisher would touch the Ninja Turtles when they were on offer in the 1980s. They simply could not accept that turtles would make viable action heroes. So in the end the creators had to fund and publish the cartoons themselves before the powers-that-be even noticed them. *Titanic* Director James Cameron actually resigned two-thirds of the way into the job because the studio cut the budget when their tests showed that the film was not looking promising. He later returned to his job, and the film went on to become the biggest box-office hit in history, grossing US $1,835,400,000, a statistic that bears witness to the many young tweens – mostly girls – who saw the movie more than twice.

Being 110 per cent direct

Today's tweens like things to be instant. They don't have the patience to listen to long-winded explanations which take circuitous routes to reach the point. They want their talk direct. They want to be engaged in an honest and frank dialogue without too much embellishment. Trying to appeal too wide, to both sexes, across a broad age segment, and across too many cultures, will result in the instant death of a brand.

So focusing on a very narrow segment, with a message that offers a direct opinion is the way to go. Once there's acceptance, the target group will become a magnet which attracts the attention of other audiences.

Being 110 per cent direct means not only showing an opinion but sticking to it. It means provoking a response in one type of audience, which will come to be admired by other groups. It means being different and being first, but not necessarily being the loudest.

Some of the most popular campaigns have succeeded by being secretive. In 2002, Nike decided to use funds they saved from sponsorship on a FIFA World Cup advertising campaign. The campaign asked groups of tweens and teens to team up and compete across the world, using the Nike site. Winning teams were asked to wear a Scorpio sign on their shirt. During the World Cup events in Korea, many people spontaneously showed their secret-sign shirts. Those in the know immediately felt a sense of belonging to the Nike tribe. Others simply missed the point. When the result of the effort was evaluated, Nike appeared to win in both brand and equity share, even though Adidas was the only shoe sponsor of the event. This reinforces the idea that once a particular group has been targeted, they're given a coded message that only the chosen group can decode. A feeling of closeness is fostered among those who understand the message. If you can't decode the message, you don't belong.

Having a 110 per cent opinion

Having an opinion is exactly what it's all about. The stronger the opinion the better. It was rumoured that SMP – an Australian brand – stood for Sex, Money and Power. The tweens loved it. Sales of the clothing brand soared within months. In actual fact it stood for Smith, Mercury & Powell.

A mineral water named Splitrock had four very small letters printed on the side of the smart, trendy label: FYGH. And so the rumours began. It was put about that they appeared there by mistake, and they stood for 'Fuck You Go Home'. The mineral water tasted like most other mineral waters. But in just four years, this has become the second largest-selling mineral water in Australia.

In a world where tweens fear mediocrity, they embrace brands which distinguish them as being different. Somehow the brand has an ability to elevate them above the grayness of the everyday and add colour to their lives. It goes further. Their support of a brand aligns them with a community to which membership is selective. Unless you get the brand's message, you can't belong. And if by its very nature the message excludes adults, so much the better!

Both Nike's Scorpio, SMP and FYGH are examples of secret brand marketing, where you ensure that initially only a very small community has the exclusive right to understand and appreciate the message.

When Absolut vodka was launched in the United States, their limited budget dictated that they opt for a low-key approach. So instead of blitzing the media and placing bottles on every possible shelf, they chose a more exclusive strategy. They only launched the vodka in two cities, New York City and San Francisco. They targeted the gay community, knowing that many a trend has begun in the urban gay neighbourhoods. Their lack of money proved to be their absolute good fortune. In less than a year Absolut was considered *the* vodka to drink. And the fact that it was only served in a few selected exclusive bars in only two cities added to its mystique and desirability.

In a short 10 years, Absolut vodka has since gone on to become the largest-selling brand of vodka in the United States. But it has not forgotten its roots. Each time a new Absolut product is created – including Absolut Kurrant, Absolut Mandarin and Absolut Vanilla – it first establishes itself in the gay community in New York City before being launched nationally. All the gimmicks that accompanied the promotions, the battery-driven badges, flashy hats and specially-designed coasters, were targeted at this exclusive audience.

Absolut vodka is now a mainstream product. It arrived in a specially-targeted community with attitude and panache. Its clear opinion of itself was a winner. However, one should be aware of the possibility of choosing the wrong audience for the message. Appealing to the gay community was a risky strategy, in that it may have backfired and been perceived as a drink for gay men only. But the risk paid off and the Absolut brand entered the larger market with ease.

Deliver more than 110 per cent

As a kid I always counted how many LEGO bricks were left over after I'd built the model precisely to the instruction manual. Over the years I realized that each box contained a few spare blocks. It took me a while to realize that this was not a packing mistake, and that LEGO was purposely giving more than what was required – almost as a gift. Their generosity thrilled me and reinforced my loyalty. I felt each extra block was a personal gift.

Some years later I got the chance to visit the factory. There I learnt that generosity was not the motive for providing the extra bricks. LEGO realized that making a successful model depended on a crucial small piece. If that small piece went missing it would be very stressful for the child who was making the model. In addition, it was a costly time-consuming exercise to follow up requests for single pieces, so they included two identical pieces as a safeguard. The instruction manual would also list other building ideas that often required the additional element. Had I not been told the practical reasons the manufacturer added the extra pieces, I would still believe it was to make kids feel they were getting a little extra.

This raises an interesting point. The cost to the manufacturer for going the extra 10 per cent is negligible. Likewise, it costs virtually nothing for Kylie Minogue to add a hidden soundtrack to her new CD or George Michael to add a free music video of *Shoot the Dog,* a music video that was banned almost everywhere. But it goes a long way to make the buyer feel they're getting something extra, it generates a huge buzz and, in the end, it inspires loyalty. And that is exactly what branding is all about – not only to create a strong personal loyalty between the tween and the brand but to make the tweens true brand advocates.

SUMMARY

▌ After September 11, 56.1 per cent of all urban tweens across the globe found the word 'religion' important. This dramatic quest for spiritual sustenance has had a very strong effect on today's tweens, making the search as much their own as their parents'.

▌ The search has been made difficult because tweens are not quite sure what they believe in. In fact, they often don't believe in anything at all.

▌ Close to half the world's urban tween population states that the clothes and brands they wear describe who they are and define their social status.

▌ This is a generation that keeps upgrading. The Sony PlayStation is an excellent example of how the desire of the have-more-have-better-have-faster generation has taken over.

▌ Tweens, like so many other groups, are the main source of inspiration for other tweens. So 80 per cent of all urban tweens state that it is important for them to feel part of a group. The group often becomes the replacement for the role traditionally occupied by the family.

▌ Everything that is at stake in a young person's life is vested in their group.

▌ Tapping into the leaders of the packs is the first important step to achieving brand acceptance among the whole group.

▌ Being 110 per cent direct, and being totally honest is the new trend. And today's tweens require everything instantly.

▌ Having 110 per cent opinion is what it is all about. The stronger the opinion the better.

▌ Deliver more than 110 per cent – in short, surprise the kids.

▌ Remember tweens want to be listened to, heard and understood.

ACTION POINTS

▶ How well do you understand your target group? Spend a day with them, in school, at home and in their clubs. Listen to their conversations, their dreams and hopes. Then consider to what degree your concept and communication plan fulfils tweens' need to have something to believe in. Would your concept and brand be able to fulfil this need?

▶ How do you intend to fulfill tweens' need to feel part of a group? Would your brand be able to perform this role, or would you have to adjust your concept?

▶ Do you believe your brand has the potential to be a true leadership brand among the group of young people you met in their schools, homes and clubs? What ingredient is needed to ensure it would be perceived as a true leader? Which elements in your product help a tween to be or feel more in control?

▶ To what degree is your brand 110 per cent direct, has a 110 per cent opinion and can deliver 110 per cent? Which elements in your communication and concept reflect these three ingredients? What activities should you put in progress to ensure that the brand would be perceived as being 110 per cent?

▶ One shot is not good enough. Can your brand be upgraded? If not, what should take place to prepare your concept in such way that it can constantly evolve and generate a new reason for the tweens to purchase the next version?

Arunas Klupsas is an Australian-based freelance photographer, who has contributed to many publications, including *Time* magazine. Arunas was asked to travel the world with his camera to catch the spirit of tweens in their bedrooms for the BRANDchild project. The brief was simple. Arunas was to ask the tweens to hold any item that they feel they cannot live without. His journey spanned 10 cities, from Sydney to San Francisco, beyond Mumbai to Manila. In each city he photographed tweens holding their chosen items. Nothing has been changed or added to these pictures. They are a true picture of tweens across the world.

Mathew Boxell, aged 12, United Kingdom

Yumiko Sakaide, aged 12, Japan

Ashmita Senguipta, aged 11, India

Shunki Tojima, aged 8, Japan

Josephine Hoiland, aged 8, Denmark

Winnie Leung, aged 9, China

Linnea Oddie, aged 11, USA

David Fanagan,
aged 10,
Ireland

Alberto Mellado, aged 8, Spain

Deniz Dilege, aged 8, Turkey

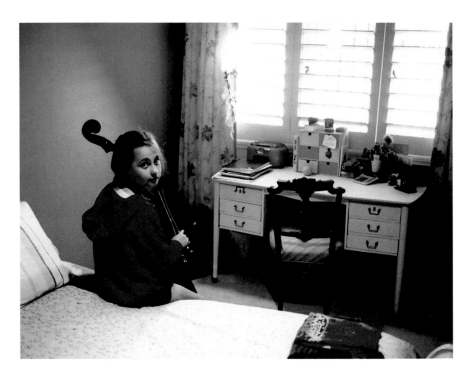

Jessica Bell, aged 8, Australia

What's on tweens' minds? As part of the BRANDchild study we asked hundreds of tweens across the globe to express their feelings about their favourite brands. No brand suggestions were given and they were not allowed to have any help from their parents. The results of this exciting exercise reveal yet another dimension of kids' relationships with brands.

Liu Zhen Yu, aged 10, Japan

Mai Wan Hua, aged 9, China

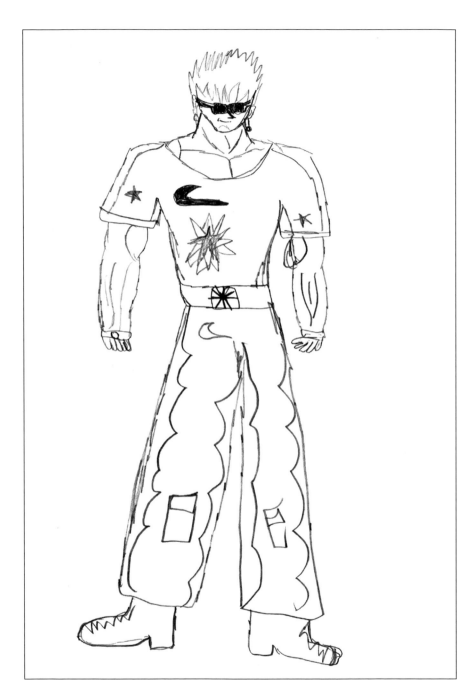

Lailon Bruno Severindviana, aged 11, Brazil

Mischa Sadgrow, aged 12, Australia

Marcus Pavlas, aged 8, Spain

Zhang Yu Chen, aged 9, China

Renan Gabriel Decarine, aged 12, USA

Albert Algreen-Petersen, aged 13, Denmark

Wang Xi, aged 11, Japan

Andreas Due, aged 12, Denmark

Michella Swartz, aged 8, Germany

Naoko Matsuo, aged 10, Japan

5

Creating imagination

Here's a question for you. In one box, there's a piece of paper with the Kinder Surprise logo. It has a picture of the chocolate egg and an alluring image, letting us know that there's also the usual mystery toy. In the other box is the real Kinder Surprise egg. You can touch the egg, hear the toy rattling inside, play with it and of course you can smell and taste the chocolate.

Which one of the two boxes would you say that kids would prefer? Stupid question, really. Of course the box which offers the best possibility to come as close as possible to the real experience will win, hands down.

In light of this, it's hard to imagine why 85 per cent of all promotion and marketing activities appeals to only *one* of the five senses. Furthermore, it's hard to understand why 99 per cent of all promotion and marketing activities in today's world appeals to just two of our senses. In fact, our research shows that less than 0.0002 per cent of all marketing and promotions undertaken in the world are designed to appeal to four or more senses.

Building brands is all about appealing to the senses. If I say Coke, you can feel the fizzy trickle down your throat. Mention Starbucks and you smell the coffee. AOL conjures up an image of a screen pop-up saying 'You've got mail'. And at the first sound of the word 'Intel', the *Intel Inside* melody will swirl around your brain. I can even ask you how a new car smells and you will be able to describe it, even though a truly new car doesn't have any smell at all. The smell you are likely to describe is artificial, and manufacturers routinely spray it into all new cars.

The more senses you appeal to, the stronger the synergy you create between them. So the more senses you harness, the stronger the brand you're likely to build in the consumer's mind. And, the younger the age, the better the hearing, the stronger the sense of smell and the more acute the vision. So tweens constitute a perfect target for sensory-enhanced messages. The preferences formed at this young age have the potential to last forever.

Building a brand in the tween segment of the marketplace should ideally involve everything bar putting an ad in the paper. It's about formulating a detailed strategy that aims to appeal to *all* the senses. So the stronger the sensory experience your campaign can create, the wider the margins allowed for the tween imagination to be indulged.

BUILDING THE SENSORY EXPERIENCE

Most people would probably think Pokémon started life as a card collection game. It didn't. Pokémon originally began as a video game. And it was on the electronic screens of the Nintendo Gameboys that tweens first met the 150 or so different Pokémon characters designed for Japanese kids.

Video games, by their very nature, offer levels of complexity and challenges, and were ideally suited to provide the perfect venue for the Pokémon characters to show their distinct personalities and demonstrate their 'powers'. The Pokémon game was the platform for the Pokémon brand to kick-start what would become the world's largest success story in the game-licensing card-collecting business. The video game gave the characters identities, the collection cards gave them powers, the movie added life to the brand, and word-of-mouth spread the news.

As with all brands intent on taking the licensing route, this not only opened the door to a billion-dollar opportunity, but also presented some very challenging decisions regarding the best way to maintain the brand.

LICENSING IS MORE THAN JUST SPREADING THE NEWS

Licensing is one of the most successful ways to add life to your brand. According to a survey undertaken by the Toy Manufacturers of America, of all the toys sold in 2001, 46 per cent were based on licensing. It's important to note that this figure does not include clothes, music and all the other gear manufactured for the children's market but not classified as toys.

Licensing has proved to be one of the most effective ways to develop the potential of a brand. Over the last few years the toy licensing business has grown by 23 per cent per annum. This makes licensing the highest revenue-generating category within the tween segment of the market.

YOU'VE GOT BRITNEY

'Britney knows my e-mail inbox better than I do!'

In 1998 AOL carved out a small piece of history when they, as the first dotcom company in the world, introduced a true integration between a branded AOL tagline and a movie. They simply licensed the 'You've got mail' phrase to the movie-making branch of Warner Bros. Shortly after, Warner Bros released a comedy based on an e-mail romance called *You've Got Mail*. The movie was a winner. It not only received global press coverage, but every time the name came up it conjured up the AOL brand and added new meaning to fresh e-mail sitting in the inbox. Now there was also romance and mystique associated with an AOL ISP account.

The AOL branding exercise didn't stop with the movie. By the end of 2001, AOL secured another blockbuster deal adding yet another dimension to the 'You've got mail' tagline. They added a voice. Not just any old computer-generated voice, but the voice of the 2001 pop sensation, Britney Spears. The dulcet tones of Ms Spears first welcome you to your mail box, let you know if you do in fact have mail, and then wish you a pleasant day when you leave. The deal was a multimedia bundle. Every purchase of AOL software sold in the United States came packaged with a copy of Britney's latest CD.

But that wasn't all. The cross-promotional deal offered AOL subscribers tickets to Britney Spears' concerts before general release, and for the lucky few there were opportunities to attend pre-concert sound checks, and special on-stage seating was also provided for the actual events. And, of course, there was a chance to chat with Britney live on AOL.

So, you may ask, what is the connection between a pop singer and an ISP? The answer is clear. Ten million tweens access AOL on a daily basis, making it the most popular ISP service for this market segment in the world. And each one of those 10 million tweens is a target audience for Britney. But this exercise was not only valuable for her. In 2001 Britney Spears was one of the best-selling artists within the tween segment. She had an enormous ability to both attract and retain visitors to the AOL site, a clear win-win situation which once again managed to position the AOL brand as the leading ISP for tweens.

THE NETWORKED BRAND

'I never see a movie without first playing the game'

Over the past 10 years, marketing aimed at children and tweens has developed beyond the odd single product to well-organized networked campaigns known as network marketing. Seemingly unrelated product categories that span gender and age segments are linked together, the essence of the brand often being the only visible connection. As one tween remarked: 'There's no such thing as a movie without a game – and there's no game without a movie. And if a movie preview doesn't list a Web site, it's death.'

The key to the success of network marketing is distribution. AOL, Disney, McDonald's and Starbucks are all brands with highly visible distribution networks. There's invaluable daily exposure with no additional costs.

In 2000 Burger King and the pop group *NSync signed what was then the world's most expensive co-promotional deal. It was valued at US $50 million. The restaurant chain offered *NSync meal packages and exclusive promotions to all *NSync CDs.

Yahoo! has also capitalized on the youth market. Their teen-targeted chats remain one of the most popular sections of their site. They also use pop stars as draw cards. Ronan Keating, Backstreet Boys and the Hansons have all interacted with fans on the Yahoo! chat channels. This co-promotion has not only generated traffic but continuously freshens an image.

Or what about Columbia Tristar, the studio that created the *Dawson's* desktop, an original Net property created as a fan vehicle for the television series, *Dawson's Creek*? Fans could access Dawson Leary's (the show's heart-throb) desktop. It came complete with an e-mail inbox, and an online journal authored by the fictional representation of Dawson Leary's computer desktop, complete with an online journal authored by the *Dawson's Creek* writing team. More than 1.5 million visitors clicked onto the desktop each week, providing fertile ground for yet another business opportunity. The desktop earned many Internet awards and broke Sony online traffic records.

It is, however, interesting to learn that the market share of the brands or the strength of distribution they represent is always enhanced when brands team up. Take Kellogg's, for example. It is the world's largest producer of cereal with annual sales of US $9 billion, and represents products like Tony the Tiger, Rice Krispies and Ernie Keebler. But even Kellogg's is forced to take the licensing route in the fight to secure market shares. The three most recent brands launched by Kellogg's are all license-based products from Disney.

BRAND + NOTHING = FIASCO

Over the past 10 years there's been a marked increase in integrated network marketing campaigns. In fact it's almost become essential to have a cross-promotion strategy in place before launching any tween-focused product.

My 11-year-old nephew, caught in the midst of the Harry Potter Philosopher's Stone game puts it quite succinctly: 'I didn't like the game before I read the books – the characters didn't make any sense at all. But now I've read the book, and seen the film and I can't stop playing the game.'

The network marketing rules are straightforward. In almost every case, tween-focused brands will only survive if they're made available on more than one channel. The good old rules about streamlining your brand are no longer relevant. There are now television channels, movie characters, pop and rock stars all feeding toy products, clothing merchandise, soft drinks, cereal boxes, video games, Web sites...

The brand chain reaction is related to the trend for game versions. As every game has a version number constantly generating new sales, so every brand needs to become part of a larger story. To stretch the metaphor: each brand is a link in the chain, and each link adds a new dimension to the story. For the story to succeed it needs to appeal to all the senses in order to secure brand channel synergy.

OFFLINE – ONLINE

'You can buy two types of water at my school – fussy water and Coke water'

In James McNeal's 1992 publication, *Kids as Customers,* the shopping habits of tweens are studied. He reveals that they visit shopping centres, on average, 5.2 times a week – which means 270 shopping centre visits a year. The study showed that children as young as seven regarded shopping as 'necessary and interesting'. Nine-year-olds go even further, regarding the shopping visit as 'a necessary part of life'. From these figures it is clear that the actual physical experience shopping offers is essential in the brand-building process. The combination of off and online marketing opens doors to a whole new way of effectively appealing to the senses.

Most recently Coke and Pepsi have concentrated on advertising their brands in a more tangible physical sense. Coca-Cola has agreed to a US $1.1 million five-year deal with the Sayerville Board of Education in New Jersey, and a US $2.4 million for a 10-year deal with a high school in North Carolina. Pepsi has entered into a contract with Reynolds High, to which they're paying US $2.7 million for similar exposure.

Ironically, neither Coke nor Pepsi is allowed to be sold in these schools, because laws limit school sales of carbonated drinks. However, the regulations mean that both Coke and Pepsi can provide fairly large non-carbonated soft drinks like orange juice, flavoured milk and mineral water. So it's with these drinks that they create a presence – a brand awareness for their more major items. Sounds strange? Possibly. But the reality is that the physical presence has proved to be more important than the revenue earned from sales on school premises.

This deal in many ways gives a clear indication of how valuable the combination of different channels have become to the brand and its sales. In relation to this deal, Pepsi has stated that further along the track, when the school kids have become adults and they're making purchasing decisions, they may very well remember the Pepsi scoreboard on the football oval or that Pepsi funded the school band's field trip. In other words, the brand is weaving itself into the life of the community. It's appealing to all its senses.

Recent figures from Forrester Research show that the effectiveness of marketing to the tween segment is increased by a whopping 200 per cent when several channels are used to convey the message. So when AOL teamed up with Britney, Yahoo! with the Hansons, and Kellogg's with Disney, they succeeded in appealing to the highest number of people via as many channels as possible.

SOUND + SIGHT + SMELL + TASTE + TOUCH = BRAND

'I love candy that talks'

Some years ago Michael Spangsberg, a young Danish confectionery manufacturer, developed a sweet brown candy. When his son saw them he exclaimed: 'They look just like dog farts!' This spawned a whole new range, and Seagull Droppings, Big Boobs and Duckweed followed on from Dog Farts.

Tweens simply loved the provocative names, and children were asked to send in their wildest suggestions. Inventing new names became the nation's latest craze. The company expanded, and in little more than two years, these sweets had become the most popular confectionery items in Scandinavia.

Most tween candy concepts succeed by appealing to several senses. Whereas traditional marketing is commonly based on what we see and what we hear, confectionery that fizzles, crackles and crunches appeals to feel and taste as well. Branding strategies are now embracing the full sensory spectrum.

Figure 5.1 *Dog Farts candy. BonBon became well known in Scandinavia for its alternative naming strategy.*

Sound

Have you ever thought about how important sound is in the Disney theme parks? The chances are you'd probably only notice it if it were missing. Yet sound is a key strategy in almost every Disney endeavour, from movies to television shows right through to the theme parks.

In fact there is a recognizable Disney sound. This has become an auditory icon for the Disney brand. Each park is packed with high-quality speaker systems which are perfectly coordinated to belt out mood music in the background, but also play an integral role in the shows, fading in and out with each passing parade.

The Disney story gets more interesting. When you visit a Disney story, you'll find them playing the same melodies as those that are played in the theme park. Ideally, the music will jog your memory and you will be reminded of the wonderful time you had when you last visited Disney World, thus creating a strong synergy between all the different brand activities, exposed via the many channels, and linked together by the sound.

The value of sound and sales was realized in the development of Muzak in the 1950s. Muzak is the unobtrusive background music that is played in supermarkets, elevators, hotel lobbies and other public spaces. When it was first introduced into supermarkets there was a 10 per cent increase in sales because it created an atmosphere of harmony which in turn increased the concentration of the shopper.

Sound has been an important part of the toy industry for the past two decades. We all remember the *woo-woo* siren on small police cars, the teddy that cries and the doll that calls 'Mama'. Understanding of the true value that sound adds to the item has increased dramatically over the past few years. No doubt current technology has been instrumental in creating new sound opportunities and many new possibilities.

Kellogg's was probably one of the first brands to enhance users' total sensory experiences by appealing to each of the five senses. This succeeds in imparting the total brand experience. The sound of Kellogg's Corn Flakes, Coco Pops, and the snap, crack and pop of Rice Bubbles are all designed and tested in sound labs so that they crunch to tween perfection. In a similar way, car manufacturers have tested and controlled the sound of a car door to ensure that its sound is fully integrated with the brand's image, just as they have done for years when testing and controlling the sound of slamming doors.

There are many who believe radio is our most imaginative channel of all the media available to us. It can reach many cheaply. It has persisted despite the introduction of ever-newer technologies. It speaks to our fantasies, but does not limit them.

Sony also introduced the Walkman. Despite every skeptical prediction, Walkmans became the latest must-have item, and now represent a market of US $2.4 billion worldwide. This huge success can be partly attributed to the excellent sound quality that Walkmans introduced. The right kind of sound is as important to tweens as the visual component of any communication.

The right kind of sound is now also available with computers. So when stereo sound on computers was introduced, it changed tweens listening behaviour in a fairly dramatic way. It was not much more than five years ago when the sound of tweens playing a computer game would be as loud as the game itself. There would be encouraging cheers and disappointed groans, a bit like what you hear in sporting arenas.

No more.

As sound has improved, making stereophonic standard and surround sound a must, manufacturers are dedicating serious resources to the production of sound on computer games.

Today there is no yelling or screaming from the tweens in the background when the play goes on. Silence is important, because too much noise will interfere with the concentration and the imagination of the player. All the current game machines like Sony's PlayStation and Microsoft's X-Box have recording and downloading facilities. This means that tweens can download MP3 music files from the Net, and listen to these via their computer console, at the very least in stereo.

No sound, no brand

It's not hard to see that a product or communication strategy that does not take in sound is probably doomed to fail. But a talking Furby or a pre-programmed melody on a Palm Pilot are not enough. The popularity of karaoke demonstrates that everyone – including tweens – loves to sing along with their favourite tunes. New karaoke products come onto the market every year. In 2002 Hasbro introduced e-kara, a device with a sophisticated karaoke controller and microphone which can connect to any television set. This arrived with a library of melodies, including the obligatory tunes from Britney Spears, the Backstreet Boys and *NSync. Toymax's VJ Karaoke Center goes a step further. It allows tweens to sing along to words on a screen while the video camera which is included in the package catches their performance.

Visit any of the top tween sites in the world, and the sound component is awe-inspiring. It is clear that streaming technology and increased memory and modem size have made it entirely possible to play music on the homepage as well as having it as an integrated element on each page.

Disney Blast (disneyblast.com) was one of the first to introduce sound-based navigation icons. Their navigation panel, which doubles as a keyboard, gives tweens the option of listening to their favourite tune while navigating the site.

Every other communication channel is clearly following this trend. In Europe alone, more than 192 million ring tones were downloaded to mobile phones. According to Forrester Research, of these 192 million ring tones, an astounding 65 per cent are being downloaded by a youthful audience between the ages of 8 and 15. The European-based Arc Group expect that by 2010 the market for personalized ring tones will be worth over a billion US dollars a year. Sound in all its many forms is clearly an outlet for self-expression. Customized ring tones can play *Happy Birthday* on your special day, and can also be programmed so that each person in your address book can be identified by their individually-assigned ring.

It's increasingly becoming a fact of life that every respectable tween will have their own digital library on their hard disk, and that every hand-held game is equipped with stereo sound. Close to 80 per cent of all tweens carry a Walkman or an MP3 player in their bag on their way to school!

Sound should be present on every channel because it creates a strong synergy between the product, the brand's value and the tween. In summary, the sound story is simple – no sound, no brand.

Sight

'When Spider-Man does a double loop, they must have used a Quantel Harry and Paintbox'

Since the mid-1990s the use of startling graphics and the time they take to download on the Net has presented a common decision-making problem for designers. Being members of the instant generation, they have never had the patience to wait for the download. Paradoxically, graphic-poor sites, games and movies have huge problems capturing tweens' attention.

Harry Potter's Philosopher's Stone was the fastest selling computer game in 2001. In little over five weeks it sold 300,000 copies. But this was far below expectations. The problem? Slow graphics. By the same token,

2001 saw a market growth of 19 per cent in collectable card games like DragonBallZ, Ninja Wars, Doomtown and Battel. According to NY Toy Fare, the second-largest trade show in New York, this growth can be directly attributed to the stunning look of the cards, which make extensive use of 3-D and lashings of gold and silver.

Ever-improving technology increases the capacity for ever-more-exciting digital visuals. In just one year – from 2000 to 2001 – memory size of computer games increased by 32 per cent, indicating that in addition to sound, the visual element is of fundamental importance. But this is an improvement across the board. The introduction of high-definition colour displays on mobile phones, sound systems, GameBoys and watches, to name only a few, has opened new avenues for marketers to communicate their brand messages to their tween audience.

So along with the right ring tone, you need the right screen. Tweens have a whole range of icons that they can download onto their mobile phones. In fact the next wave of interactive, dynamic games, downloaded and stored in mobile phone handsets, have already captured an audience of 9 per cent in Europe alone, emphasizing the growing importance of graphics.

Real image versus illustration

It is interesting to see that the balance between the use of illustration and real image does not reflect any specific age. In a tween's world, context is everything: the right style for the right message.

In James U McNeal's book, *Kids as Customers,* he indicates that from the age of 10, children start preferring real images to illustration. This preference is not fixed, because within the next couple of years, tweens swing back to favouring cartoons and illustrations that can more flexibly convey cutting-edge concepts. But cool graphics aren't enough. Animation has become a science in itself. When Nicolas Nigroponte, a professor at MIT Lab and one of the most respected commentators on technologies of the future, predicted as far back as 1995 in *Wired* magazine that computer games would create a market for game accoutrements like uniforms, guns, and maps, he was spot on. A game like Black Hawk Down offers the player the opportunity to purchase extra equipment and 'jumps', 'falls' and 'kicks' for around US $10. The fascination of a player with a special kick that no-one else has is reward enough, and adds an extra dimension to winning the game.

Graphics and animation go hand in hand, reflecting the fact that most icons, characters, fonts and commercial messages we see both online and in the radio world are booming. I recently received a seven-line message. Each letter of each word jiggled and jumped on the screen while forming its message. It was almost impossible to read – it hardly made sense.

According to an AIM/AC Nielsen research study conducted in Copenhagen in 1995, the right use of high-quality graphics on in-store displays has shown to increase sales by more than 16 per cent. Use of television screens adds an extra 7 per cent in brand awareness.

Strong visuals don't apply only to the product, but basically to every element connected with the brand. High-quality graphics are vital across all channels – the cinema, the package design, the in-store displays, the promotion materials, the Web, the games or the mobile phone.

The conclusions we draw from the visual element of branding are identical to the conclusions we drew from the sound element: no cool graphics, no cool brand.

Touch

'I love the feeling of Barbie's leather jacket – it's so cool'

Who would ever have imagined that computer games would reach a stage where they could pose a possible health risk, not only to the eyes and ears, but to the body? It's now possible to imagine that computer games have reached a stage where they are becoming potential health risks. As game manufacturers increasingly work at creating a virtual reality, so the risks increase.

In 1999 it was reported that Sony was spending tens of millions of dollars developing new ways to appeal to a third sense. Their focus was on the tactile. And with the release of the PlayStation there's a force-feedback controller that brings everyone much closer to tactile involvement in the game.

The flip-side to Sony's success was revealed when doctors at the Royal Liverpool Children's Hospital in the United Kingdom reported the case of a 15-year-old boy who was suffering from hand pains most often associated with a condition known as 'vibration white finger', previously only experienced by people operating powerful vibrating tools like chainsaws. They attributed the cause of this condition to the boy's daily use of his Sony PlayStation, where the vibrations on the rumble board transmit

Figure 5.2 *Pictures, illustrations and icons are taking over our written language. Not surprisingly, Japan leads this trend using their mobile phone's own camera facility to communicate instead of the voice or written word.*

vibrations to the hands and arms of the player, giving a 'feeling' of the on-screen action.

This case is, to date, rare, and many new computer games with just such sensory attributes are now on the market. The Digital Dance Station, which involves two players who move together on a touch-pad dance board, is proving to be one of the more popular. The game was first introduced in gaming halls, but has quickly moved into homes, conclusively proving that involving more than two senses was not only sustainable, but hugely viable.

Over the years several more traditional toy makers have successfully appealed to touch. The Touch is a board game which tests the players tactile senses as the participants race to gather a bizarre assortment of shapes and figures before time runs out. But as we know, toys rapidly lose their appeal to older children, who turn their attention to music, computer and video games.

A Razorfish study conducted in 2000 indicated that goods that appealed to our sense of touch added up to 17 per cent extra value to the total entertainment experience. In other words, to add a touch component to your product will potentially tap into a huge market of tweens waiting to embrace a more total experience in whatever they do.

There is no doubt that the technological problems posed by adding the touch component is the major reason it hasn't yet been exploited to its full potential. However, once this technological barrier has been overcome, we are sure to see more.

Smell

'I just love the smell of a fresh *Donald Duck* magazine'

It's said that the best way to sell your house is to put on some classical music, brew a pot of coffee and maybe bake a loaf of bread before potential buyers arrive. This worked well for a bank in the United Kingdom. In 1999, when their customer numbers were declining, they introduced complimentary freshly brewed coffee in all of their many branch offices. Not only did their customer traffic increase, but so did their approval rating.

Smell is the most neglected of all of the human senses. We seem to be quite unaware that almost 75 per cent of what we perceive as taste actually comes from what we smell. Using aroma as a tool to attract or retain perfume customers was first used in the 1920s in France. The technique spread to other businesses three decades later.

In the late 1950s, American movie-makers experimented with olfactory cinema. It was the movie industry's attempt to compete with the huge threat of television.

Aromarama was a system that was used in *Behind the Great Wall,* a documentary that had 72 scents which ranged from night-club smoke to Oriental spice. These were specifically timed to pump through the theatre's ventilation system on cue. Another attempt at adding the olfactory sense to cinema was called Smell-O-Vision. This was dispensed from under each seat. The idea failed to take off.

Two decades later, in 1981, underground filmmaker John Waters famously used smell as a self-satirizing gimmick in *Polyester.* Waters presented his film in Odorama, and distributed numbered, scratch-and-sniff cards to the audience.

Over the years several attempts to appeal to our olfactory sense have been made. The most successful of these 'smellable' products have been the paper perfume samples found tucked into the pages of many magazines.

As with all our senses, our sense of smell declines with age. An article published in 2000 by Discovery Communications Inc. said children's olfactory capabilities are likely to be an astounding 200 per cent better than older people's. If we cast our minds back we can remember the fascination we had as children with stink bombs, strawberry-flavoured erasers and the peculiar smells that wafted out of chemistry sets.

Imagine this: simulation computer golf games where not only do you feel the whack of the club against the ball, but experience the smell of fresh lawn on the fairway. Or how about race-track games surrounded by gasoline and burning rubber and Max Payne's underarm perspiration, tempered by the smell of burning flesh? This will be one giant step closer to achieving the ultimate virtual reality experience.

There's every indication that within five years this will be common. The company Digiscents worked with the toy manufacturer Mattel in developing an iSmell box. Before going broke in April 2001, they concentrated on designing everything from the unique scents of fire to Barbie's perfume. iSmell is a small black plastic box not much bigger than an electric pencil sharpener. A small fan blows air over tiny vials of oils that are selectively heated in response to computer commands. So in a way that's similar to a computer monitor displaying millions of colours by mixing various proportions of red, yellow and blue, so Digiscents' strategy was to generate billions of odours by blending different proportions of 100 to 200 primary scents.

Smell can be aesthetically important, because it bypasses the conscious brain and communicates directly with the limbic system. It's an opportunity for movie-makers, advertisers and Web designers to evoke emotions that are literally uncontrollable. That's the power, and perhaps the danger, of communication via smell.

Taste

'I have an eraser which smells like strawberries – it smells so good that I'm almost going to eat it'

It starts at a very young age. Blending unlikely tastes is a common adventure for most kids. They mix together flavours and textures and end up with extraordinary concoctions that only they can eat. Playing with food begins in the high chair. It's an important part of the development of play. There's barely a tween alive who has not, at some point in their lives, heard the words, 'Don't play with your food.'

Food as toys, or perhaps more accurately, candy as toys, is a venture that's become increasingly sophisticated over the years. A veteran of this venture is the Kinder Surprise organization, which has been inserting toys in chocolate eggs since 1975.

Since then numerous restaurants and fast-food chains have adopted the concept. In 1979 McDonald's introduced the Happy Meal, which consisted of a burger, French fries, a Coke and a toy all packaged together in a colourful box. It didn't take long for Burger King and Wendy's to follow.

McDonald's grew with their childhood Happy Meal eaters, and in 2001 launched a food-and-toy concept aimed specifically at tweens. Their Mighty Kids meal is served in a more mature-looking brown paper bag and is co-branded with movies and games like *Spy Kids*. Each Mighty Kid meal offers one in a range of about nine available toys in each promotional period.

So many of the new sweet treats that come onto the market come with a gimmick. Spinning lollipops that light up like lasers or play music. Candy that explodes. Each pack of Kellogg's breakfast cereal includes game cards, fake tattoos or some sort of promotional item. There are competitions to be won and free soda vouchers to be claimed – proving that the line between candy and toy is constantly blurring.

Catering to the taste of tweens has gone further. Extreme super-sour or super-hot flavours are gaining in popularity. It wouldn't be surprising to hear that someone, somewhere is working on an ice-cream that will burn your mouth. In fact, the Cornish Chilli Company, a British chilli sauce manufacturer, developed a summer sizzler – chilli-flavoured ice-cream! Apparently you don't feel the chilli when the ice-cream hits the tongue, but it gives a real kick when it reaches the throat!

IT ALL ADDS UP

Appealing to today's tween generation has become a complex business. It is all about creating the best possible concept to stimulate their imagination. The ways of doing this are only limited by the product manufacturer's imagination. But as the history of every trend indicates so far, including multiple channels and appealing to as many senses as nature has provided offers the best platform for success.

There is, however, a fine balance that needs to be struck. The broader the net you cast, the more brands you license, the less control you may find you have over your brand. And losing control of your brand is equivalent to committing brand suicide. It's important to secure brand synergy with licensing partners and maintain control over their use of it.

A child recently commented: 'I'm sick of Harry Potter. He's everywhere. For a whole year I played his games at home, read his books at school, brushed my teeth with Potter toothpaste, washed my hair with Potter shampoo. But I'm over him. I really can't see why I bothered with Potter toothpaste – it's ordinary toothpaste anyway!' He was not alone – in fact our *BRANDchild* study shows that nearly 40 per cent of tweens think Harry is fading out or past it.

SUMMARY

▌ Building brands is all about appealing to the senses. The more senses you can appeal to, the stronger the synergy you create between them, and the stronger the brand you're likely to build in the consumer's mind.

▌ The toy-licensing business has grown by 23 per cent per annum. This makes licensing the highest revenue-generating category within the tween segment. This is largely due to the fact that most of these toys appeal to several senses.

■ Over the past 10 years, marketing aimed at children and tweens has developed beyond the odd single product to well-organized networked campaigns, known as network marketing.

■ The future brand formula looks like this: Sound + Smell + Sight + Taste + Touch = Brand.

■ Sound: when sound was first introduced in supermarkets there was a 10 per cent increase in sales, because it created an atmosphere of harmony, which in turn increased the concentration of the shopper. No sound, no brand.

■ Sight: the richer the graphics, the more successful. Graphic-poor sites, games and movies have huge problems capturing tweens' attention.

■ Touch: over the years several more traditional toy-makers have successfully appealed to touch. It's predicted that touch will be the fastest growing sense of them all.

■ Taste: do I need to say more than Happy Meal? Brands building their platform on taste are true winners.

■ Smell: we seem to be quite unaware that almost 75 per cent of what we perceive as taste actually comes from what we smell.

ACTION POINTS

▶ To what degree does your brand currently appeal to all five senses?

▶ What needs to change for your brand to appeal to as many senses as possible?

▶ Develop a brand sensory strategy. Working on a sense-by-sense basis, develop a plan for how you intend to appeal to each of the different senses in the most optimal way.

▶ Conduct exactly the same exercise for your three closest competitors, as well as for a brand you simply admire.

▶ Lock yourself into a set of predefined sensory values which you use time and again, channel-by-channel, in a consistent way, no matter where. If you can not only succeed in branding your graphic design, but use sound and even smell, then you are most likely to be two steps ahead of your competitors. Remember, the more senses you appeal to, the stronger brand equity you will build.

6

How do tweens *feel* about brands?

Patricia B Seybold

When your son heads to the laundry room to grab a shirt out of the dryer to wear to school, which one does he pick? A plain black t-shirt? Or the ratty green one with the name and logo of his favorite computer game or rock band emblazoned on it?

What about your daughter? When she's getting dressed for a day of hanging out with her friends, will she pick the plain blue comfortable Lands End t-shirt you bought for her, or will she go for the worn yellow one she found at the mall a year ago, the one with the cartoon angel winking, or the purple one her friend gave her, with the 'Girls Kick Butt!' slogan on it?

You know the answers to these questions. But do you know why tweens have such strong preferences in the brands they put on their bodies?

BRANDS VS NO-BRANDS

Tweens have a deeply passionate relationship with brands. If you give a tween the choice of picking a plain t-shirt over one with a brand name, picture, slogan or logo on it, 98 per cent of them will choose the shirt with a brand or logo over the plain style.

Here's what tweens say about 'no-brand/logo' t-shirts:

▌ There are no pictures or anything to make the shirt stand out!
▌ There's nothing happy on it.

- It's just a plain shirt, with nothing cool on it!
- I won't feel as cool as I would in a shirt that had something on it.
- There's nothing to talk about on my shirt.
- Shirts with things on them show your interests.
- Not cool – nothing to distinguish me from the nerds.
- The logo/words express how I feel.

e-imagery or words on a tween's shirt are really important. It's not acceptable to be anonymous. You must express who you are by sporting an image, a slogan or a logo. No surprises there. What's really surprising is how passionately tweens feel about the imagery they wear to express themselves.

Here's what tweens say about the imagery on their favourite t-shirts:

- I feel proud when I wear it because it has the American flag on it!
- I feel happy when I wear it because I'm proud of the Titans.
- I feel good when I wear it because DragonBallZ is fun.
- I feel excited to know so much about dinosaurs.
- I feel cool because the Power Puff Girls are cool!
- I feel silly because he has a silly face and it always makes people laugh.
- I feel strong because the Samurai on my shirt is strong.

Brands are extremely important to tweens, both for what the brand itself means to them, and even more for what the brand means *about* them, to themselves and to others.

HOW PASSIONATELY DO TWEENS FEEL ABOUT DIFFERENT TYPES OF BRAND EXPERIENCE?

Using the spontaneous, emotional survey techniques developed by Resonance® Surveys and conducted by Gang & Gang Inc., we looked at three different panels of US tweens with the same demographic make-up, to measure their reactions to three different types of brand experience:

- How tweens feel about drinking their favourite brand of soft drink.
- How tweens feel about attending their school, the same public school in a Connecticut suburb.
- How tweens feel about wearing their favourite branded or logo t-shirt.

Resonance Surveys use open-ended topics to elicit spontaneous emotional reactions, then deploy a proprietary normalization protocol to gauge the relative passion of these reactions and then to link those spontaneous emotional reactions to a 'rational' explanation. After the emotional reaction, what are the phrases that turn up in the mind linked to them? What's different about the Resonance survey technique is that it is able to capture survey respondents' spontaneous emotional responses to the experience being surveyed, and to accurately calibrate these on a spectrum ranging from passionately negative to passionately positive.

Gang & Gang characterizes the degree of passion that survey respondents have as the *emotional jet fuel* that marketers can use. If the experience is passionately positive and you understand what makes it so, you have a running start. If the experience is passionately negative, and you understand why, you know what to avoid, what to fix or what to market against.

Note that the amount of passion that tweens feel in relation to the experience of wearing their favorite branded t-shirts is off the charts in terms of all the market research that Gang & Gang has done over the years. A typical level of positive passion about a favourite consumer product is in the 30 per cent range. A really strongly positive brand like Coca-Cola, Sony, Disney or A&F, may occasionally achieve up to 50 per cent passionate response among its boosters. Yet, the degree of positive passion that tweens feel about the logo t-shirts they wear tops that of even these leading brands, at 59 per cent passionately positive.

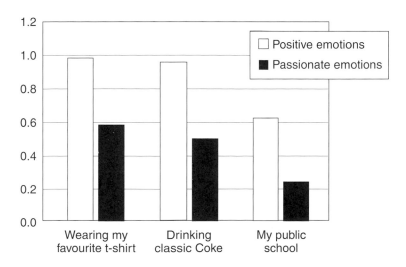

Figure 6.1 *How tweens feel about three experiences.*

When Gang & Gang asked 'How do I feel about my favourite brand of soft drink?' among tweens who are regular drinkers of that brand, their emotional response was 96 per cent positive and 50 per cent passionately positive. In response to Gang & Gang's query: 'How do I feel about my public school?' among a group of tween students of a highly regarded school in an affluent suburb in Connecticut, 62 per cent of the students had positive emotions, but only 26 per cent of them were in the passionate range. By contrast, 99 per cent of the tweens surveyed about how they felt when wearing their favourite logo t-shirt felt positive about it, and a whopping 59 per cent of them were *passionately* positive about the experience.

Steve Gang summarized the results of the branded vs non-branded t-shirt survey: 'Their t-shirt brand appears to be one of the most important brands to these tweens, based on their attitudinal responses. The emotional jet fuel provided by this branded experience is more powerful than most we have measured in other consumer experiences, regardless of age. Fully 86 per cent of these kids show levels of passionate positive emotion, above our 30 per cent benchmark for "exciting experience".'

So we can see how passionately tweens feel about wearing brands versus not wearing brands. In Figure 6.3, we dissect these feelings and see what emotions are triggering that level of passion.

Tweens attach the most emotion to how their favourite t-shirt relates to their self-image. Next in importance was how they felt about the brand,

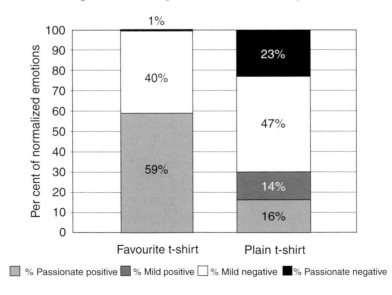

Figure 6.2 *Favourite t-shirts, logo or not?*

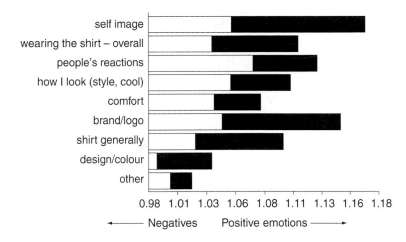

Figure 6.3 *Wearing my favourite t-shirt.*

logo, or image on their shirts. Third in importance was 'People's reactions to me'. Note that there's a lot of passion about self-image, the brand/logo and what it stands for, what people perceived about them when they were wearing the shirt and finally, the general appearance and feel of the shirt.

Here's what kids said that tells us to what extent their self-image is tied up in the brands they wear:

▎ I am brave and confident.
▎ It shows my attitude.
▎ I'm excited about myself.
▎ I like to skateboard and that's what's on the shirt.
▎ Show-off.
▎ 'Cause I just want to do lots of things.
▎ I think I am pretty.
▎ I like to joke around lots.
▎ Because I'm always nice.
▎ I like to play sports lots.
▎ I have no worries.
▎ It's kind of smart-aleck.
▎ I like to play.
▎ It's all about me!

If tweens are passionately attached to the brands they wear, what images are they wearing today? How do they express themselves through these brands?

'Personal' brands are as important to tweens as 'for profit' brands

In September 2002, we surveyed 138 tweens in what we believe is a representative sample of this tween group in the United States. The survey topic was how they felt when wearing their favourite branded or logo t-shirt versus wearing a plain non-branded shirt. The demographic breakdown was 54 per cent boys, 46 per cent girls, and 54 per cent between 9 to 10 years old, with 46 per cent aged 11 to 13, evenly distributed by gender within age levels.

These tweens' definition of brand or logo was quite varied. Less than half the t-shirts carried trendy brand names. The majority carried older brands (Star Wars) or teams (Tarheels, Yankees, Trailblazers), or simply images or slogans.

What emerged was 50 per cent of the group chose to 'self-brand' by selecting older sports teams, icons, slogans or images that are meant to convey the tween's self-image to the rest of the world. Examples are flags, angels or dinosaurs. There also appeared to be two kinds of branded experiences for tweens wearing t-shirts:

1. Tweens are billboards for well-known brands or idols. These brands – music groups, sports teams, video games – are meant to impress others. Examples of these types of brands are Jimmy, DragonBallZ, Pokèmon, GameRooster, Harry Potter, Sponge Bob, Power Puff Girls, Tweety, World Wide Wrestling Federation, Titans, Tarheels and other championship teams, the US Marines, and the American flag (this survey was taken post 9/11 in 2002). Boys appear to favour this use of branding (58 per cent, compared to 31 per cent of girls).

2. In the other case, tweens are using a more personal logo or image or slogan to express themselves. These 'brands' are meant to describe who they are. Examples of these types of brands are dinosaurs, angels, dragons and a variety of slogans. This is the kind of personal branding favoured by girls. But many boys also prefer personal brands.

There was definitely a wide variety of brands or identifiers on these tweens' favourite t-shirts. The well-known or recognized-for-profit brand names came from brands in media (24 per cent), hi-tech and games (8 per cent), retail (10 per cent), consumer packaged goods (8 per cent), and organizations/teams (10 per cent). Boys skewed toward organizations, media and hi-tech.

Other, more personal, identifiers included images (19 per cent – dinosaurs, animals, princesses, angels) and slogans (20 per cent 'Teens Rule!', 'Spoiled Rotten by Nana', 'Girls Kick Butt'). Girls skewed towards images and slogans.

Figures 6.4 demonstrates the differences in emotional motivation between kids who picked a 'personal brand' – a slogan, image, or non-commercial logo – and kids who picked a well-known commercial brand for their favorite t-shirt.

Notice that when kids select personal brands, the emotional jet fuel is primarily related to expressing who they think they are and how they want to be perceived. The importance of the brand or logo recedes.

RELATIONSHIP WITH CORPORATE BRANDS

Both boys and girls will gravitate towards wearing a for-profit brand only if it reflects how they want to think of themselves and be thought of by others. When they select a well-known commercial brand, how they *feel* about the brand image is the major factor in their allegiance to a particular shirt.

For the kids who picked a well-known brand as their favourite t-shirt, here's how they felt about the overall experience of wearing it. Notice in Figure 6.5 that the brand/logo suddenly becomes the most salient factor.

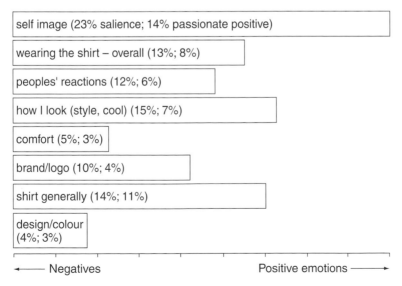

Figure 6.4 *Experience wearing personal brands, images and slogans.*

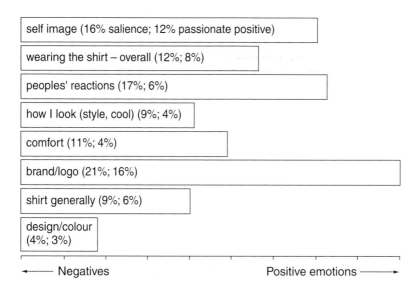

Figure 6.5 *Experience wearing well-known brands.*

So when tweens select a well-known brand, what they really care about most passionately is one that reflects how they want to be perceived. Here's what they had to say about their relationship to these brands:

▌ I like to wear shirts that have my fav character or saying on them.
▌ It's a fun TV show and I want people to know I watch it.
▌ They are a cute cartoon.
▌ I like to see them win.
▌ A&F is the best!
▌ Spongebob is cool!
▌ I like Tweety. Tweety is smiling on the shirt.
▌ I feel happy because they won the championship.
▌ I really like DBZ.
▌ Because the men on the shirt are strong.
▌ Everybody likes WWF.
▌ I like Harry Potter and it feels cool to wear the shirt.

SUMMARY

It's important to realize that tweens have a far more passionate relationship to the brands they wear than is true with any other category of consumer goods. For tweens, the brands with which they adorn themselves absolutely reflect the way they think of themselves and how they want to be seen. They use branding to stand out from the crowd as well as to fit in with their friends. They use branding to express their personalities.

Notice, however, that tweens are just as likely to express themselves by self-branding and creating personal brands that represent their self-image as they are to select commercial brands. Personal branding and self-branding are on the rise and they pack a highly emotional connection to tweens' self-image.

7

Stardust

What do milk, Tommy Hilfiger, Pepsi, Mattel and AOL all have in common? Britney Spears, of course. She promotes all their products. Her name is the most-searched for of all the entertainers on the Internet. On 19 February 2001, Encyclopedia Britannica was forced to shut down their Web site. It was their first meltdown ever. More than 19 million people were visiting. They were not after a new edition of the famous encyclopedia, and nor were they offering any special online deal. It was all about Britney Spears' belly button! Britannica.com had published the first picture.

Pepsi paid an undisclosed amount, rumoured to be more than US $10 million, to get Britney in their latest commercial. It made world headlines, ensuring that even before the commercial went to air, it received huge amounts publicity, reaching an estimated audience of more than four billion people in just over two weeks.

Ironically, all this happened in the same week as a US radio station was being sued after a fan was killed while struggling to catch a glimpse of someone she thought was Britney Spears. The 11-year-old, Susan Santodonato, died after being hit on the head. The radio station, which played a pre-recorded interview with the real Britney, hired a look-alike to sit in a limo and pretend she was really there.

CREATING ICONS WE ADMIRE

'I wanna be blonde, just like Eminem'

Many women will probably remember pretending to be one of the two girls from ABBA, in platform shoes, sparkling clothes and long hair. They probably held a hairbrush up to their lips and sang into it while the ABBA records belted out *Dancing Queen* in the background.

At some stage or another we've all dreamt of popstar fame and fortune. Over the past 10 years many a business has made their own fortunes by catering to these dreams. Tweens are a primary target. Previously, stars were made by mixing great talent with promotion, whereas now they are created by carefully calculated pop machines backed by huge corporate armies that optimize each stage of the formula. Little is left to chance.

The concept is simple. You start with 20,000 volunteers. You then look for the perfect talent recipe. They must have a good singing voice, photogenic looks, a good body and an ability to dance. Out of this enormous sample you select five, and put them through rigorous training which will shape and mould their voices, their movements and their communication skills. Then wave the magic hair-and-make-up wand and, *voila!* you have a group like Popstars.

Popstars the group is the creation of a television producer who selected those who make up the 'group', and went on to make a television show. *Popstars* the television show is now screened in 40 countries and has sold more than 10 million CDs. Its success has largely been due to the fact that it gave tweens a tangible dream and created a perception that dreams can and *do* come true.

MUSIC = DREAMS = BRANDS

'When I play music I leave the Planet Earth'

So why talk about pop stars and music as such an important phenomena? Well, according to our *BRANDchild* survey, music is important for urban tweens in almost all countries. In fact, 45 per cent would prefer to listen to music instead of watching television. India (65 per cent) tops this preference, with Japanese kids showing the least interest (19 per cent). Not surprisingly, 31 per cent of the world's tween population prefers contemporary pop music, surprisingly enough with Japanese kids leading (64 per cent), although tweens in the United States (20 per cent) and India (9 per cent) showed less interest.

The formula is tried and trusted. Music creates dreams. Dreams build brands. Music is by far the highest-ranking revenue channel within the tween segment. Music is much more than a good song. It provides a soundtrack for tweens' lives. More generally, it determines standards for behaviour, reflects opinions, and determines how they relate to one another and to the values with which they identify. Music can be a very effective tool for marketers, particularly when developing brands that will appeal to the tween demographic.

So much of branding is about creating emotions. The link between music and brand is enormously valuable in relation to any brand strategy. Just think back to when you last heard a song on the radio that you haven't heard for years. The music has the power to open a Pandora's box of memories. Not only are you reminded of the time and place where you first heard it, you're also reminded of the emotions that accompanied that place in time.

The first bird calls of spring or the gusty winds of winter also tap into a library of emotional pictures and create a particular mood.

The look of music

'My Mom and Dad love ABBA. I hate them'

Music does more than simply create emotions. It also has an interesting effect on the beginnings of trends. A song suddenly reaches the charts, but there's a whole lot of other information that comes along with the music. When tweens take to a song, they also focus on the artist who performs it. They become conscious of what the artist is wearing, they notice the artist's behaviour, they tune into their speech, their dancing style, their attitude, as well as their opinions and recommendations. A whole new language begins to emerge. This comes with a look and an attitude that taps right into the idea of network marketing.

Popular music and fashion trends have enjoyed a symbiotic relation-ship for many years. In the 1920s, dropped waists, flattened bosoms and swirling bead necklaces went hand-in-hand with jazz. Padded-shoul-dered zoot suits and kick-pleated dresses moved across the dance floor to the big band sounds of swing. Kids wearing ducktails and turned-up Levi's rock 'n' rolled in the 1950s, giving Americans their first taste of tough chic.

One could be forgiven for thinking that everything that came before was merely preparation for the style and music revolution of the 1960s.

Psychedelic colours swirled in sympathy with psychedelic sounds. There were floppy hats, embroidered jeans, mod suits, Mary Quant dresses, topless bathing suits, feather boas and Carnaby Street. The world seemed to be re-invented. New rules, new sounds and new attitudes ruled.

The early 1970s saw Annie Hall and Barbra Streisand wearing men's suits, while Diana Ross and Cher sparkled in Bob Mackie sequins. Later in the decade Malcolm McLaren and Vivienne Westwood respectively took music and fashion to extremes. The Sex Pistols made anti-music music. They wore ripped t-shirts, shredded jeans and pierced everythings – a style that rebellious youth continue to embrace.

The fashion–music mix reached its zenith in the 1980s. The reason the 80s keep haunting us is because the worlds of fashion and music mixed in a way that has rarely been repeated since.

New York designer and artist Stephen Sprouse first styled the 1980s band Duran Duran and later Nine Inch Nails. But he is most revered for his collaboration with Debbie Harry from the group Blondie. In their symbiotic partnership, Sprouse created a dynamic image for Harry that was part sex goddess and part punk poet. His recent collaboration on graffiti bags with Marc Jacobs had X-rated rappers Lil Kim and Missy Elliott reaching for the Louis Vuitton handbags.

These are music-inspired brand and fashion concept times. They promise to intensify over the next couple of years as the distribution of music penetrates into every possible channel. Not only has music continued to determine trends and generate fashion, but it's become an extremely effective brand machine. The line between the image of the icon on the screen and the person walking in the street is harder to draw. Tweens juxtapose glam, punk, disco, rap, new wave, grunge, and electronic styles to create original looks.

The BRANDchild research shows that mainstream music is about to disappear. Pop is no longer the leading genre. Rap is preferred by 29 per cent of the US tween sample. Following this trend to alternative genres are Germany and Brazil, with India standing in stark contrast against the trend. In India, film music is by far the leading genre (30 per cent). This probably comes as no surprise to everyone in Bollywood, which has the largest film industry in the world. No clear musical winner among this generation any longer exists. Many genres are now spread across all countries, covering close to 40 different styles.

MAINSTREAM HAS BECOME SUBSTREAM

It is clear that the mainstream as we knew it the 1970s and 80s is long gone. Today's tweens are reflecting a substantial diversification in their musical taste. This not only reflects a similar diversification in the bands that feature widely, but is also mirrored in the huge diversification of clothing styles, attitudes and opinions among tweens.

Music is no longer limited to radio and television, but is available everywhere. There are numerous music channels on television and whether you're after an unheard-of one-man band or the more global sounds of U2, there are quite literally tens of thousands of alternative music sites on the Net to choose from.

The similarity is that there is no similarity

Visit any tween bedroom and you will realize that the standard look you could have predicted 10 years ago – from the posters on the wall to the books on the shelves – is no longer there. Not only are the music icons more diverse, but there's an unpredictable combination of underground and commercial attractions that's almost impossible to fathom. This sets new challenges for marketers targeting this generation.

There's every style of music covering every range. There's techno, house, hip-hop, rap, glam, punk, disco, new wave and grunge – to name a few. Then with each style there are bands with opinions, values and attitudes which often represent complex and contradictory opinions that are then mirrored in the tweens' view of life.

THREE FUNDAMENTALS

Across the board, tween music contains three fundamental elements essential to the creation of pop idols, which can then gather enough momentum to go on and create products.

Dreams

Dreams are hard currency in the life of a tween. They feature in almost every aspect of their life. The success of the Popstars, Harry Potter and most Disney movies is a clear indicator that every snippet of communication, every brand and every product has to appeal to the imagination of tweens. It has to give them something to dream about.

Romance

Only a gullible few would believe it was pure coincidence that Britney Spears and Prince William were arranging to meet. The tabloid press pursued this with vigour. And, as rumour would have it, Buckingham Palace put an end to the supposed liaison. Because in addition to Ms Spears' wealth and fame, nothing could enhance her standing among her fans more than a real-life romance with a real-life prince. It's hard to find a better scenario to appeal to the dreams and fantasies of every young girl.

Every smile, every move, every piece of clothing pop idols wear is carefully crafted by their image managers, generally the creators of the band. Each comment made to magazine journalists and every utterance to radio and television is designed to fire up the imagination of their audiences. Every smile, every move, every piece of clothing the pop bands today expose to the world is carefully crafted by their creators.

A result of the planning behind bands like *NSync is patently obvious in an interview that Justin Timberlake, the front man for *NSync, gave to *CosmoGirl*. You can bet that every girl reading this interview would believe that she'd be faithful. She's convinced that she'd be true, and she's pretty much certain that she'd be just the right girl for Justin!

> COSMOGIRL: Well, how do you show a girl love?
> JUSTIN: There are all kinds of little things you can do.
> COSMOGIRL: So you tell them you love them, you give them things, you do things for them...
> JUSTIN: All of the above.
> COSMOGIRL: Do you call them 24/7?
> JUSTIN: Well, I'm not annoying. I'll do things like put cards in their drawers... I mean dresser drawers. And scavenger hunts – I'll hide clues, and they'll follow them to the gift.
> COSMOGIRL: That's so sweet! Is it true that one of your girlfriends cheated on you? She must have been totally crazy!
> JUSTIN: Most of the girls I've been with have cheated on me.
> COSMOGIRL: But you don't think all girls are like that, right?
> JUSTIN: I'm trying not to. But I went through a period where I was disgusted. I'd totally give myself to somebody, and she took it for granted

and I was like 'What is anything worth?' I kinda felt like it was all just a game, and I wasn't into playing the game. So I despised women for about a half a year.

Rebellion

'Grunge is not only about music. It's also about showing my friends who I really am'

Over the years, many celebrities have deliberately announced and shared their opinions with the world. U2's Bono based the band's world tour, ZOO, on a range of political messages. By establishing an advanced communication centre behind the scenes, and allowing satellite access to the world, Bono called powerful politicians and other influential leaders from the stage. At each concert he confronted them with tough, opinionated questions which boomed across the concert hall and were broadcast live to his global satellite audience.

The ZOO concerts were instrumental in elevating U2 from a pretty good rock 'n' roll band to one with courage and attitude. Their appeal has encompassed millions of people across the world who are seeking something they can believe. U2 has become much bigger than a band of five men. They're now a fully-fledged brand.

The U2 phenomenon reached new heights in February 2002 when their singer, Bono, became the first popular icon to be invited to join the World Economic Forum in New York. There he rubbed shoulders with the world's richest and most powerful. He discussed world peace with the likes of Bill Gates, and later secured a healthy financial pledge for furthering his work after meeting with US president, George W Bush.

It's getting younger

Younger children are exposed to more issues and conflicts than ever before. As such there's an attraction for them to opinionated performers, and they are drawn to the brands with which their icons are associated. Eminem, the bad-boy American rap singer, is probably one of the best examples of an opinionated artist who succeeds in appealing to kids, tweens and teens. His core audience are white, middle class tweens and teens who live out their rebellion in the heart of suburbia. His meteoric success surprised everyone. Over a three-year period he ranked as the second most successful music artist, with a turnover of close to US $155 million in CD sales alone.

Like U2, Eminem has emerged as more than your basic musician. He has become a brand. His platform is simple: it's all about anger. And millions of tweens across the world – particularly in the United States – identify with the anger he expresses in his lyrics, and his overall take on society and life in general.

A key ingredient in Eminem's success is probably his directness. The tweens have endless admiration for someone who ignores the unwritten rules of society. In fact, this disregard for authority is what elevates his status among tweens. His fans perceive him as a non-commercial singer who cannot be manipulated to serve anyone's goals but his own. He certainly isn't going to kowtow to his record company nor be manipulated into what the image-makers believe he should be.

BRANDING IS ALL ABOUT PERSONALITY

No matter how diverse their music may be, Britney Spears, *NSync, U2 and Eminem all have one important element in common. They all have strong personalities. The biggest challenge for the marketers is (and always will be) to ensure that each and every one of these characters stays true to themselves and to the brand they've created. That way they (and their brand) will continue to have value, and to communicate with the fan base that they've built based almost entirely on the values and standards for which they originally stood.

When Mariah Carey announced on her Web site that she was physically worn down and had to be taken to hospital, the dialogue was structured in such way that it came directly from her and needed to be communicated to her greatest asset – her fans. Rumour had it that even her public relations manager tried to suppress the news, but that she insisted on sharing the details of her problems with her fans. In the days immediately following Mariah Carey's announcement, sales of her CDs doubled.

Similarly, when George Michael was arrested in Los Angeles when an undercover policeman observed him performing a 'lewd act' in a public toilet, it made headlines across the world. He was arrested, charged, then released on US $800 bail. Three days after his arrest, Michael decided to talk with CNN about his arrest and also chose to acknowledge that he was gay. He said, '...This is a good a time as any... I want to say that I have no problem with people knowing that I'm in a relationship with a man right now. I have not been in a relationship with a woman for almost 10 years.'

George Michael implied that the events of his arrest initiated his self-disclosure. He went on to say: 'I don't feel any shame. I feel stupid and I feel reckless and weak for having allowed my sexuality to be exposed this way.' And then shortly after his arrest, he released a music video featuring men dancing in tight black leather uniforms. It also included a scene with two policemen kissing. This release topped the British charts for six weeks and generated more fans than ever.

Let's make no mistake here. It's not that mental breakdown or lewd behaviour in themselves generate sales. Rather it's all about creating brands with which people identify: brands that are human, that have opinions and attitudes, and that can honestly portray strengths and weaknesses.

Another controversial release from George Michael came in 2002 with his heavily political song, *Shoot the Dog*. This was accompanied by a video that graphically depicted George W Bush and Tony Blair's calls for war. In his press release, he states: '*Shoot the Dog* is intended as a piece of political satire, no more no less, and I hope that it will make people laugh and dance, and then think a little, that's all.' No need to add that his point of view was embraced by the world, reflected in huge sales.

The reason why some tween brands succeed and some fail is because of the need to capture the elusive territory of the tween heart. When Mariah Carey revealed that her bright star was wounded and vulnerable, there were thousands of girls able to immediately identify with her. This sympathetic attitude showed up in the sales figures of her latest CD. Similarly when George Michael showed his fans that he, too, was human, and like everyone else could make mistakes, his fans adored him for not hiding anything.

What both brands did was honestly reveal another aspect of their personality. This created an even stronger bond between them and their fans. In all probability, neither of these two scenarios was planned by their public relations machine, but honestly depicted their life dramas.

If Mariah Carey had chosen to deny her breakdown, or if George Michael had continued to gloss over his sexuality, both would probably have very different images today. There would not be the honesty that is now seen, and without it, there would be doubt about conflicting press reports and the public personalities of both.

EVERY BRAND IS A HUMAN BRAND

The difference between the personal branding of established pop stars and traditional branding is not huge. Giving a brand a personality is very important when appealing to tweens. The rule is quite straightforward: the stronger personality a brand has, and the stronger the dialogue it can establish with its users, the stronger the loyalty the brand will create. Almost every successful tween brand proves this theory.

Some years ago Arnotts, a popular brand of Australian biscuits, learned the necessity of appealing to personal values. The company was faced with a threat by an extortionist who claimed to have poisoned some of the product. Experts advised Arnotts that such a threat was to be treated with the utmost seriousness. The extortionist gave them just three days to respond to his demands. So Arnotts immediately recalled their products from every supermarket shelf, destroyed them, and produced a new and totally different package design. Within days it was ready to re-launch the Arnotts brand, one that Australians had known for generations.

In the meantime, the public relations department spun a story designed to appeal to Australian consumers' sense of loyalty and patriotism. They spoke of the danger of local companies being lost to overseas interests, and the possibility of a well-loved Australian company buckling to the will of international competition. The strategy worked. It garnered plenty of community sympathy and support, and prepared the way for a hugely successful relaunch.

The brand survived. It fact, it underwent a renaissance never seen before as people empathized with it and its values. During several campaigns, it managed to position itself as the personal brand of the Australian people. Their loyalty was assured.

BEING DIRECT

When Lester Wunderman wrote about the strength of one-to-one communication in his book *Being Direct*, it probably didn't occur to him that tweens would create a twist on his definition. Increasingly more brands have succeeded by reflecting an 'attitude' – not only in their products but in surrounding communication as well.

Basically, brands can be placed in two different categories: cause-related and attitude, depending on their values.

Cause-related brands

Kellogg's, Mattel and McDonald's are examples of cause-related brands. Typically the brand seeks to find charity organizations or even create their own charity programs, supporting their target group through problems, illnesses and challenges. Ronald McDonald House is a good example of this. Over the past 20 years, McDonald's has established Ronald McDonald Houses across several countries, so helping families stay close to their seriously ill children.

Then there are attitude brands which raise a certain topic or theme in communication. They seek primarily to be provocative. In the 1990s Pepsi used its commercial base to provoke its traditional rival, Coca-Cola. Pepsi did this until its brand was sufficiently mature to be able to speak for itself, and could independently rely on a firm testimonial strategy.

You would imagine that younger children are less affected by cause-related marketing, but the *BRANDchild* study clearly shows that products with a cause are substantially more effective than was first anticipated. Of all the urban tweens surveyed, 84 per cent stated that products that are harmful to the environment should be banned. Brazilian tweens rated highest with 91 per cent sharing this view whilst in contrast 70 per cent of American tweens and 65 per cent of Danish tweens shared this opinion.

The fact that McDonald's devotes a certain percentage of their revenue to good works not only goes a long way to impressing parents, but is also valued by tweens and teens. Interestingly, this does not necessarily mean that they are prepared to pay more for a product or service. But if there's a similarly-priced choice, they will often make their decision based on the cause-related marketing twist.

Cause-related marketing

It is important to stress that cause-related marketing is not a charitable donation. It is a strategically-planned marketing effort designed to increase a company's sales or improve its position in the market place through actions that also benefit a charity. A new report conducted in 2001 by Profitable Partnerships took a representative sample of over 2000 British consumers, and showed that 96 per cent were aware of the mutual benefit of partnerships between businesses and charities or causes such as schools. Increasingly, more companies who wish to appeal to kids and tweens have initiated a cause-related marketing program as part of the brand-building strategy.

For example, Kellogg's has established several programs across most of its market, not only generating loyalty and revenue but also benefiting charities and community organizations. Since 1998 they have sponsored Kids Help Line Australia. Over three years, Kellogg's has allocated A $1.5 million to raising awareness of the service. Each year more than 60,000 kids, tweens and teens between the ages of 10 and 15, dial their number. The organization employs 85 professionally-trained counsellors around the clock to answer calls.

The kids' problems are many and varied, from serious troubles at home to a hard day at school. The service is designed to help them cope with a range of issues, from confusion about relationships, troubles with authority, school bullying, and alcohol and drug problems. They come to Kids Help Line Australia for confidential support, practical help, confidence-building or just to hear someone listen and care. This program not only engenders loyalty between parents and the Kellogg's brand, but also generates loyalty between the Kellogg's brand and kids.

Tesco, the UK's largest supermarket chain, with Walkers Crisps, leveraged this knowledge by introducing the Tesco Computers for Schools and Walkers Crisps for Schools partnership. These two programs alone managed to raised over £100 million for schools.

The concept was simple. The idea was to provide schools with the opportunity to acquire much-needed resources. At the same time consumers were given the chance to make a positive difference to the schools in their community by going about their regular buying activities. All they had to do was give their check-out receipt to the relevant collectors.

Attitude branding

'Diesel hates advertising, so I love Diesel'

From about the age of 12, attitude-based brands start to have a distinct appeal. Cause-related brands still have a place, but now there's a combination of cause-related brands and attitude brands, depending on the product.

Benetton started a whole trend by launching their United Colors advertising campaign. This campaign first shocked, was later loved and then came to be intensely disliked by most people around the world. The brand displayed full-on attitude based on the concept of 'united colors'. Over a period of 20 years the attitude has gained in strength and visibility. It took its message to the limit and occasionally tested boundaries.

Through its advertising campaigns, Benetton brashly offered opinions on everything from religion, sex, illness, racism and politics. It went as far as to photograph prisoners on death row in the United States. It showed seriously disabled people wearing the stylish Benetton brand. Often the press generated on each campaign was ten-fold in value compared with the money spent on advertising. Frequently the ads were banned from tube stations in London or on the streets of Rome.

But over the years it's clear that some of the most successful tween and teen campaigns have succeeded exactly because they had an opinion and were not afraid to share it with the world.

The clothing brand Diesel has given its 2002 spring/summer catalogue a name. They call it 'Happy Valley'. Come 'this way to Happy Valley, home of Donald and friends'. It shows a Ronald McDonald-like character on the cover. As in the Benetton ads, if you didn't know the Diesel brand you would have difficulty identifying the message being pushed. But as with Benetton, the opinion creates the brand.

On the first page of the Diesel catalogue there's a message. It reads:

Hi Friends,
My name is Donald. Donald Diesel. I'm the mascot for Diesel, the fashion brand that keeps on smiling.
I'm here to take you by the hand to a place called Happy Valley, the happiest valley on earth.
Happy Valley is a place where love leaps and sadness sleeps.
A place where the sun always shines and the rain is only allowed in to make rainbows.
A place where all the animals are happy to be eaten and where the entrance fee can be paid in any currency.
Above all, Happy Valley is a place where the only emotions you're allowed to experience are the nice ones.
And it's all sponsored by those kind people at Diesel.
So what are we waiting for. Bring a smile on your face, a song in your heart and a major credit card in your pocket. And let's take a ride through the wonders of Happy Valley.
Love
Donald Diesel.
Bringing pleasure to the masses.

Crossing the 'fine' line...

'I love the commercials that shock my parents'

These days a gay couple shopping for a dining room table is not an unusual occurrence. But as recently as 1994 such a scenario had never

DONALD SAYS GOODBYE:
"Friendship lasts forever, because there is no 'end' in 'friend'. Except at the end of the word friend."

Figure 7.1 *Donald Diesel. Diesel's attitude campaigns have turned 45.5 per cent of the world's tween population into admirers.*

been played out on television. Ikea, the Swedish furniture retailer, broke ground by portraying just such a scene in a TV commercial. Although it aired briefly in just a few cities in the United States, it became international news.

In the northern summer of 2001, Virgin Cola stepped into the fray and added a gay kiss to part of its Say Something campaign. Although the ad was aired on 32 stations, six major US television markets, including San Francisco, New York and Los Angeles, refused to carry it. This is all about determining when to cross a fine line without committing brand suicide.

Calvin Klein knows this well. Through risqué publicity campaigns it has given the house edgy cachet and trend-setting status. Wearable mainstream clothing is what has made the fashion brand Calvin Klein what it is today, but useful notoriety has also come from the publicity surrounding its outré advertisements. First, there was the pre-pubescent Brooke Shields in tight jeans suggestively claiming that 'Nothing' came between her and her Calvin's. Then came the Obsession perfume ads with supermodel Kate Moss and hunky Marky Mark erotically pressing up together against a wall.

However, in 1999 Calvin Klein was forced to cancel one of its campaigns. When Calvin Klein launched its underwear range in partnership with Warnaco, Inc., the ad which was featured on a billboard in New York's Times Square featured semi-naked toddlers posing in Calvin Klein underwear. The public outcry led by the New York City Mayor, Rudy Giuliani, put a quick end to the campaign.

Building brands for tweens requires a delicate balance. The line is, however, moving as we speak. What wasn't tolerable yesterday is acceptable today. What was in yesterday is out today. However, the fundamental ingredients that we've discussed remain constant, no matter what year we're talking about.

SUMMARY

▌ Pop stars and music are the most important phenomena influencing tweens, across the globe. The formula is tried and tested. Music creates dreams. Dreams build brands.

▌ Music determines standards for behaviour, reflects opinions, and determines how tweens relate to one another as well as the values with which they identify.

▌ Mainstream music is about to disappear. Tweens' musical tastes are reflecting a substantial diversification. This sets new challenges for marketers targeting this generation.

▌ Dreams are hard currency in the life of a tween. Every brand and every product has to appeal to the imagination of tweens. It has to give them something to dream about.

▌ Creating romance is a formula that still appeals to girls, and is likely to continue.

▌ Rebellion is attractive. Tweens are attracted to opinionated performers, and are drawn to bands with a rebellious image. They have endless admiration for those who ignore the unwritten rules of society. In fact, this disregard for authority is what elevates the rebellious groups' status among tweens.

▌ Branding is all about personality. The biggest challenge for the marketers is (and always will be) to ensure that each and every one of these characters stay true to themselves.

▌ Brands that are human, have opinions and attitudes, and brands that can honestly portray strength and reveal weakness will be the survivors.

▌ Attitude branding is on the rise. From about 12 years old, attitude-based brands start to have a distinct appeal.

ACTION POINTS

▶ Does your brand target a broad vaguely defined tween group or does it zero in on a specific well-defined segment?

▶ Identify which type of music your core audience is listening to. Based on this, try to re-evaluate the description of your existing target group. The results might very well reveal a totally different description to your initial one, allowing you space for expansion.

▶ What values are being portrayed by the music to which your audience is listening? Who are their heroes and what do these heroes do to maintain their position? Create a list of the 10 points which you believe will bestow hero status among your core audience.

▶ Using the hero list as your basis, convert this into your existing concept strategy. How would you convert each of the 10 hero guidelines into 10 golden rules for your brand and your communication strategy?

▶ Now check your list against these three points: dreams, romance and rebellion. In short, what is the attitude of your brand, and how would you describe its personality if it was a real person?

▶ What five key actions would this person – your brand – be known for? What would your brand do to make tweens talk, discuss its attitude and love it forever?

8

The peer factor

In 1999 an 18-year-old student named Shawn Fanning dropped out of college and changed the music industry forever. His idea was a file-sharing program called Napster. It seemed simple: a program that allowed computer users to share and swap files, specifically music, through a centralized file server. His response to complaints about the difficulty of finding and downloading music over the Net was to stay awake for 60 hours straight. In that time, he wrote the source code for a program that combined a music-search function with a file-sharing system and, to facilitate communication, instant messaging.

This is not a story about how Shawn Fanning was the first person to shake up the music and entertainment industry to such degree that share prices fell for giants like EMI and Sony. It is, however, a story showing how peer-to-peer marketing became a reality. It's based on something that has existed forever in every school playground, shopping centre and sports club. The difference is that now, because of the existence of the Internet, information can spread like wild-fire across the globe.

Since the appearance of the Internet several successful concepts have succeeded because they are based on ideas about interconnection. Hotmail is probably one of the most successful dotcom examples. It was the first free e-mail site to promote itself in every single e-mail sent using the service. So every time a message went through their server, they included an ad inviting the receiver to sign up. Today Hotmail represents 110 million users and they process more than a billion emails a day. And each email promotes the Hotmail brand. It just gets stronger and stronger.

Why has peer-to-peer marketing proved to be such a powerful tool? Is it a fad, or is it here to stay?

In a paper published in 1983 called 'Socialization in the Context of the Family', Eleanor E Maccoby and John A Martin strongly implied that the physical environment that parents provide for their children has very little impact. Psychologist Judith Rich Harris took this one step further in her 1998 book *The Nurture Assumption*. Here she concludes that ultimately kids are far more affected by their peers than by their parents. Harris cites accents of migrant children as an example. It is very rare for these kids to adopt the accent of their parents, and in almost every case they embrace the language of their peers. Harris says: 'When children go out, they leave behind the behaviour they acquired at home. They cast it off like the dorky sweater their mother made them wear.'

It is clear that even though parents can affect their kids to some degree, their strongest opinions, attitudes and interests are primarily created outside the home.

In theory, peer-to-peer marketing has always existed. The introduction of newer, quicker and more effective communication tools, however, has enabled tweens in particular to spread information faster and faster. Suddenly news is no longer restricted to peers in the neighborhood, but available to everyone sharing e-mail addresses, chat room space or owning a mobile phone.

USING PEER-TO-PEER MARKETING TO BUILD BRANDS

 Visit DualBook.com/bc/ch7p2p to learn more about the latest trends in peer-to-peer marketing.

Almost every successful tween brand today has a peer-to-peer component on which it is based. By analyzing this it's clear that a range of guidelines can be identified to maximize the possibility of success. There are three key ingredients common in successful campaigns: *community exploration, peer-to-peer marketing* and *viral marketing*.

Community exploration

The first step is to identify a community with strong characteristics.

Peer-to-peer marketing

Next establish a peer-to-peer program which targets the leaders of the community.

Viral marketing

Let tweens take ownership of the brand by building and spreading it themselves.

The process of peer-to-peer marketing typically involves 10 steps:

1. Identify a community.
2. Map the behaviour of the community.
3. Identify alternative distribution channels.
4. Identify the leaders of the community.
5. Build a peer-to-peer marketing program around the leaders.
6. Place tweens in the centre – not the brand.
7. Support the community with unique initiatives.
8. Develop viral marketing tools enabling the tweens to market for you.
9. Let the outside world know about the community success.
10. Spread the brand to audiences outside the community.

1. Identify a community

The people who are best at identifying strong communities are those who were once part of them. Contrary to general belief, age, gender and demographic correlations are not necessarily the primary factors that determine a community's membership. Often it's an interest or a passion that proves to be the uniting force. Common aspirations are equally powerful in creating a community spirit.

To some extent this undermines everything that classic marketing courses have taught us. Notions of target groups based on age, gender and demographic may not prove accurate if planning a campaign based on peer-to-peer ideals. The communities we're seeking to target are often established by a series of coincidental factors. We're increasingly seeing communities established with the help of commercially driven organizations interested in creating new identifiable market segments.

Strong passions and extreme behaviours publicize, unite and identify communities. This, in turn, becomes a self-fulfilling prophecy. The stronger the voice, the more attention it creates, further strengthening community membership.

The surf culture in Australia is a good example of how powerful a community can be in developing new brands. All year round hundreds of thousands of surfers take to the waves up and down the Australian coast. Over the past 20 years there's been literally an ocean of new surfing brands. It's not surprising that these brands have been created, manufactured and managed by current and former members of the surfing community.

One of the most successful surfing brands is Billabong. It was begun by Gordon Merchant in 1973, and today is sold in 60 countries with an annual revenue close to A $400 million. Initially Billabong was promoted exclusively in Australia, and despite the fact that almost no advertising money was spent internationally, it became well known among surfer communities all over the world. Regardless of geographical distance, travelling surfers took news of the brand to their own communities creating a solid foundation for the Australian company to go global.

Not only did Billabong tap directly into a surf fashion aesthetic, it also managed to appeal to a very clear, very well-defined peer group that gathers on beaches and loves to ride waves – no matter where in the world they're based. Billabong's low-key marketing strategy was to maintain its presence by sponsoring sporting events.

The Billabong brand helped the surf community create a very strong identity never seen before. Up until the 1980s, surfing was not regarded as a trendy sport but rather one for outsiders – beach bums. However, Billabong has been one of the driving forces mapping surfing as a desirable sport. Not only does it add a strong sense of belonging to the surfing community, but it has successfully attracted attention outside its community. Now it is mostly worn by people who have never so much as sat on a surf board. The brand has moved from a strong community brand to one independent of its core community. But the Billabong brand also remains faithful to its roots, maintaining the core spirit of the brand and keeping the vision alive.

Similarly another clothing brand, FUBU, succeeded by appealing to a well-defined segment of the community. The clothing is made 'For Us By

Us', with the 'us' being African-Americans. FUBU was one of the most popular clothing brands in the 1990s. It has become synonymous with US hip-hop culture and has spread across the world.

Ironically, FUBU is now hardly worn by the community for which it was once created. It's been embraced by tweens all over the world who identify with urban culture. Tweens as far away from African-American cities as Asia have adopted the loose baggy fit, the dreadlocks and the break-dancing. The global spread of US urban culture allowed FUBU to capitalize on growing awareness of the brand, enabling them to position it as youth-oriented instead of something exclusively worn by the African-American community. FUBU trades on the assumption that most kids – regardless of location – identify with its inner-city cutting-edge designs and concepts.

2. Map the behaviour of the community

Understanding a community is the key to success. It is essential to understand what's driving it. There needs to be intimate knowledge of what motivates each member of the community. Almost more importantly, marketers need to know what turns them off. What are their passions? What are their dreams? How do they spend most of their time?

FUBU is an excellent example of a brand that succeeded because the founders were themselves members of the community for which they were catering. The brand began in 1992 in Queens, New York. According to one of the founders, Daymond John, he became so fed up with the lack of suitable urban gear in his neighbourhood retail stores that he devised a scheme to launch his own label. With a US $100,000 mortgage on his home and the assistance of three neighbourhood friends, J Alexander Martin, Keith Perrin and Carl Brown, John turned half of his home into a factory. The other half became living quarters for the group. Thus was born one of the fastest-growing African-American owned companies in today's fashion industry.

The right combination of brand signals, apparel combinations and distribution was essential for the FUBU brand's success – a strategy only people very close to the community would have been able to create. They started out with men's t-shirts, rugby shirts and hockey jerseys, and baseball caps, all emblazoned with the FUBU insignia. Over the past decade the range has grown to include accessories, shoes, hats and a full range of women and children's clothes.

The FUBU brand has spread its wings outside the community, but like Billabong it remains faithful to its core audience and continues to cater to the spirit of the brand.

Both Billabong and FUBU are brands which began catering to a very narrow market segment represented by a particular group of teens and tweens. They had clear-cut features characterized by passion and a strong community feeling. This attracted a wider audience who went out and bought the brand. In both cases peer-to-peer communication was one of the key factors creating and growing the brands.

The viral effect pushed the brands into new markets before the actual product was even targeted at them. Thus a reverse marketing technique came into play which created an attractive brand that was almost impossible to obtain. But this made it even more desirable to tweens. Both Billabong and FUBU successfully avoided the in-your-face style of campaigns. These tend to have a negative effect on tweens, who love to feel the ownership of brands that they've searched out and found on their own.

3. Identify alternative distribution channels

Peter van Stolk founded the Jones Soda Co in 1996. He felt that tweens might accept a new soda brand if they felt they had discovered it themselves. For this reason Jones Soda Co initially established what they called an alternative distribution strategy. The drinks were always placed in their own cooler bearing their signature flames. The coolers were placed in unique venues: skate, surf and snowboarding shops, tattoo and piercing parlours, individual fashion stores, national retail clothing chains and music shops. These are all places where tweens tend to hang out, making the association between brand and place a positive one.

A by-product of this unorthodox distribution strategy was that it had the added advantage that no other competitors were present. The only drinks available in the shops were Jones sodas. Once this distribution strategy was in place, Jones began placing their product in convenience and food stores. Then finally the company moved into the larger chains like Starbucks, Safeway, Albertson's and 7-Eleven.

Peter van Stolk's tactics were based on a strategic choice of distribution channels which not only avoided the classic struggle to gain access to established supermarket shelf space, but generated a buzz in the market at which it was aimed.

Distribution is, not surprisingly, a key issue in the success or failure of most new brands. Ben & Jerry's ice cream became well known for its tactics in securing supermarket space in a hugely competitive environment. They perfectly followed the second peer-to-peer marketing step – appealing to a carefully-selected community. And it was the community which helped the brand gain enough local support to ensure it had space in selected communities. They in turn helped the brand gain enough local support to ensure space in stores.

As more and more products jostle to secure shelf space, focusing on a selected community is essential for a new brand to survive.

4. Identify the leaders of the community

Jones Soda Co's promotion machine is based almost entirely on peer-to-peer marketing. However, before this can take place, it's essential that you are thoroughly familiar with the rules of the community you're targeting. Every community has spoken and unspoken rules. If your brand plays by these rules then it is more likely to be accepted. Making this possible is essential. You need to be completely familiar with the dynamics of a group, to know what is acceptable and, just as importantly, what is not.

One of Jones Soda Co's core strategies was to build a peer-to-peer program around their brand. They created the Soda Pro Riders team. This consists of 14 tweens and teens who are each passionate about a sport. Jones's mission is to support these team members so they perfect their skills. The surfers, cyclists, wakeboarders, skateboarders and skiers are selected because of their passion. Each has a strong persona and can speak articulately on their sport – as well, of course, on their favourite soda!

Jones has avoided traditional sponsor techniques to promote the Soda Pro Riders team. Securing a tight connection between the Pro Riders and the brand, the Jones Soda label has become the media of communication to the outside world. Selected Pro Riders have created their own Signature Series label. This is a very rare series where only a few thousand bottle labels have been produced, each dedicated to a specific community and featuring a leader of that community. So besides showing commitment to the community, it's also showing how much it values it by making it exclusive. This appealed both to the yen for exclusivity and the idea of collecting so prevalent among tweens. This marketing technique is making the Jones Signature Series even more attractive, drawing attention to the community and highlighting the skills and talents of its members – all the while focusing on the Jones Soda brand.

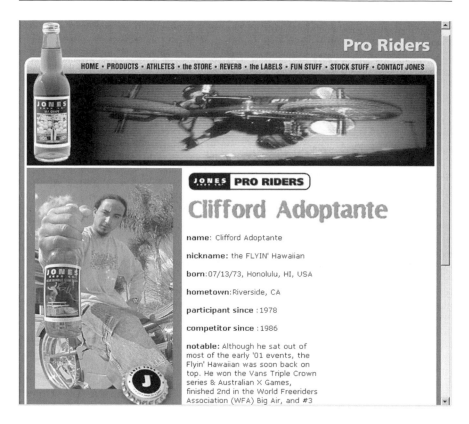

Figure 8.1 *A Jones Pro Rider. An alternative distribution strategy combined with a solid peer-to-peer programme were the main ingredients in Jones Soda's launch success in the United States.*

Jones Soda has created a brand by using the tweens themselves. Additionally they've built on a notion of community similar to that used by Billabong and FUBU, and established a devoted customer base.

5. Build a peer-to-peer marketing program around the leaders

The Jones Soda peer-to-peer marketing program continued to build on its success. As a part of the Jones Soda philosophy, the brand sponsors fascinating people from a very young age, ensuring that any new Jones Soda event spreads quickly by word of mouth.

Josh Sundquist is sponsored by Jones Soda. He spreads the message that life is cool, even if cancer cost him his leg and almost killed him when

Figure 8.2 *The Jones community. Jones Soda managed to turn its target group into true brand ambassadors over just a few months by, amongst other things, releasing individual labels promoting unique people among their audience. So far, 10,000 tweens have signed up to receive their own label at JonesSoda.com.*

he was nine. Sundquist was signed up when he wrote Jones Soda a fan letter back in 1997. He never expected even a reply. But much to his surprise, four days after mailing the letter he got a call from the CEO, who hired him as a Jones Soda spokesperson.

The Seattle soda maker with a cult following sponsors upbeat, motivational speeches that Sundquist delivers to rapt tweens. Jones Soda pays thousands of dollars for Sundquist's equipment and his travel costs. In exchange, Sundquist wears a Jones sweatshirt and swigs on a Jones Soda wherever he talks.

Tweens like to spend, but they don't like being told on what! Everything is focused on letting peers market to peers, establishing an individual connection, or going for one cool crowd at a time – or one hip happening here and another there.

Mountain Dew executives have called this phenomenon the Pavlovian connection. They hand out samples of their drink at surf, skateboard and snowboard tournaments. They build a connection between the brand and the exhilarating experience. Drinking 'the Dew' isn't a rush because of the added caffeine and sugar. The rush comes from the location which is hip and home to a community.

But like any other people-driven activity, peer-to-peer marketing is hard to establish and even harder to maintain. Such marketing programs catch on when the community perceives the brand is talking with their voice, thinking similar thoughts and sharing their interests. And, most importantly, the passion the brand exemplifies has to be trusted and true.

The failure of thousands of brands across the world who struggle for acceptance in particular communities is testimony to the fine line that exists between displaying the passion that exists in a community or simply appearing bogus or overdone. The support of community members in the process of developing a peer-to-peer marketing program is essential. Even more important is to ensure that the people helping get this message across are the right ones, those who are respected, admired and followed by their peers. It is often here that the process fails.

6. Place tweens in the centre – not the brand

The list of brands which systematically avoid mass communication in favour of peer-to-peer marketing techniques is growing. Hydrogen Records directs its fans to popular chat rooms to talk up new music. Vans, a sports shoe manufacturer, cosies up to tweens by building zippy skateboard parks. Common to all these brands is that they establish trust by using other people, often close friends, to recommend the brands. By doing this marketers avoid the classic dilemma of communicating directly to an audience which basically hates to be communicated to – directly, anyway.

A brand like Vans can still be seen on MTV, but the *real* competition for tween attention and trust building takes place in 12 indoor skateboard parks that have been constructed by Vans across the United States, from Orange County in California to Orlando in Florida.

It is also clear that single products cannot and do not stand alone. It's all about projecting a lifestyle. This is no longer focused on a single soda, item of clothing or computer product. The product has to appeal to every element in the tweens' lives, offering an array of totally branded lifestyle product selection.

One of the first and probably most successful brands to create a lifestyle is Nickelodeon, which many have identified as one of the most important recent phenomena in the history of American pop culture. Nickelodeon began in 1979 as a video comic book showing cartoons from around the world on *Nickel Flicks* and *Pinwheel*, hosted by a human with a bevy of puppets. The brand has since gone on to become a 24/7 channel with a focus that never wavers from providing tweens with a place on television that's just for them.

Nickelodeon is not alone when it comes to spreading its wings and securing a 360-degree appeal to its audience. Today this technique includes appealing to every dimension of life. 'Nice to have' is no longer sufficient. If a brand is to succeed in the tough tween market it has to be stamped 'must have'.

FUBU, Pokèmon, Jones Soda and Vans are all good examples of how important it is to let the brand drive the product's development across all possible categories as long as the values reflected can tie it all together. In 2001 Vans decided to expand their peer-to-peer strategy by initiating Warped Tour. This establishes a close association between popular music and extreme sports. Vans is also a majority shareholder in *Dogtown and Z Boys*, a skateboarding movie that is regarded in some tween circles as the coolest film ever made. Vans sells the shoes and clothing worn in the movie, as well as building its own music label with tween bands like Too Rude and Western Waste.

7. Support the community with unique initiatives

'Run with the little guy... create some change' is the FUBU creed. But in reality almost all community-created brands are based on positioning tweens in the centre and allowing them to feel they are the keepers of the brand rather than the manufacturer.

Now I haven't yet told you the full story about the Jones Soda label strategy. Besides using the labels to create attention among selected community members, the labels have also become accessible to all Jones Soda drinkers. In fact Jones Soda offers their customers their own five minutes fame via the Jones Soda Web site. This invites loyal fans to send in a photograph of themselves for possible use on a Jones Soda label. So far more than 60,000 labels are ready for production. The odds for selection are low – only 40 are picked annually – but for tweens the lure is irresistible. The image chosen is often as far removed from the usual corporate soda label as possible. It's silly enough to create even more support among the tweens, and so generate even stronger brand loyalty to the Jones brand.

A major characteristic of Jones Soda is that the brand consistently builds on a 'Me brand feeling'. This is designed to make the consumer feel 'I found the brand. I invented the product. I own the brand. I recommend the brand.'

The fascinating part of this thinking is the complete reversal in brand theory. Brands are no longer owned by the manufacture, but by the audience. The first true example of this was seen back in 1985 when New Coke was launched. The strategic product re-launch was a result of a constant decrease in market share, from 60 per cent just after World War II, to under 24 per cent in 1983. This was due mainly to Pepsi's steady success. But customers rejected New Coke. It simply couldn't replace the old Coca-Cola with which they were so familiar.

Brand trends over the years have changed dramatically. Today it's almost impossible to develop a product or a service, off or online, without seeing a competitor offering the same within a few days of it appearing. In response, brand building has moved from its focus in the 1930s, which concentrated on the brand's unique selling proposition (USP), to what I call the 'Me selling proposition' (MSP). That progression took place through the development of the 'emotional selling proposition' (ESP), the 'organization selling proposition' (OSP), the cult-dependent 'brand selling proposition" (BSP) right up to the MSP.

It is clear that the larger the ownership the tween audience feels for the brand, the stronger their loyalty. In the late 1980s, surfers felt that Billabong was their personal brand. They believed they had invented the

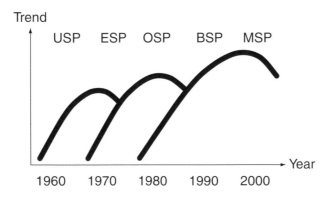

Figure 8.3 *Brand trends over 40 years. Today's brands are MSP brands (Me selling proposition). MSP brands are brands that are no longer owned by the manufacturer, but by the consumer.*

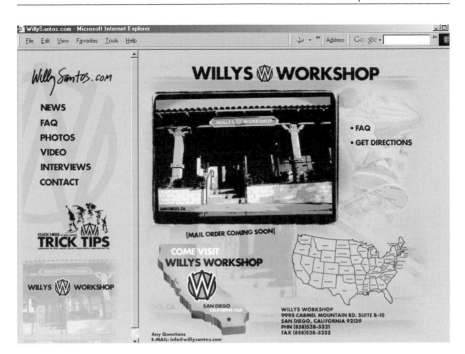

Figure 8.4 *Willy Santos's Web site. Jones Soda has kick started new brands – brands owned and run by their peer-to-peer audience.*

idea, they lived the philosophy behind it, and they wore the clothes that made Billabong the success it is today. And they're probably right. Exactly the same can be said of the FUBU community. In both cases these brands have been smart enough to stay loyal to their roots despite the fact that they are also now catering to a much broader market.

MSP is about to take things even further. Driven by the popularity of reality television, the dream of five minutes of fame is more achievable than ever. And as brands tie their fortune to their consumers' desire for just that, so the notion grows.

In some countries Pepsi has offered drinkers an express access ticket to join the obsessively watched television show *Big Brother*. Not surprisingly, Jones Soda has taken the concept of MSP brands even further by turning real people into real brands. Take the case of Willy Santos.

Willy Santos was born in 1975, started skateboarding when he was 10, and has been a pro skater for seven years. Willy has his own merchandising line covering shoes and bags and – you guessed right – targeting his own peers. Willy is also owner of his own signature label series at Jones

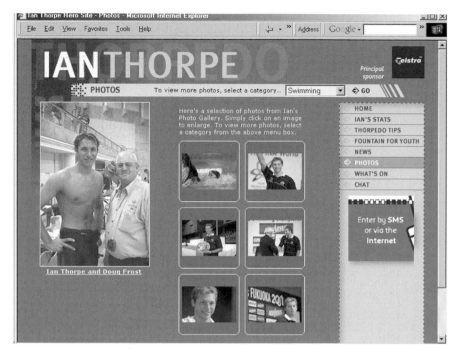

Figure 8.5 *Ian Thorpe's Web site. Ian Thorpe, the Australian world-class swimmer turned his achievement into a merchandising exercise. Only time will tell if he succeeds.*

Soda, helping him to promote his own sales, while at the same time promoting Jones Soda as a cool brand.

Real people – people we all can relate to – have become the spokespeople for real brands. These are generally the brands all tweens can relate to, understand, appreciate and above all, find cool.

The Olympic gold medalist swimmer Ian Thorpe is another example of an icon transformed into a brand. He captured the world's attention at the 2000 Sydney Olympics, where he won five medals. He was quickly signed up by Telstra, Australia's national telecommunications network, which immediately gave Thorpe his own identity in a Telstra-created online environment. He's already become his own brand, and if he goes on to duplicate his outstanding Olympic record a few more times, his brand will be set in gold.

8. Develop viral marketing tools enabling the tweens to market for you

Today no marketing budget based solely on traditional communication will be enough to secure a successful brand launch. However, since the advent of the Internet, viral techniques have proved to be one of the most effective methods of creating and maintaining attention among tweens.

Viral marketing characteristically includes a message which is adapted and transmitted by the audience themselves. The challenge has become to design a message in such a way that it doesn't take the brand off track. Once it has been released into the ether, it will be just like a virus – unstoppable and too late for any last-minute treatment.

Over the past decade, thousands, if not millions of attempts at viral marketing have spectacularly failed. Lured by the fact that it is an easy and cheap marketing approach, they fail because the details of the message and the objectives of the campaign don't match the nature of the viral idea.

We've all engaged in viral communication. Think of the jokes, the images, the chain letters and anecdotes sent by friends and family members based all over the world. With a click of the Send button we sometimes forward the message on to friends and family members because it strikes a chord and we want to share it with other members of our community.

The Blair Witch Project, the movie we've already discussed, demonstrated just how effective true viral marketing could be in creating a high level of awareness that translated into unprecedented numbers of people going to the cinema.

Pokèmon didn't go as far as *The Blair Witch Project* but established a campaign that combined traditional marketing with viral elements. Pokèmon didn't want to establish their whole campaign on viral marketing, despite the fact that most of the Pokèmon brand's success in Japan was viral. The Pokèmon consortium was afraid that a viral campaign could spin out of control. They needed to be careful. The Pokèmon scenario is a complex one. There are characters and relationships that all have specific functions, roles and relationships. There was a danger that the viral effect could become contaminated.

Pokèmon was invented by Satoshi Tijir, a 33-year-old 'geek' who based his concept on a childhood memory of collecting bugs. He combined this with monsters he saw on Japanese television and invented a video game for Nintendo which inspired a global card-trading frenzy, making it the most successful toy craze the world has ever seen.

The game was first launched in Japan. It was when video sales topped 10 million copies and licensed product neared the 1000 mark that the United States first took notice. The Japanese success was clearly due to the power of word of mouth. Tweens were telling tweens. The effect was pervasive. Previous experience in the United States with the Tamagotchi virtual pet from Bandai America and the Beanie Babies from Ty Inc. – both from Japan – indicated that a peer-to-peer launch strategy would work well. It was decided that TV would be the best medium to get the ball rolling.

From the very beginning it was clear that all the networks were doubtful about the future of Pokèmon in North America. At first, no-one would take it on. Ties with Kellogg's and other tween-focused brands failed. In the end, Nintendo bartered, using their advertising budget as leverage to get local stations to take the show, which was given away in return for a cut in advertising revenue. The rest, as they say, is history.

9. Let the outside world know about the community success

The real test for a community-based brand comes when the community can no longer fulfil the growth needs of the brand. This is a precarious phase because when the brand needs to spread its wings, it's in danger of losing the basic community's support. This is the brand's challenge.

To some extent Pokèmon had managed to appeal to a small start-up group, but the real test was if the brand platform and product could hold when expanded to a nationwide audience. A technique previously used for Nintendo proved to be extremely effective in this case. Before the video game and television show were introduced, a special video was produced, an infomercial that initially introduced the concept to kids who were not yet aware of it. The 14-minute teaser was mailed to 1.2 million US households. The mailing list was derived from the GameBoy owner database supplemented by retailers' lists.

The video showed kids explaining what Pokèmon is: a GameBoy video game where the trainer collects and trains little monsters and overcomes the forces of evil to become a Pokèmon master. Based on the slogan 'Gotta catch 'em all', tweens immediately embraced the idea and set out to collect every one. The video introduced the characters and was also adapted to the different markets in different time zones, telling each audience when they could catch the show on TV.

'*I like Pokemon clothes best*', Ding Si Jia, aged 11, China

The video was mailed out the week before the first show, which aired on 5 September 1998. Three weeks later, Pokèmon Blue and Red GameBoy games, each priced at US $29, arrived on retail shelves. Sales of the role-playing monster game hit 400,000 cartridges within a few weeks of the launch.

But the secret of the enormous success of the campaign was the integration of every element. All the product pieces supported each other. The teaser video announced that a weekday morning cartoon would provide hints to players that would help them master the video game. By watching the TV show closely, gamers picked up tips that allowed them to succeed at the video and card games. A fleet of Pokè Cars – 10 yellow Volkswagen Beetles customized to look like the Pokèmon character Pikachu and equipped with interactive gaming hardware – was sent out to drive around tweens' neighbourhoods. Nintendo ran an in-school promotion where tweens were given free Pokèmon book covers.

Alfred Kahn had helped popularize Cabbage Patch dolls. He was appointed by Nintendo to bring Pokèmon to the United States. He says: 'We weren't the only one doing the marketing. The kids would watch the tape, watch the TV show, play the game, and "pass it on". It was like the kids were marketing it to each other. The video became "the thing to have". It took on a life on its own. Our team had created an underground universe of terminology. Everyone was talking Pikachu, energy, Pokedex, trainers. It was amazing!'

By 2000 Pokèmon's revenue had reached a startling US 2.8 billion. Over 400 million trading cards were in circulation. The Pokèmon song was the all-time Number One children's song listed by *Billboard* in 1999.

10. Spread the brand to audiences outside the community

What started out as an 'around the way' project for FUBU has subsequently evolved into a US $850 million business, with Samsung America, the tenth largest company in the world, assisting FUBU with its production and distribution needs. And it's grown tremendously in the last decade. FUBU is now sold in over 5000 stores worldwide and online.

Now FUBU is heading east to capitalize on its popularity in Asia. It currently has freestanding stores and wholesale distribution in both Korea and Japan, with upcoming ventures in China. FUBU is also in the process of arranging distribution licences to open a total of 34 stores in Singapore, Indonesia, Malaysia, Thailand and Taiwan. It has become a formidable presence in the retail industry in both the United States and Asia.

The newest challenge for the founders will come in their spreading into the music and film industry. In December 2000, FUBU launched FB Entertainment and FUBU Films. The team has also collaborated with Universal Records to release a hip-hop and R&B compilation CD, as well as co-producing the feature film *The Crow: Lazarus* starring rap and movie star DMX.

Billabong, Jones Soda, Pokèmon and Vans have followed the same successful strategy, beginning with a narrow but very concentrated focus on a community and then spreading the message to other even more attractive audiences.

It is clear that successful peer-to-peer marketing is all about building on a passion, appealing to a shared dream, talking the language of the audience and finally making that audience do the work of marketing the brands – to themselves. Once the brand has been adopted in their world, there's every indication that there will be two winners: the community and the brand.

SUMMARY

▌ The introduction of newer, quicker and more effective communication tools has enabled tweens to spread information across the globe.

▌ Parents' influence on their kids behaviour is minimal. Their kids' opinions, attitudes and interests are primarily created outside the home.

▌ Almost every successful tween brand today has a strong peer-to-peer component.

▌ There are three key ingredients common to successful campaigns: community exploration, peer-to-peer marketing and viral marketing.

▌ The process of peer-to-peer marketing typically involves 10 steps:

1. Identify a community. The people who are best at identifying strong communities are those who are, or were once, part of it.

2. Map the behavior of the community. It is essential to understand what's driving it.

3. Identify alternative distribution channels.

4. Identify the leaders of the community. However, before this can take place, it's essential that you are thoroughly familiar with the rules of the community you're targeting.

5. Build a peer-to-peer marketing program around the leaders.

6. Place tweens in the centre, rather than the brand.

7. Support the community with unique initiatives. Make people to whom the audience can relate the spokespeople for the brand.

8. Develop viral marketing tools enabling the tweens to market for you.

9. Let the outside world know about the community's success.

10. Spread the brand to audiences outside the community. Successful peer-to-peer marketing is all about building on a passion, appealing to a shared dream, talking the language of the audience and making the audience do the work.

ACTION POINTS

▶ How can your brand play a role in a tween's family in order to create a relationship in a deep everlasting way?

▶ Identify the parents' influence on your target group. Do parents have a substantial influence, or would their positive opinion dilute the brand for their tween children?

▶ Map five characteristics of tween behavior. Find out what motivates them, what makes them laugh, and what energizes them.

▶ Identify the rules of the community. What are the 'guidelines' for outsiders to be accepted? And most importantly, what would this group hate to be identified with?

▶ Identify the leaders of the community, and then build a peer-to-peer marketing program around the leaders.

▶ Based on the rules that you've identified, develop a program that supports the community with unique initiatives. The golden rule is to have real people become the spokespeople for your brand. Then establish viral marketing tools that will facilitate tweens marketing the brand themselves.

9

Cyberchild

When the movie *The Truman Show* was released, many were impressed by the originality of the plot. Its main character, Truman Burbank, grew up and lived in a fake town full of actors playing town folk. The town itself was situated in a giant dome decked out with hi-tech simulations of sun and sky. The rain and wind came courtesy of the special effects department. The drama lay in the fact that only Truman was unaware that he was living his life on a stage set. He goes about his daily business as the cameras focus on him, making him the main player in an ongoing drama that makes our current understanding of reality television seem tame.

In March 1999, a place called Norrath was founded. It is not unrelated to the town in *The Truman Show*. Norrath has a population of around 12,000 people – although up to 60,000 can be there at any given time. The nominal hourly wage is set at about US $3.42 an hour. Each day the population grows. People come in from all around the world.

WELCOME TO A NEW TWEEN REALITY

Like the tidy town in *The Truman Show*, Norrath is not real. A group of software engineers in San Diego began building a vast virtual world with the vision of creating a place where people would prefer to live. Inspired by the popular role-playing game Dungeons and Dragons, their plan was to build an environment large enough to accommodate nearly 500,000 visitors a year. They named their world Norrath and floated it off the California coast.

Norrath is in fact owned by Verant Interactive, a division of Sony Corporation. Since the early 1980s, Sony saw the potential of online games and virtual worlds, and they pumped money into projects like Norrath. It is now a massive, never-ending, online role-playing game set in a fantasy world similar to Middle Earth in *The Lord of the Rings*.

The Norrath project is called EverQuest, and it took six years and A $28 million to create. But why bother? Norrath could be perceived as a silly game similar to the science fiction worlds created in movies like *The Matrix* and *Total Recall*. Perhaps not. Professor Edward Castronova from the Economics Department at the University of California, Fullerton, estimates that revenue from online gaming alone will grow to over US $1.5 billion in 2004.

EverQuest: you are in our world now

EverQuest is only one of several role-playing games – also known as multi-player games – that have been around since the mid-1990s. To date, more than half a million people have subscribed to the virtual world, and at any given time there are about 60,000 people playing simultaneously.

A virtual world is characterized by three key components:

1. *Interactivity*. It exists on one computer but can be accessed remotely and simultaneously by a large number of people. The command inputs of one person affect the command result of the others.
2. *Physicality*. People access the program through an interface that simulates a first-person physical environment on their computer screen. The environment is generally ruled by the natural laws of Earth, and is characterized by a scarcity of resources.
3. *Persistence*. The program continues to run whether anyone is using it or not. It remembers the location of people and objects, as well as keeping track of ownership.

In short, EverQuest represents an entire world with its own diverse species, economic systems, alliances and politics. It's possible to choose from a variety of races and classes, customize the character and begin the quest in any number of cities or villages on a number of continents.

In a similar way to *The Truman Show*, EverQuest creates a reality so detailed, so accurate and so engaging that the signals indicate it has become a permanent world for its citizens. According to Professor Castronova's study, the average Norrath citizen spends 36 hours a week

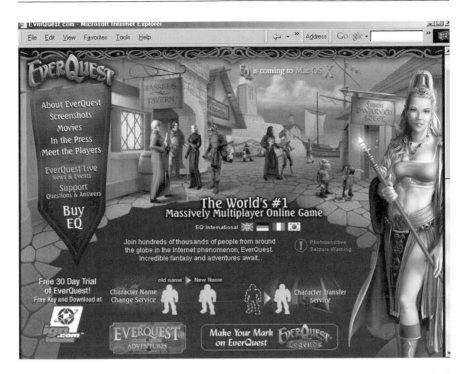

Figure 9.1 *Welcome to the world of EverQuest. 60,000 people earn a full salary from the computer game EverQuest by selling their avatars on auction sites like eBay and Yahoo Auctions.*

inside its virtual walls. What's more, about 93,000 people spend more time in Norrath in a typical week than they do at their paid work.

The fascinating part is that, contrary to general belief, virtual worlds are not necessarily isolated. Strong communities have been established at EverQuest and many players have developed complex systems of trading. Digital products such as weapons, magic power and armour are sold for real cash in the real world – the outside world, that is.

Shortly after the launch of EverQuest, its players began trading the game's internal currency, the platinum piece or PP as they call it, for real dollars on Internet auction sites. The problem got so bad that Sony requested these sites stop trading. However, as in the real world, the trading simply relocated. Today there is still an official exchange rate between EverQuest's platinum piece and the US dollar, and the deals are steadily growing.

Other games have similar currency exchanges. In Dark Age of Camelot, a consortium of professional players is suing the game's owners for the right to sell the game's currency on the open market. In an odd take on the real world, players have issued a bill of rights for citizens of all virtual worlds.

The day the virtual world became visible on the map

'I couldn't stop laughing the day I bought an EverQuest laser weapon for a thousand bucks on an eBay auction'

According to Professor Edward Castronova, EverQuest is now the 77th wealthiest country in the world – sandwiched between Russia and Bulgaria. His research shows that virtual internal markets, combined with illegal online trading on auction Web sites, mean that at the end of March 2002, Norrath had a Gross National Product per capita of $2,266, which is larger than China or India.

Professor Castronova tracked thousands of EverQuest transactions on Internet auction sites to determine the economic value generated by the inhabitants of Norrath. This allowed him to calculate how much each character is worth if sold on the open market. If telecommunications costs were less prohibitive, it would be more productive for the average Bulgarian citizen to play EverQuest than to go to work. Experts predict that a steady increase in computer processing power would further improve virtual economies, thereby playing an even bigger part in real world financial stakes over the next decade.

EverQuest is not the only virtual world that's experiencing enormous success. There are an astounding 2.5 million Koreans who play Lineage, and more than 5 million worldwide who subscribe to other online virtual worlds.

CREATING A NEW TWEEN IDENTITY

'When I speak Norrath to Dad, he flips out'

For those who've never played virtual role-playing games before, the rules are very complicated. The instruction books run to hundreds of pages, informing the would-be player of the rules of the new society, the skills and the language used. Players communicate via an internal language that uses similar abbreviations to text messaging. To the uninitiated, just getting another character to say 'Hi' in Norrath requires an immense effort.

Since you choose your own identity, your own world and your own role, this type of game has enormous appeal. Compared to life in the real world, virtual worlds offer equality of opportunity. And even though you may not be able to run in the real world, once in the virtual world your character could race across a desert with effortless ease that would be the envy of trained Olympic runners.

The game is to survive – in the real world

Statistics analyzing virtual worlds reveal that approximately 20 per cent of Norrath's citizens already consider it their place of residence. They simply commute to earth and back. Players at the top level of these games spend almost all their time there. They earn enough money in the virtual world to do what they want, but their principal problem in life is how to make enough money in the real world to support their time in a world like Norrath. Not surprisingly, there's an EverQuest widows' club, and more than anything else, this shows the dark side of the game, which so far has been responsible for several thousand marriage break-ups – in the real world, that is.

It is not surprising that there are literally thousands of people who depend on these trading opportunities. The going rate for characters at online auctions ranges from US $400 to $2,000. College students tend to spend a fair amount of money purchasing the skills and equipment to advance their play. There is also a group, who although not quite in the professional player league, still make a couple of hundred dollars a week.

It's interesting to note that Professor Castronova's research indicates that EverQuest players can earn on average US $3.42 an hour playing the game. This is only one dollar below the standard minimum wage in the real world of the United States.

The intrusion of real dollars

The income capacity of the online gamer is beyond the scope of the manufacturer. In fact, as mentioned, since the beginning of real money trading, Sony has attempted to put a stop to it. According to Sony, real money trading simply ruins the virtual experience, because if one is prepared to pay they can purchase power and jump ahead of all the other players who are diligently following the rules of the game.

Many games manufacturers seem shy of the real world economies their games create. It has been observed that Sony, effectively the government of Norrath, is fighting a war of trade restrictions that no real world government has ever won. But what if the makers of virtual worlds tried to stimulate such economies? In Sweden, a private corporation called MindArk (mindark.com) has just launched their version of a futuristic virtual world. The major difference between MindArk and RealQuest is that MindArk actively seeks the infusion of real money into the game.

Despite the fact that Sony does not support the intrusion of hard currency, it is clear that most new virtual worlds will be based on real money trading. Warhammar Online is a good example. As a part of the induction process, you go onto one of the Web sites, fill in your credit card details over the Internet, and then arrange to meet the people you'll be trading with in the game. You then log on and meet in a tavern or in a town. The virtual you meets the other players who will hand over the gold, or the sword. But essentially the whole transaction occurs in cyberspace.

This is only the beginning. More advanced online games are in the making. Sony is teaming up with Lucas Arts to create a virtual world which already has a mass following. It's estimated that within a year, Star Wars Galaxies (starwarsgalaxies.stationsony.com) will have at least a million subscribers.

Closer and closer to reality

Electronic Arts is planning to release The Sims Online, a Net-based follow-up to the popular computer game that has already sold seven million copies. The online version of the game will cater for groups of up to 30 players per server, to interact and role play in real time. Players will participate in a truly interactive soap opera, with themselves as the virtual stars.

In The Sims Online, players will build houses, open bars or run shops. Electronic Arts has announced that there will even be a whiff of passion, although we're assured there will be nothing more risqué than kissing. The game, which is based on psychologist Abraham Maslow's hierarchy of human needs, offers a welcome change from the blood-thirsty environment of EverQuest, and points are scored for good neighbourly behaviour.

Virtual clicks-and-mortar

To combat the development of currency markets, players will be able to purchase digital artifacts in the game directly from the company. It's only a matter of time before other companies succumb to the attractions of creating virtual worlds. Leading market analysts believe many games, for example Project Entropia, are well suited to providing the foundation for a bricks-and-mortar company. And it's entirely within the realms of possibility that we will soon see the establishment of virtual 3-D stores in virtual worlds.

MARKETING IN MANY VIRTUAL WORLDS

'I love the service in the Wal-Mart virtual stores'

Professor Edward Castronova's survey indicates that the average EverQuest player spends four hours a day, and more than 20 hours a week, playing the game. In fact, many people used the term 'addiction' to describe their behaviour. They perceive their time in the virtual world as in serious conflict with their activities and relationships in the real world. Interviews with online game participants indicate that many a relationship has ended because of the time a partner devotes to their virtual world. The flipside of this is that there are people who are meeting and getting married in ceremonies conducted in the virtual world.

Given the statistics of online game playing, we must conclude that the virtual world is offering something more than mere entertainment. Virtual worlds are not only enticing, but create a dependency, where spending time there becomes compulsive. They are offering an alternate reality, a different country where one can live most of one's life, exactly as one chooses. Life in a virtual world is extremely attractive to many people. So when faced with the choice between the real and virtual worlds, life on Earth often now comes off second best.

A marketer's dream?

It's important that marketers pay attention to the virtual world phenomenon, because these worlds may soon become one of the most important forums for human interaction, alongside the telephone and e-mail. It's also possible that virtual worlds will introduce many changes in the way organizations communicate in the real world.

Virtual worlds are flourishing and their growth seems likely to continue. They already represent an area of Internet commerce that is booming while other sectors are faltering. The attraction of virtual worlds lies in their ability to replicate the physical and economic world of Earth – with slight but significant changes in the rules. These include granting people the freedom to customize their appearance and take on whatever skills they desire, and are sufficient to generate a society that is hugely attractive to thousands of people. About 22 per cent of Norrath's citizens express the desire to spend all their time there. More and more are signing up.

Welcome to the world of virtual branding

'Mom will love this place – it has heaps of parking'

Project Entropia, created by a private Swedish company MindArk, is likely to hold a monopoly on virtual reality 3-D commerce. The 'game' will come free of charge, and access to it will also be free. Here's the catch. Project Entropia gamers will be able to buy things for their avatars using real currency and credit cards, which they can then sell on.

Free software and free access to the virtual world will encourage more and more people to join Project Entropia, where they can socialize with one another and shop with their avatars. The reward systems that we're familiar with – airline points, credit cards, hotels and car rentals – will be a major feature here. The greater the loyalty you show, the greater the rewards. So if you and your friend spend, say, 800 hours developing avatars in Project Entropia, you'll be hardly likely to switch to another competing world. Your loyalty is assured. This is where the situation becomes interesting. In the not-too-distant future, Project Entropia and other virtual worlds will encourage bricks-and-mortar-based brands to establish virtual 3-D stores in their worlds. So if you want to buy a hat for your avatar, and a matching one for yourself, you will go to the virtual hat store.

MindArk takes the concept further. They foresee the emergence of virtual employment. For example, Wal-Mart might pay a gamer to use their avatar to sell avatar clothes in the virtual Wal-Mart.

Believe it or not, it doesn't end here. Since all tweens are thoroughly familiar with communicating in cyberspace, they're not bounded by the borders of nation and distance, as their parents are. There's not much difference between chatting with friends on the Internet or chatting with a person they've never met, or chatting to a person in a virtual game.

Already 24 per cent of all urban tweens globally use the Internet as their primary tool to communicate with their friends, ahead of face-to-face communication and the telephone. And 21 per cent state that the Net is the easiest way to find new friends. But the most surprising statistic to emerge in our survey showed that it was the Chinese tweens (44 per cent) who considered the Internet the easiest way to make new friends, compared to 11 per cent of tweens in the United States. It's not unusual for tweens to have more than 40 Net friends in their address book.

The true fusion of clicks with bricks

So far most game developers' creativity has been limited to online-based activities within their virtual worlds. A bridge between virtual worlds and the rest of the Internet has been limited. And a bridge between virtual worlds and the real world – based on true clicks-and-mortar thinking – has so far been out of the question. There's every indication that this is about to change.

Just think about it. Who says you can't receive an SMS message from your virtual world telling you that someone has approached your avatar and wants to purchase your virtual service? Or that some danger is waiting for you and you had better return to the game to solve the challenge?

When the Internet first came into being, online and offline were quite separate. No longer. There's now a merger between them. In the same way, a merger between real and virtual worlds is about to happen. The question is how this will affect the way marketers communicate to tweens across this virtual divide. Will the classic marketing techniques still have relevance?

The 'dual' personality of tweens

I have an old marketing text book that instructs: 'You have to identify your audience, their age, their geographic and demographic data before planning your advertising campaign.' This is no longer possible. The average player in RealQuest has 2.3 personalities, or in the language of the virtual world, 2.3 avatars. This phenomena is called dissociation and has become an increasingly stronger trend over the past five years.

The *BRANDchild* survey reveals that 36 per cent of wired urban tweens have at least two different avatars. It may be interesting to note that as many as seven per cent of the world's tween population have up to 10 different avatars! Chinese tweens hit the top of the list with 46 per cent representing up to three different avatars in their daily life, followed by US kids (37 per cent). There are only 10 per cent of Japanese kids who have up to three different avatars, which is ironic given the fact that this is the land where most characters, games and avatars are born.

The big question is to what extent today's young tweens are able to distinguish and separate fantasy from reality. According to Edward Castronova's report, 20 per cent prefer the virtual world to the real world. The implications of this are yet to fully reveal themselves. Only time will tell.

But no matter how big an influence these dramatic figures have on the tweens, none of the old market criteria hold true, because the lives of tweens span many worlds, and are represented by different ages, genders and behaviours. So what methodologies can we adopt to communicate to future generations?

One brand, which might be popular among the tweens in one school, might be regarded as totally uncool by the same audience in a virtual world. Online dynamics are different. The audience is behaving under different conditions. Their identity may be changed, and they have different needs and different friends. There are different rules, and different dynamics between the players. Thus they may adopt completely different attitudes towards brands that will appear contradictory. What's perceived as totally cool in the real world can be considered quite nerdy in the virtual world.

This complexity presents even more challenges.

The virtual world of EverQuest is divided into zones, and auction chat can only be accessed within a particular zone. As a result, shrewd avatars do most of their selling in zones where demand for their goods is likely to be high. Shrewd buyers travel to zones where the goods they seek are abundant. At the same time, the bazaar-like nature of the haggling requires that trade be concentrated in space. The result is a pattern of markets in predictable places. Some places are less popular, since they represent player-killer areas where, because of the frequency of murder and robbery, property rights are weak and the prices for things are constantly low.

Reverse direct marketing

To date, very few brands have established a presence in the virtual world and then succeeded in moving it offline. One brand that's come close to this sort of success is Red Bull. Much of its success is due to its online strategy. In fact, a large part of its launch was based on a virtual world presence.

Red Bull teamed up with Sony PlayStation, and secured product placement space in their games. Once you reach a particular level, a message appears promoting the Red Bull energy drink as a good way to take a break between levels. No official data has validated that this component was a key factor in Red Bull's success among its target market. However, interviews conducted with tweens clearly indicate that most of the Sony PlayStation players remember the Red Bull promotion in the games. In fact, they felt it was cool that a brand had finally managed to create a direct dialogue with the avatars playing the game.

Inventive new marketing approaches indicate that future brand platforms aimed at a tween market will involve a combination of different worlds. It's quite possible – even probable – that things will work in reverse. Brands will first appear in an online environment, and in time, they'll move offline.

So far no corporation has succeeded in establishing their brand exclusively in an online world, but it's merely a matter of time. Brands using this option will establish substantial goodwill among the players, since they will regard it as recognition of their world. But no matter if a brand is created solely in a virtual world or an offline environment, the clicks-and-mortar brand platform will need to take a range of different facts into consideration.

Targeting the mercurial personality

Creating a clear profile of your tween audience is no longer a straightforward marketing exercise that falls into simple categories. The only common denominator that exists in this group is the fact that they are all tweens. The similarities stop there.

Take, for example, a 12-year-old dedicated to extreme sports who skateboards after school and hangs out with fellow skateboarders. They all talk, walk and dream of skateboarding. They may even be health conscious, since this supports their competitive skills.

Another tween of exactly the same age is just as likely to be spending six hours after school in front of the computer, playing EverQuest or other virtual games, eating junk food and chatting to friends over the Net – friends they may have never met. Traditional demographics of these two contemporaries are the same. However, in the real world, there's barely one thing in common between them.

It's just such contrasts that form the character of the tween world. The sheer number of musical styles available on the market are testimony to this fact. But a good rule of thumb is that you'll find as many tween characters as you'll find music genres.

Unfortunately, the challenges don't stop there. You also need to take their media choices and brand preferences into consideration. Additionally, you will need to take account of the Internet, chat rooms, mobile phones, games and virtual worlds where tweens have the ability to change image and characteristics several times a day.

Judith Rich Harris, a leading behavioural psychologist, says that a tween often has one type of image at home and a totally different image at school. In her book *The Nurture Assumption*, she says it's common for children to behave in an entirely contradictory way at home and school. We need to identify just how complex the multi-image personality phenomenon is. Are there any common denominators between each tween image personality? Or is a lack of common denominator the reality? The answer probably lies in the fact that it's a bit of both.

As virtual games integrate their worlds with the daily life of tweens, we are likely to see the them increasingly separate their own values and brands, depending on what life they're living at any given moment. Whatever we may think of this, the trend is probably unstoppable.

From a marketing perspective, this raises a number of challenging questions. First and foremost we need to find a way of identifying a target group that is never the same.

The tools are there, but they still aren't good enough

Over the years a range of different personality tests have been applied to various segments of the market. There's AC Nielsen's RISC, Europstyle and Target Group Index (TGI) developed by BMRB. These tools are designed to identify certain market segments and find common denominators across the traditional geographic and demographic indicators. TGI is an example based on 10,000 interviews conducted annually, with each interview lasting between two and three hours. It helps marketers under-stand the behaviour of an ever-changing target group.

We see these tools in action when we go to sites like amazon.com and Barnes & Noble. As soon as you select a book from their databases, it immediately matches your choice with an array of similar or related titles. Sometimes this is useful, but sometimes it's irrelevant. Although these tools are helpful, no technique has so far has been able to grasp the unpre-dictability of the tweens who tap into new channels that are barely known to traditional market researchers.

EIGHT GUIDELINES FOR TARGETING TWEENS

One target group description is never enough

When formulating a marketing plan aimed at tweens, it's important to remember that you will need more than one or two fixed descriptions of this group. By the same token, one or two good strategies will not be enough. In order to be effective, you will need to have at least eight descriptions of your target group, with just as many marketing approaches for the brand you wish to launch.

Red Bull's global launch reflects this thinking. The energy drink identi-fied alternative distribution channels – like local gas stations – where their target market tended to hang out. Their strategy was spot-on. The largest distribution channel for energy drinks in Europe is gas stations. Red Bull fills up metres of refrigeration space and it's surrounded by other energy drinks that have cottoned on to the process.

Similar to the Absolut vodka strategy that we have already described, Red Bull chose to enter the global market catering first to a specially-targeted niche group. Unlike Billabong and FUBU, Red Bull did not start its brand life within a community. Rather it had to create its own, and once that was done they relied on it to drive the product's success. Instead of relying on the traditional channels of TV and print media, Red Bull chose to diversify its message and use direct marketing as its major tool. This enabled them to constantly alter the message to fit the type of audience with whom they were communicating.

In New York City they used easily-recognizable Red Bull cars carrying a Red Bull can on the roof. They recruited teams from their target audi-ence to drive from district to district handing out samples.

In Austria the slogan 'Red Bull Gives You Wings' created the basis for a competition where tweens and teens competed to see who could fly for the longest time. And fly they did. They used all their physical creativity to jump from a ramp. A panel selected the person judged to have the longest flight.

These events were supported with in-store promotions, the Internet, and as we discussed earlier, product placement in the mid-levels of Sony PlayStation games.

The common denominator of these campaigns was the word 'energy'. Later on the slogan 'Gives you wings' was added. But the interpretation varied according to where in the world the message was being received. This flexibility allowed the message to stay relevant, no matter where it was being broadcast. Take, for example, the word 'cool'. Everyone uses it, although the interpretation is as different as its user. In Australia surfers may consider the particular curve on a wave as cool. In New York City it can be applied to a dance party, while in Denmark a new ring-tone on the mobile is also cool. As we cross the continents, the value of the word is the same, but the expression takes on a totally different form.

Tween marketing is very similar. Our *BRANDchild* research shows that you can't expect what a Japanese tween finds cool to be regarded as cool in Germany. The only safe ground you can be sure of is to focus on a few well-chosen values to drive the campaign across audience types, and help you ensure consistency.

You must be prepared to run several different campaigns in the same region, appealing to different tween audiences. This may be confusing, but the interesting fact is that tweens will easily understand that their favourite brand takes on a different tone of voice according to who it is addressing. The golden rule is to ensure that the core values of the brand remain consistently the same.

Be out there

As you will notice, almost all the successful tween campaigns I've referred to are based on direct marketing methods. Event-driven activities, at least for the moment, seem to be the major driving force in launching a new brand aimed at reaching tweens. Over time, when the brand's profile and image have been established, the story might be different.

They all do it…

▌ Billabong sponsors surfing competitions around the world;
▌ FUBU holds rap competitions;

▌ Jones Soda runs singing, surfing, skateboarding and gliding competitions;
▌ Adidas organizes basketball competitions for sons and dads;
▌ Nike arranges secret soccer matches;
▌ McDonald's arranges soccer shows.

These brands will all have two or three brand values in common across their promotions and event activities.

Despite the fact that the tween audience is extremely diverse, your brand values should not entirely reflect this diversity. The more concise the values message of your brand, the better the opportunity to spread your message across several channels, personality types and countries, ensuring it is appropriately adapted to the situation so that there's synergy across the brand platform.

Another point to remember is that in order to be successful, it's important that the market feels it has ownership of the brand. This ownership, as we have already pointed out, can help establish your brand, far and wide. There's a distinct danger in trying to appeal to tweens unilaterally. Keeping it local, and running a direct campaign aimed at the tween market has shown to be the single most successful way of establishing a new brand.

Creating relevance

Once you have succeeded in building a solid brand platform, relevance becomes the next point of focus. This process is difficult. It's complicated by the fact that you're looking at it with adult eyes, and what's relevant to you will most certainly be irrelevant to a tween. Conversely, they would be equally stymied if asked to create a relevant campaign for you!

Some years ago, a small brand managed to win acclaim by distributing cheat codes on the Net. These help players navigate the intricacies of the game so they can progress at a much faster rate than they ordinarily would. However, accessing these codes required more than simply finding the site. You had to combine a code printed on the back of a soft drink label, with another code on the Internet site to solve the mystery – and crack the code! Over a period of weeks, thousands of tweens logged on to the site, and they promptly went out and purchased the code-labelled drink. Within a few months the soft drink became a major seller and cheat codes were available everywhere!

This activity would be irrelevant to almost every adult one can think of.

Relevance varies according to the particular tween group to whom you are talking. Gamers might love you if you happened to be a virtual avatar. They'd guide you through difficult challenges in a virtual world. Or they might find you relevant if you happened to build skate parks, or if you followed Nokia's example. Nokia built a hospital where you could urgently replace the cover of your phone or change the ring-tone.

It is essential that the link between product, brand value, event and relevance is clear. One weak link in the chain, and you can be sure that tweens will disregard you. Even if the event is relevant, the product may be too difficult to find – and then you are almost guaranteed they will leave for good.

In a recent *BRANDchild* conversation about mobile phone brands and a neighbourhood event, a tween was heard to comment: 'They gave away free skateboard wheels – cool. But hey, what does that have to do with mobile phones? Well I don't care, I took the wheels and left – who can resist free wheels? One thing is for sure: I'll never change to that brand – their campaign was stupid. I bet their prices are really high because they're giving away all these wheels.'

Relevance therefore has two dimensions. First, in relation to the particular personality segment you are addressing, and second, to your core brand values. If you don't fulfil both aspects, it's more than likely you'll end up in the same category as the mobile phone company who gave away skateboard wheels – tuned out and turned off.

Creating synergy across channels

As more media opportunities open up, the issue facing marketers is not only which media channel is most appropriate to carry a brand's message, but also how to secure brand synergy across multiple media channels so you don't fragment the message.

Here are a couple of principles that will help you avoid disabling your brand's message.

Channel synergy

Your brand should enjoy synergy across a range of passive and interactive media. For example, if you use TV, a passive channel, you could use the medium to direct your audience towards an interactive medium, such as the store. Then, make sure the in-store promotion harnesses the traffic generated by the televised message. If it doesn't, failure occurs and synergy is lost. If you decide to run a radio promotion, use the airwaves to direct your audience to your Web site. Likewise, in all your print messages you can encourage interaction via your SMS service.

The fundamental principle is to shift between passive and active media, always ensuring that you link the channels' traffic together. This spreads your brand's message as widely as possible and ensures that consumers have somewhere else to go or an action to take – a fresh avenue that will keep them involved with your brand. If there's no immediate action then the ad and memories of the brand go into long-term memory.

The passive/interactive channel combination allows for immediate response. It offers another possibility in the cycle of consumer action and response.

'I hate 1800 numbers – you can't SMS them!'

In my part of the world, the TV show *Big Brother* was a hit. Viewers voted on who could stay in the *Big Brother* house and who had to leave. Viewers called a phone number to vote.

Most of the *Big Brother* audience falls into the 14 to 28-year-old age group. Most have mobile phones and Web access. Despite the fact up to 80 per cent of the audience prefers to use e-mail or SMS to vote, these options aren't offered. Why is that? Because the television station earns a few cents on every call. How many potential voters is the station losing by forcing viewers to use one communication channel? Why doesn't it leverage the fact that SMS or Internet voting would generate other advertising and revenue opportunities and, possibly, 25 per cent more viewers?

Choice of medium should not be based on what's convenient for the marketer but what's convenient for the consumer. If consumers prefer e-mail, give them e-mail access. If they prefer paper coupons, give them paper coupons. In the end, your choice of channel will affect your traffic and brand loyalty.

Building virtual brands in virtual worlds

Building a virtual brand in a virtual world presents a dream scenario for marketers, because in a virtual world you can track every action, dialogue, purchase and behaviour pattern. Any product used to enhance an avatar's role would itself be virtual, so there would be no need for warehousing or inventory management.

On the other hand, a host of new challenges are very likely to present themselves – challenges that are yet to be worked through. First, there's the challenge of positioning a brand in a virtual community. Take, for example, Nike shoes. You will need to pay real money for a pair of virtual Nike shoes, which you can only use in a virtual world. How could you justify paying the money? How would you position your brand in the virtual community? What would possibly justify paying money for nothing? The brand! Is your brand strong enough to enter such a test? And how would you differentiate your brand from other competing brands in such a world? Will your Nike jump over hot coals? Can they walk on water? Will they help you fly? And then, most importantly, will these extraordinary feats be compatible with your real-life brand platform?

This may sound fantastic, but it's important to remember that the biggest entertainment market for tweens and teens is about to become the gaming industry. According to NPD Fun World and NPD Tech World, in 2001, the gaming industry had a turnover of US \$6.35 billion in the United States alone – a figure that's estimated to be close to US \$17 billion worldwide. And as we speak, 145 million people are playing computer and video games in the United States (Peter D Hart Research, 2000). On average, tweens spend close to two hours a day on games – which in all likelihood will become four hours within the next three years. This is the same amount of time that they spend in front of television.

As graphics become more sophisticated, and download times quicker and quicker, so the experience in the virtual world will become ever-more enticing. This makes the likelihood of virtual brands a foregone conclusion – particularly among the tween segment of the market. We need to focus on how to build a virtual brand platform. The answer lies in staying firmly committed to the brand's core values.

We need to remember that the predominant feature of virtual worlds is their persistence. The communities exist all day, every day, and take on a life of their own. In the early days, virtual communities consisted of sparse graphics, short cuts and text-based messages. So when the more sophisticated virtual worlds forced Microsoft's pioneering Meridian 59, or M59, to close, hundreds of people mourned its loss. There was a strong feeling that M59 had been a significant part of their lives. People had made friends that they didn't want to leave. Since then, black market versions have sprung up and are being maintained in Germany, South Korea and Russia.

Avoiding brand suicide

If you initially choose to commit to this type of audience and not maintain this, you are committing brand suicide. Building a virtual brand presence is like building a real one. This may seem an exaggeration, but it is the fact: a virtual presence must be treated as seriously as a bricks-and-mortar one. If you dabble here and there in virtual communities and online worlds, this will reflect a brand unable to commit to its audience.

Adapting your language to fit the audience

Since 1949, when George Orwell published his novel *1984*, it has remained the harbinger of doom for ultimate totalitarian state control over the masses. As we forge ahead into the new millennium, 1984 has been and gone. A prophecy unfulfilled. But relief may be premature. In an appendix to *1984*, Orwell wrote of an even more ominous date. In 2050 the ultimate technology for thought control would be in place, he predicted, and the common language for this will be Newspeak. It will provide a form of expression for the new world-view. It will supersede Oldspeak by inventing new words with clearer, more controlled meaning.

Welcome to TweenSpeak

Have you noticed tweens sending messages on their phones? Their thumbs move across the numbers with nimbleness and speed. They hardly need to glance at what they're writing. Word prediction programs allow whole sentences to be conveyed with a few touches. They call it texting.

Since the arrival of chat rooms and mobile phone texting, tweens have adapted a language suited to the technology. It is not necessarily a product of this technology, but a mixture of technological barriers and impatience. Tweens have no desire to spend several minutes composing a grammatically correct sentence. Forget about it! Those days are gone. We would be mistaken to assume the language has evolved because the screens on mobile phones can't accommodate fuller sentences. Even when tweens have access to full screens and keyboards – as they use in chats – they continue to write in abbreviated form.

Steven Pinker, a professor in the Department of Brain and Cognitive Science at MIT, says in his book *Words and Rules* (1999), that although language is in a constant state of change, it is happening faster than ever before. The point of adoption is, however, the same. Change makes most headway through the young of any society.

Speeding up the evolution of TweenSpeak

The instant nature of the tools at hand is impacting on the language, and the change is more instantly apparent than has been seen with previous generations. Abbreviations and acronyms permeate TweenSpeak. Correct grammar is considered nerdy. This 'typo-infested, acronym-speckled language' is youth-specific and has a distinct global accent.

The *BRANDchild* study shows that 64 per cent of all urban tweens globally change their language when texting. Half of these claim it's because it's quicker, but the remainder do it because they think they sound more cool or it reflects a better image. What's interesting is that it is the countries with high mobile phone penetration that are the ones who aim for a cooler image. The countries with low penetration – like China, Brazil and the United States – say they change the language for the sake of speed.

Without a doubt tweens understand this language well. They have no need for dictionaries or grammar texts because they've invented it. Is it here to stay? I asked Steven Pinker, and he said:

> The typo-infested, acronym-speckled epistles that fill our electronic mail-boxes will not fatally infect speech and writing. A century ago, the telegraph did not lead people to omit prepositions from their speech or end every sentence with 'STOP'. People adjust their language depending on whom they are addressing (children or spouses, friends or strangers) and how they want to sound (casual or official, orotund or businesslike).

However, there are three main reasons why this language shift might be much bigger than first anticipated:

1. Every tween 'speaks' the language. And if they don't, they'll have to learn it quickly if they want to join the conversation. Telegraph wires were only used by a few, and were by their very nature confined to a fairly specialized group of people.
2. Increasingly, acronyms have advanced into words. We have lasers (light amplification by stimulated emissions) and we talk about ATMs (automatic teller machines), and everything we do is required ASAP. It's almost impossible to imagine a slower-paced world evolving

where we'll begin writing material for your information – instead of FYI!

3. We cannot discount the domino effect. The new language is not restricted to chat rooms or mobile phone displays. It has penetrated everywhere. It appears in ads, on billboards and in tween magazines. You hear it in songs and commercials. It's also entered day-to-day tween conversations.

Whether the language is here to stay or disappears in a few years time, tweens who don't speak it are at risk of being labelled nerds.

Preparing your message for new channels

Let me ask you a difficult question. How on earth would you build your brand on a canvas smaller than a matchbox? And to further limit the situation, imagine using only one colour (say, black on green), having no scope for graphics, and the consumer is paying by the second to receive the text message.

These are the current limitations on radio branding, and knowing how quickly it could arrive, you should start making plans for it. Forgive me for comparing this with a cigarette brand, as this shouldn't have anything to do with kids, but the Silk Cut example is too good to pass over. In the 1980s, this English brand brilliantly prepared for the blanket government ban on cigarette commercials. All cigarette companies knew that the ban was coming and had plenty of time to prepare. But only a few used this time well. Silk Cut's marketing campaigns continued unabated. They did this by cultivating an image, using luxuriously rumpled purple silk with a gaping slash through it. By the time the ban was upon the tobacco corporations, no-one needed to see the words 'Silk Cut' to know what the ad was saying. It effectively became a recognizable image. Colour and style became the communicator. Billboards with racing cars in the distinctive purple livery spread the word. No-one even noticed that the brand name did not appear.

Marlboro is another brand that successfully bypassed the cigarette advertising restrictions. The cigarette retained its client base and communicated with potential smokers by promoting its Marlboro Country clothing brand.

Both brands managed to creatively navigate the strict limitations placed on them. Likewise a tiny one-colour screen can display a logo, but that would not justify a consumer paying for it. One way around the problem may be to work on a product placement arrangement that would ensure your brand is exposed whenever it's relevant on the news, or as a movie ad.

Another possibility would be to develop your brand's language – to use phrases that the consumer would recognize as being the voice of your brand. Companies are already developing phrases that are associated with their brands. Over the past few months Coca-Cola has been heavily promoting the word 'Enjoy'. Intel Inside has a specific melody, which could easily signify their brand when played on a mobile phone. Both companies have created identifiers around their brands which can, independent of their logos, names and images, remind the consumer about the brand and all it stands for.

But many, many more brands haven't yet been as inventive. And despite the fact that we may feel we've recently seen many new interactive channels appearing, there are undoubtedly many more to come. A solid brand strategy is all about creating a value proposition that can be carried across multiple media, using few tools in a very creative way. If you don't have any tools, create them fast, because the race for branding phone display real estate has already begun. And at this early stage, there's already not much space left.

Figure 9.2 *'Dial a Coke'. The local Australian telecommunication company Telstra and Coca-Cola ran one of the world's first test trials in Sydney enabling consumers to order and pay for a Coke using their mobile phones.*

The future is all about branding everything – including language

Brands that manage to reinvent old terms and new abbreviations are not only likely to appeal to the tween audience, but also tend to own the word – at least for a while. The Commonwealth Bank of Australia ran a campaign based on the question 'Which bank?'. The ads were so strong that after a while the bank no longer needed to answer with its name. The question alone automatically brought them to mind. If the same principle were to be applied to the tween world, it would open the door to some interesting possibilities.

In theory your brand name would present itself every time the word was mentioned on the mobile phone display, in the chat rooms, or of course in your own ads. As yet there are no established rules and the terminology is evolving so the language is yours to command!

How far do you go?

Let's dispel a myth. A brand doesn't need to speak in the same tones across every media. Some media channels are more receptive to relaxed voice, while others prefer more formal and detail-oriented tones. In fact, it's likely that you could destroy your brand if you try to force a certain tone of voice on a medium that's not sympathetic with that channel. So, for example, you only have eight words at your disposal on a mobile phone screen. To speak formally means you've outworded your message. So it will need to conform to the quick, simple and erasable style associated with the message carrier.

I don't mean to imply that your message can be inconsistent across communication channels. On the contrary, brand consistency lies in core values, key words and identifiable style – not in copy. By the same token, copy can no longer remain static in every brand manifestation. The range of media at your disposal requires your brand's tone of voice to be flexible.

What are the guidelines?

Whatever we may personally feel about TweenSpeak, it's here for at least a while. So it's important we start dealing with it. Your tween campaign should use at least 5, if not 10, different media channels. Of these, it's likely that 80 per cent will be based on written communication. It might be useful to begin considering how to approach your own brand's language.

What's your brand's language?

Like Coke and the Commonwealth Bank, does your brand have its own slogan or phrase? Would tweens instantly recognize it as yours? Have you spread your brand across many channels? Do you appeal to tween audiences in numerous ways using several different messaging styles?

It is more important than ever to exercise as much control as possible over your few branded elements. Language is an inherent part of this. The more synergy you can create in your language, the better. It's important that you identify certain terms and particular words, and then repeat them across the relevant channels.

You should also define the essence of your language, then operate within those parameters. For example, you have one way of talking and another of writing. This changes according to the person you are addressing. In some cases you might talk in a business context, while in friendly situations you tend to speak more casually. But despite the different environments, there is consistency in your style. And it's this consistency that will unite the different channel strategies for your brand, making it recognizable across a mobile-phone display, a billboard, a TV commercial, a virtual shop and a banner ad without necessarily stating the name of your brand.

In order to reach this synergy there are a number of questions you need to answer:

▶ What gender is your brand?

Is it masculine, feminine or neutral?

▶ Which terms does your brand like – and which terms does it hate?

Does it favour repetitive phrases that represent its image and opinions? What terms work against it?

▶ Does your brand use metaphors? And if so, what type of metaphors?

Metaphors are effective in representing your brand, its features and its services.

▶ Does your brand identify as casual or formal?

Your company's formality, or lack of it, can be seen in simple things like an e-mail address. Do you use the first name of a person, or their last? Would your name translate equally well on an SMS message or a letterhead?

► Is your brand witty, to the point and direct?

Does your brand have a sense of humour? Can it react to current events, or is it isolated from the rest of the world?

► Is your brand visual in its language, or is it reliant on words?

Do you need to explain a lot about who you are?

► Is your brand action oriented in its language?

Is a call to action implicit in your brand, or does it passively leave the action up to the consumer?

IT ALL COUNTS

Building brands in the future will become a much more complex process than it was 10 years ago. The number of new communication channels, a substantial rise in new media alternatives, the appearance of a much more diversified audience, the emergence of interactive media, virtual worlds and even a new language are all setting the stage for new rules, which need to be followed in order to control the total brand presence.

You might not yet be planning to open a virtual world in MindArk next year, or to run a radio campaign launching your new products. But you should be prepared for this, so you can build your brand platform for when the day comes that your brand needs to take the next step. This way you can ensure that you are perfectly placed to embrace many channels and can thus avoid the negative 'nerd' label spelling death to your brand.

SUMMARY

▌ It's important that marketers pay attention to the virtual world phenomenon. Virtual worlds may soon become one of the most important forums for tween interaction, alongside the telephone and e-mail. Within five years they will become the key component in every marketing plan.

▌ Role-playing games, which are also know as multi-player games, are based on interactivity, physicality and persistence, and have been shown to be the most addictive and time-consuming game type.

▌ Games will most likely become the main driver in many tweens' lives. Studies show that spending time playing games becomes compulsive. Why? Because tweens choose their own identity, their own world and their own role. It is here where tweens can truly feel themselves at the centre of the world.

▌ Within the not-too-distant future, virtual worlds will encourage bricks-and-mortar-based brands to establish virtual 3-D stores in their worlds. This will force your brand to develop a 'virtual' brand platform.

▌ Classical marketing approaches, such as identifying your audience's age, location and demographic, are no longer possible. Each tween will in future represent several different profiles, or in worst-case scenarios, several different personas.

▌ Adapt your language to fit the audience. A totally new tween language has appeared. It's called TweenSpeak and will most likely change your brand's tone of voice.

▌ M-branding will follow gaming. Most likely your next campaign will run on a mobile phone display.

▌ The future is all about branding everything – including language. Theoretically your brand name will present itself every time the relevant word is mentioned on the mobile phone display, in the chat rooms, or of course in your own ads.

ACTION POINTS

▶ Identify your audience's use of electronic media, including mobile phones, chat rooms, the Internet and gaming.

▶ You have realized that electronic media will be a major part of tweens' lives, so it is essential for your brand to start developing a strategy to integrate your communication to make it appropriate to these new channels. In short, how will you ensure that at least 10 per cent – preferably 20 per cent – of your total budget will be spent on interactive channels over the next two years?

▶ Identify the many personality types your tween audience represents when playing games and chatting. Then turn these into five or six audience categories on which you can base your communication strategy.

▶ It's alpha omega to control your brand values. Develop a virtual brand platform that enables you to spread your message across multiple interactive channels and still control the brand's 'personality'. Develop the brand's tone of voice, and a graphic that can adapt to mobile phone displays, computer games and chat rooms, with a vocabulary that is unique to your brand.

10

Personalized brands build strong businesses

Patricia B Seybold

Tweens – youngsters between the ages of 8 and 14 – have a strong desire to put their personal brand on the things they wear and share with their friends.

How do you build a business around tweens' desire for self-expression? Ask Maxine Clark, the CEO of Build-A-Bear® Workshops. Since 1997, she has built a successful retail empire of 100 stores, with revenues-per-square-foot hitting a surprising US $700, compared to the US national average of $350 per square foot in a shopping mall. Build-A-Bear will be rolling out internationally in 2003.

What's the secret?

Clark has succeeded at tapping into a combination of tweens' values. These are:

▌ let me express myself;
▌ let me have fun;
▌ let me do my own thing;
▌ let me get my friends involved;
▌ let me host a great party;
▌ let me show off to my friends and family.

Build-A-Bear Workshops are interactive retail outlets, stores to which tweens (mostly girls) flock after school to craft their own personalized stuffed animals for themselves and their friends. It's an interactive, hands-on experience. It's one you can share with your friends or do on your own.

The result is a highly personalized teddy, dog or other cuddly animal, stuffed with qualities to which most kids' aspire – hugs, happiness, love, and friendship – custom-dressed in an outfit they make up, with a voice and a message they can select or self-record.

Build-A-Bear's interactive retail formula has built-in cross-selling and upselling, as well as built-in viral marketing. A companion Web site has a Build-A-Bear configurator, a party planning scenario, the ability to send customized greeting cards and an e-newsletter to flesh out the offerings.

KIDS HELP TO DESIGN AN INTERACTIVE RETAILING CONCEPT

Maxine Clark's retailing career began at the May Department Stores Company, where she started as an executive trainee, and quickly became valued for her ability to spot emerging retail and merchandizing trends. At the May Company she initiated merchandizing partnerships with Disney, American Greetings and Mattel. Clark then moved on to become president of Payless Shoe Source from 1992–96, turning Payless into the Number One seller of children's licensed footwear in the world.

As she was considering her options in early 1997, Clark thought about a 'make-it-yourself stuffed animal' store. She tried out the idea on two tweens: Katie (13) and Jack (10) Burkhardt. They were enthusiastic. 'They loved the idea and wanted to help me with it,' Clark recalls. As she fleshed out the game plan that eventually became the first Build-A-Bear Workshop store in St Louis, she recruited 20 children, aged 6 to 14, to serve on a customer advisory board. She called it her Cub Board.

WHAT'S THE BUILD-A-BEAR EXPERIENCE?

Tweens flock to the stores after school and on weekends. 'It's mostly girls and younger boys. Once boys get to be 13 or 14, they think they're too cool to build a bear,' explained one avid bear-builder. 'But you should see the older guys! Eighteen, 19 and even 20-year-old guys come in and cavort around, building animals for their girlfriends. And then there are the wedding bears,' she said dreamily. 'A lot of couples come in and make custom bears for the bride and groom.'

So how does the in-store assembly line work? You start at the Choose Me station, by selecting a slightly pre-stuffed but mostly empty animal skin. You can choose from dozens of styles of bears, as well as cats, leopards, tigers, bunnies, puppies, elephants, horses or dogs, including the popular black Labrador.

Next, you move to the Stuff Me area, where you select the hypo-allergenic stuffing that gets blown into your bear with the help of a Master Bear Builder (store associate). The stuffing comes in several flavours, labelled Hugs and Kisses, Love, Kindness or Friendship. By pushing buttons, you custom-fill your animal with just the right amount of each. Then you pick a heart to put inside your bear. The heart contains your bear's unique-in-the-world bar code.

You can even add optional sound to your bear or other stuffed toy at the Hear Me station. These can be pre-recorded sounds, like a Happy Birthday song, or *The Bear Went Over the Mountain*, or seasonal ditties. Or, best of all, you can Build-A-Sound by recording 10 seconds worth of your own song or message in your own voice, through the magic of Voice Express technology. Many customers retire to the bathroom to record their messages in private. 'We call it our Flush Me studio,' Clark quipped in an interview with the *St Louis Post Gazette*.

Next you move on to give your newly-created furry friend an air bath, to blow excess stuffing and fur off, and brush its plush fur. You can stop there, and just add a free ribbon to adorn your furry friend. But the majority of customers opt to dress their animals, selecting from a wide variety of costumes. You can dress your bear as a hockey player, a ballerina or a monster. There's a constant range of new garments from which to choose, including branded items, like Skechers shoes.

Once your fuzzy friend is completed and dressed, it's time to register and name him or her. In the Name Me area of each store, there's a set of customized computer workstations with large kid-friendly keys. You sit down, fill in a form to name your friend and print out his or her birth certificate.

Then your toy gets its very own cardboard house in which you can take it home or give it away at the final Take Me Home stop.

Of course, this registration process lets Build-A-Bear keep track of each bear, each bear builder (customer) and each bear owner. For the customers, the advantage is that Build-A-Bear keeps track of errant bears. If you lose one, the chances are good that someone will return it to a nearby store, where store associates can look it up and return it to its rightful owner. For Build-A-Bear, the bear registration process gives it a great start on its customer database. More prospects and customers sign up on the Web site to receive the company's ongoing e-newsletters and coupons.

The entire Build-A-Bear experience typically lasts for 20 minutes. That's enjoyable time spent creating a unique and highly personal branded toy for yourself or a friend or family member. There's no better way to express your unique and quirky personality! But, of course, the Build-A-Bear experience doesn't stop after you've built your first bear.

BUILT-IN UPSELLING AND CROSS-SELLING

Most Build-A-Bear customers come back over and over again. 'There's one family that comes in every weekend to get everything that's new.' The average Build-A-Bear customer typically builds and clothes at least five toys per year. Many continue to accessorize their toys by shopping online at Build-A-Bear's Web site. The site has a huge selection of ever-changing outfits and accessories for the well-dressed bear (or dog or kitty). Among tweens, it's common to create a new custom toy for each friend's birthday. 'I have one friend who goes in often to build bears to cheer her friends up, or to celebrate a special event, like winning a game. Another one saves up all her spending money until she can build a new bear,' one customer explained.

BEARY VIRAL MARKETING

'I got my first bear for my birthday. I'm an ice skater, and it came dressed in a complete skating outfit. I fell in love with it, and I went looking for a Build-A-Bear store so I could have the experience of creating my own bears. Now I have everything: bears, kitties, dogs, I just want to have them all!' explained one enthusiastic customer. 'Now I build bears for all my friends' birthdays and I bring them to the store and send them to the Web site.'

Beary birthdays

Birthday parties are a key part of Build-A-Bear's viral marketing approach. It's easy to arrange a party – you can call and reserve a spot, drop into the nearest store and make your selections, or you can use the Build-A-Party planner on the Build-A-Bear Web site. Usually parents make the party arrangements, deciding how much they're willing to spend per child, and pre-paying. Some Build-A-Bear Workshop stores have a separate party room. Others just herd the flock of kids through the assembly line. Each party group has its own dedicated Master Bear Builder to walk kids through the process and to help them stay within the parents' budget. Build-A-Bear even helps you arrange the rest of your party – the pizza or hamburgers, ice-cream and cake after the bear-building event, through partnerships with restaurants in each mall.

This Plan My Party scenario is a great example of a customer ScenarioNet, something that includes other companies offering services to help the customer achieve what she wants. Build-A-Bear makes it really easy for the parent and the kids to plan and execute a great party, by linking in all the different companies and brands needed to pull off the Pawfect party.

Recruiting store associates

With over 100 stores, it's a challenge for any retailer to recruit, train and maintain a knowledgeable workforce. Build-A-Bear has a built-in recruitment engine. Avid customers become enthusiastic Master Bear-Builders. As soon as they come of age, kids who used to drop in after school to hang out and to build their own bears are encouraged to apply for a position as a Bear-Builder. Not everyone makes the cut. You need to have a positive, bubbly, outgoing personality. But if you're selected, your friends think you're really cool. Master Bear-Builders attend a three-week training class to learn the company culture, lingo and attitudes. 'It's a lot like working at Disney World – your attitude is everything. We want our customers to have fun!'

KEEP THE HONEY FLOWING AND THE BUZZ ALIVE

Build-A-Bear has a great and growing set of after-market offerings that keep its customers coming back for more. You can earn and redeem, you can give Bear Bucks gift certificates (to redeem in the store), or use digital

Bear Bucks certificates (to redeem on the Web site). You can send a Bear-o-Gram (pre-dressed holiday or special occasion mini-bears) to a friend from the Web site, as well as design your own customized HoneyCard electronic greeting. There are several lines of collectibles, a book club, a library, downloadable screen savers and lots of games and contests.

STAYING ATTUNED TO CUSTOMERS

Everyone at Build-A-Bear stays tuned to customer feedback. Maxine Clark personally reads most of the e-mails and other feedback the company receives each day. 'They tell me where to locate the next retail store, what colour outfits they want, and what's working and what's not.'

SUMMARY

What does Build-A-Bear Workshops tell us about the future of retailing? By looking at this highly successful and profitable business model – one that was designed by tweens, for tweens – we can note several key critical success factors for winning the hearts and minds of these consumers while they're in their tweens, and as they grow older.

Here are the key success elements of the Build-A-Bear success story:

▌ start by listening to your customers. Get their help in designing the offering and the customer experience;

▌ build customer feedback into your planning process;

▌ offer products that customers can brand with their own personalities and aspirations;

▌ offer a fun, entertaining, interactive in-store experience;

▌ support and enhance the in-store experience with a complete interactive online experience;

▌ offer a massive assortment of products and services on your Web site – things that you couldn't possibly stock in every store;

▌ give your customers easy ways to tell their friends about their experience;

▌ recruit your sales associates from your best customers;

▌ focus on your customers' key scenarios: planning and hosting parties, celebrating a special event or rewarding an accomplishment. Design your customer experiences around those key scenarios, incorporating partners who can offer complementary services;

▌ create a fun-filled, honest corporate culture!

11

Santa's nightmare

Tweens are described as the 'richest generation' in history. Certainly those living in the Western world are. There's an endless variety of disposable goods and leisure products designed specifically for them. They're sophisticated consumers, and thus a marketer's dream. But the dream has a harsher side, more akin to a nightmare.

These are the facts. An average child in the United States, Australia and the UK sees between 20 to 40,000 commercials a year (Leonhardt and Kerwi, 1997). According to a study done in 1999 by the Annenberg Public Policy Center, US children spend 60 per cent more time watching television each year than they spend in school. Children's spending has roughly doubled every 10 years over the past three decades. In 2000, teens aged from 12 to 17 spent a record US $155 billion. In 2001, children aged 4 to 12 spent an estimated $35 billion in the United States. Contrast this with the 1960s, when children influenced about US $5 billion of their parents' purchase. By 1984 that figure had increased tenfold, to US $50 billion. By 1997 it had tripled to US $188 billion, and in 2000 their purchase power had reached a whopping US $290 billion in the United States alone. Globally, their total purchase influence is an astounding US $1.88 trillion.

At six months of age, a baby begins imitating simple sounds like 'Ma-Ma'. Babies are also forming mental images of corporate logos and mascots. In Dr James U McNeal's book *Kids as Customers*, he estimates that brand loyalty can be influenced from about the age of two, when babies are forming these mental images. Children as young as three can recognize brand logos, and experts say that each lifetime consumer may be worth US $100,000 to a retailer, making effective cradle-to-grave strategies extremely valuable.

Has all this resulted in information overload? Probably not. In fact, I believe that information overload is not relevant to today's tween. It's a term that's more applicable to an older group who saw television and radio stations grow from two to 2000. We saw a proliferation of magazines and newspapers, and witnessed the emergence of the Internet, a place which in just over seven years contains close on 40 billion pages – if this can be estimated at all!

What we tend to forget is that this proliferation of media has always been around for today's tweens. Have you ever observed a tween surfing the Net? You will notice that they rarely have one window open at a time. They have 10! And this is happening while the television runs, the CD player plays and they have a friend on the telephone line. This is tween relaxation time!

So it's not surprising that this dramatic increase in tween communication is reflected in the toy industry, which has found it increasingly challenging to create and maintain visibility in this market. The daily challenge lies not only in the fact that television as the primary media for marketing has become a bottle-neck for most brands. The increasing media diversity across the Internet, mobile phones, games and magazines has created a communication challenge that's never been seen before. Marketers not only have to keep up with the steadily increasing media market, but to target this audience one also has to keep up with a fragmented tween audience, which constantly shifts behaviour according to the most recent trends.

ADDING LIFE TO BRANDS

It is clear that more and more tween brands are looking to Hollywood to add life and emotions to their product. They're increasingly emulating a glamorous tone of voice for the ever-growing ads targeting the tween market. Ironically, over the past two years, almost every studio and film distributor has embraced the Web as a critical marketing tool, and one of the most effective means of reaching audiences directly and creating a conversation about a movie.

The Web has also been used to secure a clicks-and-mortar synergy for print media wanting to gain the tween audience's attention. The dramatic increase in linkage between electronic media is reflected in the whopping usage figure of six-and-three-quarter hours a day among 8 to13-year-olds. It is clear that in order for a brand to survive, it must have an interconnection-based strategy. For a toy to survive it will need to develop an integrated movie, television show and possibly computer game strategy in its media plan. The motion picture, whether it is on television or in the cinema, has become the lifeblood of tween brands.

The death of toys as we knew them

When I was 12 years old, my bedroom was filled with toys. You could hardly see the floor for LEGO bricks, cars and monsters. Visit any 12-year-old's bedroom today, and you will see things have dramatically changed. Toys are gone. They've been replaced with CD-ROM covers, movies and CDs. So based on this we can assume that once a child has reached the ripe old age of 10, traditional toys have become irrelevant. This significantly reduces the life span that toys once enjoyed. In fact if a toy does happen to reach a 10-year-old's shelf, it is likely to be a spin-off from a movie or a game that's a result of a clicks-and-mortar toy strategy.

In order to understand this phenomenon, we need to look to Japan. The Japanese market has a tradition of integrating toy products with games and movies that dates back to the 1970s. Almost no serious game is released in Japan without toy merchandizing and movie back-up. Likewise, no toy is released without a strong connection to an interactive game or motion picture.

Toy companies have seen the importance of integrating their product with the entertainment industry to add 'life' to the concept. Today's successful Bob The Builder is a television show, a game, a toy and an international touring road show. We now have Yu-Gi-Oh!, DragonBallZ, Medabots and Cardcaptors, which are cartoon card collection systems that succeeded in reaching the US market by becoming 'advertainment' TV shows. From April 2002, Yu-Gi-Oh! could be seen six times a week on all major US television channels, similar to what the world saw two years ago with Pokèmon.

It is increasingly clear that the role of toys has changed. They are now but one of the cogs in the big entertainment industry, taking their place and creating their identity alongside films, games and television.

WHERE IT ALL BEGINS

Let's take a closer look at some of the motivators driving today's tweens. It's sad – but unfortunately true – that fear and pressure are the two most common elements characterizing the daily lives of tweens. In many parts of the world, this is undoubtedly fuelled by higher divorce rates, increasing crime and threats of war. But it is aggravated by the advertising industry, which structures its messages on fear-based elements in order to capture new markets. There are two main sources that generate fear in a tween's life: the schoolyard and peer pressure.

Schoolyards have turned into brand showrooms. This highlights economic divisions among groups. In a discussion, an 11-year-old girl commented: 'I love brands. Brands are my life. Brands not only tell me who I am, but also protect me from problems with the others in my class.'

A *Seventeen* magazine survey conducted in 1999 revealed that 44 per cent of tweens reported pressure to achieve academically; 29 per cent felt pressure to belong socially; 19 per cent felt pressure to use alcohol and drugs; and 13 per cent revealed that they felt pressure to be sexually active. The survey also indicated that, in general, girls experienced more pressure than boys.

Furthermore, the survey revealed 2000 female tweens and teens, representing 46 per cent, saying they were unhappy with their bodies; 35 per cent saying they would consider plastic surgery, including breast augmentation; and 7 per cent claiming to suffer from eating disorders.

So although this may be the most affluent generation to walk the planet, it also has the dubious distinction of being the most insecure and depressed. And whatever faith they seem to have, it's all invested in the power of the brand. Brands have become a contemporary expression of devotion. As formal religion in the Western world continues to erode, so brands move in to fill the vacuum. You could say that tween culture and media culture have merged to such an extent that it's almost impossible to tell which came first – the anger or the marketing of anger!

A Millward Brown study reveals that there are seven major factors that contribute to the fear and anxiety of US tweens. These are:

1. Identity seeking.
2. Fish streaming.
3. Quick to adopt, quick to reject.
4. Hate to be sold to and love to be respected.
5. Broader in scope, shallow in detail.
6. Been there, done that.
7. Community dependency.

Identity seeking

Consider television. Television networks discovered that tweens tune in at specific times. For example, summer days attract a large tween audience. Even the daytime soap operas alter their story lines and feature younger actors more prominently when school is out. So summer viewers are more likely to see commercials for acne medicine than arthritis relief.

If you happened to visit Ginger's Web site on cooltoons.com you would quickly learn that the characters in this show aired by Nickelodeon are based on real-world tween personality stereotypes.

For many years it has been claimed that tweens establish their identity via the media, and it has become increasingly clear that this is a fairly accurate assertion. Everyone from music promoters to television executives to movie producers besiege today's tweens with pseudo-authentic marketing pitches. And tweens increasingly look to the media to provide them with ready-made identities based on today's notion of 'cool'.

So, rather than empowering youngsters, the incessant focus on their wants and desires leaves them adrift in a sea of conflicting marketing messages. In many ways you could say tweens today feel frustrated and lonely partly because they are *encouraged* to feel that way.

Almost every brand, whether it is the Japanese Yu-Gi-Oh! or the United States's Britney Spears, are all products offering tweens a ready-made identity. Yu-Gi-Oh!, a role-playing game, offers tweens a new identity giving them special powers and strengths when exchanging cards. Britney creates a version of the ideal and offers distinct guidelines for how to look and behave.

Although it could be said that advertising has always exploited anxiety, this trend has steadily increased over the past few years. We have all seen the commercials telling girls that they're not pretty enough, don't have the right friends, and that they will be losers unless they're cool. However, today's reality is even more specific: the brand creates the values, the look and the acceptance, and unless you adopt the values embodied in the brand, you'll be a nobody.

Fish streaming

Tween brands focus on the tween market because tweens are trendsetters – not only for one another, but also for the population at large. Younger children look up to tweens to identify and adopt the latest fashion.

Plugging into this cycle of admiration is the key to establishing tween loyalty. Using direct marketing techniques focused on high school events is exactly what The Nouveau Group, a US production company based in Orlando, does. The company created a high school marketing program called Planet Gruv, which brings state-of-the-art concert sound and lighting, video jockeys and video screens to local high school dances. Sounds cool, but there's a catch. The event is sponsored by national advertisers who want to reach teens.

Teen People recently renewed its sponsorship contract with Planet Gruv. The relationship allows the magazine to give its national advertisers an opportunity to sponsor the high school tour, essentially plugging directly into the tween stream. The result has been that hundreds of high schools, which initially rejected on-campus promotions, are now opening their doors for the very first time, offering advertisers a primary position from which to communicate with the tween audience.

High school events are not the only way to plug into this generation. Heeling Sports Limited is a Texas-based shoe manufacturer which produces Heelys, a sneaker-like shoe that rolls like skates. They strictly limited access to the shoe to a select group of tweens and teens. The scarcity of the product made them utterly desirable and created a buzz wherever the Heelys-wearing representatives, known as 'riders', appeared. Initially, Heelys were also hard to find and were distributed through only a few stores. The limited number of skating shoes made them even more desirable and created a buzz and jealousy around the shoes. The limited release was followed by major retail distribution. Participating retailers reported Heelys flying off the shelves as quickly as they were stocked.

Bearing The Nouveau Group and the Heelys experience in mind, it is clear that the behaviour of tween groups is very similar to the behaviour of fish streams. They are closely linked and similarly influenced across the group, based on a clear-cut hierarchical system. This behavioural hierarchy has always existed.

From what used to be a local group extending only as far as a couple of neighbourhood streets, tween networks have now spread their wings to encompass the world. Due to the global scale of this group, narrow niche interests have now become popular. Where once only a few activities would be of interest – parties, sport, movies or make-up – now we see the rise of many niche interest groups. Tweens can connect with junk craftsmen, raising and showing computerized pets and duct tape artists. These passions can now be shared, on a daily basis, with anyone anywhere who has an online connection.

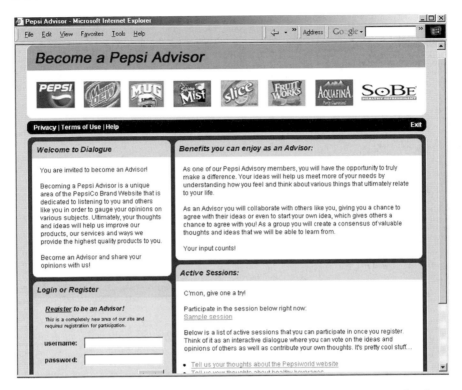

Figure 11.1 *The Pepsi dialogue. Pepsi goes 'MSP' by inviting its drinkers to develop future soft drink products for Pepsi & Co.*

A tween fish stream involves extending influence to the other side of the world. One only needs to look as far as Pokèmon to get a good idea of the reach. When Pokèmon was first launched in Japan, it became increasingly clear to Nintendo that the characters – their names and their roles – had to be dramatically adjusted to the US market.

The recent introduction of Yu-Gi-Oh! was different. The game is in many ways similar to Pokèmon or Dungeons and Dragons, but many American tweens had already discovered it long before it was launched in the United States. This is because there is already a proliferation of Web sites dedicated to informing tweens about current Japanese trends. As a result, there has been a much less dramatic change in concept than occurred for Pokèmon. The kids had already familiarized themselves with the characters, learning from their mates in Japan.

Constantly seeking confirmation

The fish stream trend is also characterized by the fact that tweens constantly seek confirmation that they are on the right track. The biggest fear of all is to stand out – alone! However, the complex problems associated with the average adolescent's need to belong cannot be simply targeted. A regular car ad which manages to confirm a new purchase as well as tempt a potential buyer will not work on your average tween. Tweens respond to indirect promotions. They respond to popular icons or to situations that they feel they've invented. Just three months after Britney Spears signed up with Pepsi, aligning the brand with 'cool', its sales moved into the Number One soft drink spot.

Similarly, Red Bull distributed their drink to a carefully-selected group of trendy people in Sydney and Melbourne – free of charge. Each selected person quickly became an icon for the drink, and attracted a crowd who purchased and supported the brand. In this case the famous person was simply replaced with acknowledged and respected people in the local community.

Quick to adopt, quick to reject

Up to now it has been widely acknowledged that early brand exposure generates long-term loyalty – it's the cradle-to-grave marketing strategy. To what extent a positive brand experience among tweens will affect their later brand choices is debatable. All indications show that there will be little influence. Tweens are an audience that has shown no particular brand loyalty. They simply follow other indicators based on group choices, rather than individual commitments. But it's important to ensure that key members of the group are comfortable with their choices.

Tweens are a generation that fears commitment. After all, if they're committed to a particular brand they will have less flexibility to change. At the same time, if they are slow to adopt a brand, they may be perceived as weak, and a weak reputation will leave them isolated and conspicuously alone.

The turnover of items on each tween's wish list has undoubtedly increased dramatically over the years, no one item lasting longer than a couple of months. In many cases they have not lasted longer than a couple of days. It's a list that is constantly changing. Another feature of the basic tween wish list is that you will rarely see general items like Nike shoes or a Nintendo game. It is now very product-specific – although still reflecting some degree of loyalty to the umbrella brands, much less so than would have existed 10 years ago.

Over the last decade, tweens' personal identity has shifted focus from the psychological to the physical. You are what you eat, what you wear, what you see and what you play. Brands help create an identity based more on what they represent rather than what they are. And the trend we're so familiar with from the adult world is perpetuated. It is not uncommon to see parents purchasing Gucci shoes for their 7-year-olds or Prada jackets for their 12-year-olds. Brand dependency has been, and will continue to be driven by both the kids themselves and their parents.

Where does this leave the marketers? Well, it dispels the cradle-to-grave myth that marketers have believed for years. There is no such thing. Creating and maintaining brand loyalty across the generational spectrum is a challenge that's never been successfully addressed. Naturally, brands that exclude tweens are likely to face a few challenges when the tween gets older. I remember as a tween wanting to open a savings account – my first bank account – and being rejected. Needless to say, that bank never saw me again. But these cases are rare today. Most brands are clever enough to act politically correct, or at least create an aura of exclusivity, leaving the impression that this is one to bear in mind for 'when I get old'.

Whatever the case, the fact remains that creating strong brand loyalty in the tween segment bears no correlation to any loyalty they may have when they're older. However, brand loyalty remains a tangible concept for older segments of the consumer market.

Hate to be sold to and love to be respected

Tweens have a strong resistance to the commercial machine. There's a Detroit-based group who call themselves the Insane Clown Posse who play a genre of music that's become known as rage rock. When tweens are asked to describe what they find most appealing about this music, they talk about how they feel that the group and its music belongs to them. The Insane Clown Posse, whose music is loaded with profanity, violence and misogyny, hasn't yet been taken up by the music corporations and sold back to them at the mall.

But it won't take long for marketers to find a way to overcome this challenge, because rage rock is becoming big business. The Insane Clown Posse has a carefully orchestrated plan. They're basing themselves on the bigger rage acts like Eminem and Limp Bizkit who are now making big money from big sales and are even winning industry accolades in the form of Grammy nominations.

The popularity of Insane Clown Posse is entirely due to tweens and not some external marketing arm of a corporation that is pumping millions of dollars into an experiment. The fact that the tweens feel a sense of ownership of Insane Clown Posse creates a sense of loyalty between them and the group. Tweens support the philosophy behind the group and share a passion for the music. In other words, they feel Insane Clown Posse is authentic. And that's what tweens want: the real thing. Uncut, untested, unplanned and unpretentious.

Many companies today are aiming to achieve similar authenticity. However, if you represent a well-established corporate brand it will be much harder to create trust in the tween market. Pepsi managed to overcome their previously distant image. They re-launched their Web site, aiming to create a dialogue with the tween audience, and went as far as involving them in the process of developing new products. The Pepsi Adviser invites tweens to develop new tastes, discuss their lifestyles, share their interests and talk about trends including, of course, their favourite brands.

Here is our message – but hey it's up to you!

The challenge for any marketer taking on a group like Insane Clown Posse would be to launch the brand in the mass market without losing its authentic flavour. Insane Clown Posse is a perfect reflection of a brand basically stating: 'Here is our message – but hey it's up to you if you want to purchase it.' Most importantly, it doesn't push the tweens.

The days when slogans and commercial messages induced people to 'Buy it', 'Try it' or 'Drink it' are long gone. Brands are now placing consumers in the centre. Diesel says 'Successful living'. Xbox advises 'Life is short, play more'. Coca-Cola tells us 'Life tastes good', but to Nintendo 'Life's a game'. These slogans clearly frame human attitudes outlining the pathway to a better and more fulfilled life – not to mention the personal happiness to be gained from using precisely *that* brand.

Freedom to choose – and change

Your brand will be on shaky ground if you don't offer tweens the opportunity to opt out. Successful brands offer the opportunity to choose – and change, if necessary – since the notion of only having one brand at their disposal can create panic among even the most patient tween.

What is evident is that brands position themselves by offering an opinion about their environment. So when Nintendo says 'Life's a game', or Xbox tells users that 'Life is short, play more', they're promoting an attitude that is not only cool, but may also be quite controversial with parents. By choosing a brand, you choose a lifestyle, and all the better if that lifestyle choice happens to conflict with your parents' point of view. What's more, the bigger the contrast, the better.

Broader in scope, shallow in detail

Where the only reality worth bothering with is one that's instantly accessible, and where freedom of choice is an inherent part of identity, there's not much room left for depth. The speed of movies, games, events and music has created a generation where broad scope has become paramount, enabling tweens to scan their options and instantly select the best possible choice.

Single-stream concepts are on the way out. A movie is no longer just a movie, but a platform to a merchandizing program. To narrow a concept in such a way that leaves no room for continuity or merchandizing opportunities is equivalent to brand suicide. It's no coincidence that 60 per cent of the revenue earned at pop concerts comes from the sales of merchandise. Record sales are down for a number of reasons. There's diversification in music taste, as well as pirated copies to contend with, so any brand owner has to focus on alternative revenue channels such as merchandizing.

Toy Story 2 and *Spider-Man* are two movies with one thing in common – they were both written and directed with merchandizing as the central focus. Hollywood no longer considers a film on its own merits. It has to come along with firm merchandizing revenue streams. So if a story is considered on its own merits, the merchandizing is necessarily limited. Whereas if the premise begins with the products that can be sold as an offshoot, then the story can be crafted to optimize the merchandizing opportunities.

Been there, done that

In the same way that people in their late 30s are gaining interest in pop music, so youth are expanding their musical tastes to include rap, R&B and heavy rock. Rap and hip-hop are the fastest growing genre in the youth market, but there's a distinct fall-off in interest beyond the 25+ age group.

A lot happens in a tween year. There's a voluminous amount of change and development. So much gets packed into a 12-month period. One only needs to look at the huge differences between 10-year-olds and 12-year-olds – who are in turn very different from 14-year-olds. But we tend to lump them all into a single age-defined category called tweens. But if you're running a campaign for this age group you will need to be conscious of exactly who your target market is in order to customize your message and presentation to make it appropriate to the specific group. Each stage offers a huge receptive market, but you need to carefully identify who they are and what interests them.

Community dependency

One of the most consistent creators of community is the entertainment industry. No single industry has explored the value of the Internet to the extent that movies have. According to Jupiter Media Metrix there will be 26.9 million children under 12 online by 2005 – and this figure only takes account of the US population. This represents one of the fastest-growing demographics on the Web.

According to research done by the MPAA, 8 to 24-year-olds accounted for more than 40 per cent of the movie-going public in 1999 – and these figures are growing. Equally significant, teens go to the movies more regularly than any other group. Close to half of those between the ages of 8 and 17 consider themselves to be frequent movie-goers, meaning they travel to a cineplex at least once a month.

Almost every movie released over the past several years has had a complementary Internet site with details about the movie and its stars. What's changed is the attention studios are now giving these sites, and what the sites are trying to accomplish. Ever since Artisan Entertainment used savvy Web marketing to elevate *The Blair Witch Project* from a campy teenage fright flick into a mega-hit, studios have embraced Web promotion as the fourth pillar in their marketing strategies. What started out as a marketing experiment is now an essential aspect of a studio's television commercials, newspaper ads and publicity efforts. And movie sites are no longer afterthoughts. In fact, most studios are launching movie sites months before the opening date as part of creating a pre-release buzz.

The most innovative studios are using the Web as extensions of the movie itself. Sites for movies like *X-Men*, *The Lord of the Rings* and *Series 7* have tangential plot lines, special footage, and countless other features to deliver an experience that captures the essence of the movie. Some studios are going as far as hiring independent Web designers and hosts to put up fake fan sites as part of stirring up excitement over the forthcoming attraction. Marketers all agree that the one-on-one communication that the Web delivers achieves an intimacy that a blaring 30-second ad simply cannot.

New Line Cinema is pouring millions into its big budget movie of the J R R Tolkien classic, *The Lord of the Rings*. At lordoftherings.net, New Line constructed another world online, complete with fantasy tales, teasers and scenes from the making of the movie. New Line's marketers plan to roll out new content weekly through to 2004, when the last film in the trilogy will hit movie screens.

Industry insiders note that *The Blair Witch Project*'s marketing worked so well because of the sense of investigation and discovery the site conveyed. The strategy was to make people feel that they had invested in the story and so owned a piece of it. And as word-of-mouth took over, box-office sales sky-rocketed.

When visitors log onto the Web site of *Center of the World*, a film about love and sex in the technological age, they are led through a strip club. *Raw Deal*, a film about a rape in a college fraternity, has constructed a site where visitors are invited to give their opinions on the case and are encouraged to interact about its theme. The technique has been so compelling that many consumer goods manufacturers are emulating the studios and building interactive sites to reach their targeted demographic.

Most marketers judge their results holistically, and as yet have few yardsticks to measure the effectiveness of their Web efforts. But new research by the University of Southern California marketing professor Fred Zufryden suggests Web site use and ticket sales are directly related. In an article published in the *Journal of Advertising Research* in 2001, Zufryden asserted that Web site traffic is statistically significant in predicting the box-office take of a new film. He combined data from several movies including number of screens, film grading, critics' scores, time of release, production budget and seasonality, together with Web site traffic data, to build a model that accurately predicted the life-span of several popular films. Although his results were empirical, they showed that a spike in Web site traffic soon after the release of *Space Jam*, for instance, corresponded to an increase in the box-office take for the movie.

Where better to spread the word than on the Net? And yet, Hollywood is not as compelled as it may seem to be. Despite the rising budgets of most movie studios, Web marketing expenditures are barely a ticket stub compared with the money spent on other media. According to the Motion Picture Association of America (MPAA), in 2000, Internet marketing costs amounted to only 0.7 per cent of the average US $27 million spent marketing each movie. While that figure is up 40 per cent, from only 0.5 per cent in 1999, it's a number that could be missed entirely on a balance sheet. In comparison, 23.8 per cent of the US $27 million was spent on network television, 18.3 per cent on local television spots, 15.6 per cent on newspaper ads and an additional 6.4 per cent on trailers.

Yet the Web is far from foolproof. As Web marketing grows, movie marketers may find some of their efforts backfiring. Ironically, what made *The Blair Witch Project* so successful barely helped its sequel, *Book of Shadows: Blair Witch 2*, which bombed. According to various reports, the backlash began months before the film opened. Negative Web reviews on the same chat lines that helped elevate *The Blair Witch Project* to fame and fortune now decried its sequel as 'just another slasher movie', and movie-goers stayed away in droves.

WHERE DOES ALL THIS LEAVE THE TWEENS... AND US?

It is clear that what we learned about tweens only 10 years ago is now significantly out of date. The role of the classic toy is gone – in fact when did you last see kids playing on the street? Toys are increasingly digital. They involve electronic screens, pocket computers, mobile phones and personal computers. And accompanying everything is the Internet. Merchandizing opportunities have taken centre stage, and brands straddle online and offline worlds. In fact this bridge that brands create helps secure the life of a product so that it can extend beyond the three-month average for any fad. Successful entertainment products won't survive this electronic new world unless their foundations are firmly planted in at least one or more of the seven motivators outlined, because for tweens, perception has become more important than reality, and in many ways, that's what branding is all about.

SUMMARY

▍ Tweens in the United States, Australia and the United Kingdom spend 60 per cent more time watching television each year than they spend in school.

▍ Hollywood will increasingly become the focal point of brand inspiration when marketers build new brand strategies.

▍ Traditional toys are a disappearing phenomena. They've been replaced with hand-held computers, movies and CDs.

▍ For a toy to survive it will need to develop an integrated movie, television and computer game strategy in its media plan. The motion picture, whether on television or in the cinema, has become the lifeblood of tween brands.

▍ Schoolyards have turned into brand showrooms.

▍ Characteristics of future tweens include:
1. *Identity seeking.* For many years it has been claimed that tweens establish their identity via the media. It has become increasingly clear that this is a fairly accurate assertion.
2. *Fish streaming.* Younger children look up to tweens to identify and adopt the latest fashion.
3. *Quick to adopt, quick to reject.* The cradle-to-grave marketing theory is dead.
4. *Hate to be sold to and love to be respected.* Tweens have a strong resistance to commercialization. Your brand will be on shaky ground if you don't offer tweens an opportunity to opt out.
5. *Broader in scope, shallow in detail.* Single-stream concepts are on the way out.
6. *Been there, done that.* This is a generation that will try everything, but are incredibly impatient.
7. *Community dependency.*

ACTION POINTS

► Picking up on the marketing strategy you have worked on so far, how do you intend customizing it so that your message will stand out among the 40,000 other television commercials that tweens are currently exposed to each year?

► List five points that will enable your competitors to differentiate their message.

► To what degree are you able to ensure that your concept and communication strategy will be entertaining?

► Will your audience find your communication appealing and not characterize it as a traditional commercial with only one objective – that is, to sell?

► Have you allowed your audience to opt out at any point?

► What surprise elements does your tween strategy include? What will take them by surprise and make them love your brand?

12

The essence of being a child

Yun Mi Antorini

These days, marketers and researchers struggle to get inside what it means to be a child. In the past, it was fair to expect some coherence between one generation and the next. Values and a sense of identity would be inherited, and predictions such as 'like father, like son' would still make sense. Today, with the notion of post-modernity, gone are beliefs in absolute truth, along with notions that we can control the present and predict the future. The concept of self is no longer a given, but is something we all have to invent. This includes children. Depending on how you see it, you either have the wonderful liberty or the daunting obligation to write and live your own script in life. Individually, we set the scene and decide the moral codes and the rules that will guide us. Dead scary for some, an adventure for others – particularly for children, since they have no preconception or fear of something they don't know and haven't experienced.

Since there is no longer coherence between one generation and another, knowledge about what it means to be a child can no longer be extracted from the past. It now needs to be created in participation with today's children, since they are the only true experts in what the world means to them. Edward De Bono once compared children and grown-ups to tadpoles and frogs. One creature, but two completely different forms of life, each requiring an environment utterly different from one another in order to develop and thrive.

Just recently, the core identity of the LEGO Company – its reason for being – was revisited. Pursuing this initially required us to discard the superficial clichés and the here-and-now tendencies, and instead search deep for the eternal and timeless characteristics of what it means to be a child. During this work, based on many conversations with children, studying many theories regarding childhood, and participating in many qualitative and quantitative global research studies, it became clear that the core of what it means to be a child is somewhat the same as it has always been. We reaffirmed the sense that any child has an inbuilt urge to learn and to progress, and this takes a leading role from birth, determining the actions and interests of the child.

To want to learn and progress is in fact a major characteristic of being a human being, and it will continue to be so, since our survival depends on it. Through time, the means and materials used by children to learn and progress have changed. Technological possibilities evolve and fashion changes, but the motive to play, communicate and interact remain the same. Yes, we will probably continue to see children's culture converge on a global scale. And yes, the speed of fashion and technology trends will accelerate. The future will probably bring more abstract learning possibilities, and we will probably see children abandon the more traditional play experiences typical of industrial society in order to move to experiences more suited to our own times. The pressure on children to excel and stand out will probably also get more intense, and a more fragmented everyday life with even more tasks to complete will certainly be a fact of life for many. Yet beneath these changing trends, a child's need to learn from activities or experiences will continue to motivate them, whether they are born in Denmark, the United States, China, Africa or Russia. As marketers and producers of children's products and services, we have an obligation to create what MIT's Dr Seymour Papert calls 'learning-rich' environments. In doing so we not only prioritize the needs of children, we also invest in our common future.

TARGETING CHILDREN TO BUILD A BRAND

A few years ago most companies had to rely on offline activities in building a brand. Traditional media like television commercials, print ads and the like, were prime push-related platforms for building and positioning brands. Marketing thinking was dominated by price, place, promotion and PR. Those who got the best block on kids' channels and the best placing in the store would win the battle. A quick glance at today's children-targeted brands confirms that most companies still use very traditional branding, marketing and communication strategies to reach children. The 'more-of-the-same' formula seems to rule the way companies treat children's brands, making brand building a non-creative and dull exercise. This is a real shame, considering the energy and curiosity that this particular group can muster.

Things are about to change

Underneath the 'more-of-the-same' surface, interesting things are starting to happen, primarily as the result of new technologies and the Internet. Communities created around children's interests are blossoming, allowing children to interact and communicate in whole new ways and on a global level. The Global Community of LEGO enthusiasts (lugnet.com), The Unofficial Harry Potter Fan Club (harrypotterfans.net), the community Web site for *Star Wars* (starwars-rpg.net) are just a few examples of brand communities driven by users at a professional level. The official company Web site often cannot match the enthusiasm and level of detail and knowledge put into the site by the non-paid, yet utterly committed users.

In offering spaces where people can connect, bond, retrieve information and share rituals and traditions, these so-called brand communities will undoubtedly become a major way for companies to connect with their markets. Brand communities may very well become the preferred virtual playground of tomorrow, as they not only allow for meeting others with the same interests, but also offer children a place to participate in important social structures.

Brand power to the people

Communities offering ways for children to come together on a voluntary basis will forever change the balance between companies on the one side and the consumers – the children – on the other. According to Tim Frank Andersen, co-founder of Networkers and FramFab, one of the biggest challenges companies will have to face is the fact that they will no longer hold the power over the brand. Up until now, companies alone have decided the direction and the content of the brand. In future, direction and content will be negotiated between the company and the market, in this case the children. Thus they will be an important stakeholder group in forming tomorrow's brands. This is new. Compared with only a few years ago, children will not only have to be heard, they will become part of the design and creation of brands.

As primary stakeholders, one can imagine that children will have a big say in the strategic direction of a company, production methods and investment plans – everything involved in running a company. Today, many semi-public institutions are already delivering information to children about how and where to shop for healthy and environmentally-safe products, and how to choose the best alternative among the many product choices. Children are raised to become conscious consumers, and are empowered by the information and education they receive through brand communities, institutions and schools.

To win children, you've gotta have children

A natural next step for children will be to use their buying power and their knowledge to have their say on the brands and products that so greatly influence their lives. This brand-content negotiation between company and children can, for example, be witnessed at lugnet.com where direct discussions between LEGO Direct's managing director, Brad Justus, and the community (most often older boys) takes place. In contrast with Brad Justus's own people, the lugnet.com community does not get paid, they have no obligations, and they do not belong to the company culture. They are free to love, criticize, praise or hate whatever they see coming from the company, and in sharing these feelings they offer the best, most valuable information a company can ever dream of having. But this does not really come free. These guys want to be heard, and they want to see some action based on their inputs. And when they see action, they become in return even more dedicated enthusiasts and even more loyal customers.

What this direct dialogue between companies and children will mean for the way future companies operate and organize themselves, and how companies will use this valuable knowledge, one can only speculate. But whereas the key to the children's market used to be the products, the branding and the marketing, tomorrow's winners will be those that first find ways to make children true stakeholders of the company and so part of the company's destiny. Tomorrow's winners are those that realize that they need children to reach children. Children will bring totally new perspectives on brand building and brand loyalty, which is much needed if branding and marketing as theoretical concepts are to move on and find new and contemporary content.

BUILDING KIDS' BRANDS

Basically, what will make or break a child-targeted brand is pretty much the same thing that will make or break an adult brand. Brands that are complicated, lie, try too hard or offer inferior quality will fail. Brands that are straightforward, have integrity, believe in themselves and are attractive and of good quality will succeed!

1. Accept and learn to work with paradoxes. It is a children's market, yet children do not want 'kiddie' stuff. Price competition is fierce, yet poor solutions are not going to help your business thrive. Children strive for social recognition, yet seeing 'their' brand all over the place will turn them off. Between these paradoxes create your own crisp vision of what is you, what nobody else brings to the market.

2. Expect disloyalty! According to Frederick Reichheld, author of *The Loyalty Effect*, on average, US corporations lose half their customers every five years, half their employees every four years and half their investors every year. Children will leave your brand to try new stuff. But do not panic. If your core benefits are still relevant and attractive, new kids will come on board. Instead, spend time analyzing how you can strengthen your brand proposition, and hit back hard.

3. In a child's world there is only room for a few players. So go for market leadership. Create a brand different and fascinating enough to make it to the top, and have the guts to execute your plan accordingly (or don't go at all!).

4. Avoid being too complicated. Express your brand proposition in such a way that children get what your brand is all about. Tell them how it is different from all other brands. Describe the brand proposition in a timeless, traditional way. Hold on to the proposition in everything you do.

5. When defining the brand positioning, find inspiration among the archetypical and classical themes. Avoid being tempted by the quick and the superficial. It is said that Pokémon took seven years to develop into a game, and that the inventor was inspired by his childhood love of collecting and classifying insects and small animals. The inventor of Pokémon put all his love and all his passion into it, and from this emerged an obsession that ruled the world and inspired children to use their skills to do one of the most important things humans do, namely categorize and create order among things. Many parents only saw the amount of money their children spent on the game and

therefore labelled Pokémon bad. They failed to see the extensive learning that took place while playing the game.

6. Be clear on what you want to use as 'holding power' to make children come back to you for more. Is it the story? Is it the product functionality? Is it the symbolic value possessed by the brand? Is it the community belonging to the brand? Whatever it is, find ways of being innovative and keeping your proposition alive so that you never repeat yourself. Yet at the same time, remain loyal to the brand proposition.

7. Work with the best people around. Never be afraid to join forces with people with no experience – with children – as long as they understand what makes different and fascinating brands.

8. Do not be tempted to think you know all about children just because you have worked within the field for years and have read all the books. Go and talk with children on a regular basis, and see how they live their lives.

9. Think of brand building as a way of creating a relationship with children. Relationships are based on trust, so never lie and never go for inferior solutions. Apply quality in everything you do. A line of small plastic figures recently created a major collector buzz in Scandinavia. It was rumoured among children that while the first series of figures was produced in Israel, now they were being made in another country known by children to produce inferior quality toys. Therefore children did not want to own the new series of figures. Talking to kids about this phenomenon, I clearly sensed that it was not the quality issue that bothered children, but the fact that they had been cheated, lured into buying something different from what they had been promised.

10. Last, but not least, have fun and enjoy the ride. It shines through, and children will love you for it!

13

Pump up the volume

In 1996 Abbotts Kids' Village, the world's first mall catering exclusively to children, opened its doors in Alpharetta, Georgia in the United States. This 41,270 square foot shopping centre contained only stores that catered to children. It proved the concept skeptics completely wrong. The originally risky venture has turned into a gold mine all on its own, and ever since, kids' villages have sprung up all around the country. What was originally a simple idea has encompassed the total village concept, and now skating rinks sit alongside ice-cream parlours, there are kiddie hair salons and family photo shops, toys, clothing and swimming and computing facilities.

These are often open air venues with rainbow-like awnings, sidewalks painted with hopscotch games and tic-tac-toe grids, and everything's adorned with brightly coloured signage. Everything's designed to attract the attention of the ever-demanding tween consumer group.

The success of the kids' village concept doesn't necessarily reflect a general trend among the toy industry, which is struggling at targeting an ever-changing market. The days of toy trains, miniature cars and stuffed animals are long gone. An estimated 20 million tweens in the United States alone are far more interested in fashion, electronics and videos which cater to the tweens' increasingly sophisticated tastes – so much so that the average tween would be at a loss if asked directions to the local toy store.

The spending power of tweens has grown to such an extent that the toy retail sector has been forced to re-evaluate its business platform. Most recently, the large US-based toy retailer, FAO Schwarz, aiming at the tween market, has upgraded their messenger bags and now offer electronic password journals. In fact, in 2001, FAO Schwarz opened separate tween boutiques at five of its biggest stores, and also entered the event business, holding a concert outside its Manhattan store featuring Dream Street, a young sugar-pop music group.

Another huge US toy retailer, Toys 'R' Us, has created separate electronics areas for tweens in 600 of their stores, while K-B Toys, a 1,300-store chain, has dramatically expanded its sports products, including 20-inch BMX bikes and skateboard accessories. They've also focused on the hi-tech market with items like karaoke machines. This phenomenon reflects an 'age compression', which over the past five years, has presented the major challenge for an industry that has been forced to lower the age they've defined as the time children stop playing with toys.

Age compression is apparent in every move tweens make. Girls, for example, are over Barbie at the tender age of eight. This used to be around 11 or 12. Boys of 10 are no longer interested in LEGO. Age compression is also reflected in a generation which shows great skills with technology. They're naturally comfortable with the likes of hand-held computers and cell phones. These kids are similarly aware of their shopping options. As a result they're spending less time in the toy shop and more time at retailers like CompUSA, which have expanded their video game areas.

Quite simply, the definition of toys has changed. Every statistic emanating from the *BRANDchild* study indicates that adult brands are substantially more admired among tweens than first anticipated. Tweens are attracted to lifestyle products, and they're going to go wherever they can to find them.

THE YOUNG AND THE RICH

There are diverse signals emanating from the tween sector signifying an overall confusion. On the one hand kids' villages are very successful, while on the other the total business concept of big toy retailers is on decidedly shaky ground.

This is the reality: tweens are becoming more sophisticated at a younger age. Along with this sophistication comes greater purchasing power. They have an estimated US $24 billion at their disposal. The toy industry can't afford to lose them, and courting them requires an ever-more delicate balance.

Labelling wishes

Research conducted by Dr James U McNeal, a professor of marketing at Texas A&M University, shows that children from as young as 18 months are able to recognize corporate labels. About a year later they are able to associate the items in their world with specific brand names. For example, when they think about juice, they don't think just juice, they think company.

Between the ages of two and three, kids begin drawing brands. Generic items don't feature. Their dolls are Barbies and their computers are Dells. And by the age of five, tweens are ready to make their own purchases with their parents acting as their financiers. By seven years old, they are totally in control.

Where does the money come from?

The nature of money, or perhaps more accurately tweens' perception of money, has changed. It's no longer a reward but an expected revenue channel – an entertainment allowance. Since the average 21st century household requires two incomes, both parents work. Guilt about hours spent away from home is appeased by spending money on their children's every wish. The thought of nagging in the precious time a family has together is enough to open the parental wallets to appease any potential tantrum.

If we add the fact that 50 per cent of kids travel between divorced parents, and that often the contact between child and father is limited to every second weekend, money goes a long way to grease the cogs in a very part-time relationship. It's not too big a leap to understand that the sometime father will happily provide whatever's close to their tween's heart, whether it be computer games, the latest CD or a nifty skateboard.

It's one thing for tweens to have access to cash. It's another for them to spend it on whatever they fancy at the moment. Much of what they desire is available on the Internet. But in order to purchase online you need a credit card. Many parents sign their kids up as second credit card holders.

Credit card companies have perceived this gap and have gallantly stepped in to fill it. American Express and Visa spent three years in the planning of tween and teen-targeted debit cards. In 2000, Visa Buxx was launched. This is a parent-controlled payment card intended for older tweens and teens. You have to be 13 years old to use it.

The Buxx card uses a bank-hosted value storage mechanism, as opposed to Smart Card chip-based storage. This is similar to the gift cards that merchants are increasingly adopting. One major difference with a Buxx card is that it's accepted everywhere the Visa logo is displayed, including online merchants who accept Visa, ATMs and, of course, over the Internet.

The Buxx card looks and works like any traditional magnetic strip Visa card, and has the teen's name embossed on the front. Parents can load the card with whatever value they choose and the balance can never be exceeded. Additional value may be added to the card via the Web site or a toll-free number. Parents can use the Web to track their teen's spending, and can also exercise their option to remove value from the card, should they deem it necessary.

Shortly after Visa launched their Buxx card, American Express brought out the Cobalt card. Despite American Express claiming that the card was a success, they withdrew it from the market less than a year after it was launched. According to American Express, it was forced to close down when Zowi Corporation, their strategic partner, ran out of funding. American Express say they remain steadfast in their belief in the potential of the tween and teen market.

Despite start-up hiccups in a tween credit card, interest remains high. Just prior to the release of the Buxx card, about 500,000 people visited the Visa Web site which was set up to promote it. The company now gets 5,000 to 6,000 requests a day for information about the card. American Express believes the main reason why tweens have embraced it is because it gives them full access to engaging in e-commerce transactions on the Internet.

360-DEGREE TWEEN BRANDING

In the 1980s and 90s, tweens were far more naïve when it came to differentiating a commercial message from a non-commercial one. The powers-that-be in the marketing world tended to exploit this blurring of perception. But these were the early days of marketing brands to tweens, and commercial messages were restricted to the odd television commercial – or perhaps an ad before the movie feature.

Depending on where tweens live, laws and restrictions will vary. Scandinavian countries probably have the most restrictive in terms of marketing to tweens, whereas the United States offers the most accommodating legal environment for advertising. But no matter what the local regulations say, commercial messages are becoming more and more integrated into the lives of tweens. Tweens in the United States have the most exposure to brands, and they have access to brands 24 hours a day, seven days a week.

A day in the life of a tween

It's 7.00am as tween Peter and his sister Ann awaken on Yu-Gi-Oh! sheets. Peter dresses in his Spider-Man underwear and Dick Tracy t-shirt. He sits down to a plate of Yu-Gi-Oh! breakfast cereal. Ann prefers Kellogg's Winnie the Pooh cereal. Peter grabs his Simpson's school bag, while Ann tosses her Coke bag over her shoulder, and they head out to catch the school bus. By 9.00am they're watching Channel One, *the prepared-for-schools news, along with its obligatory two minutes of ads.*

Infotainment

Infotainment can be defined as any program where the boundary between entertainment, information and advertising is blurred. The controversy over advertising masquerading as information seems to be an ongoing unresolved issue in the United States. A large number of tweens and teens – 43 per cent – are exposed to messages sponsored by television programs like *Channel One,* which carries advertising directly to students. *Channel One* is a 12-minute news program produced specifically for schools. Its two minutes of ads, which come courtesy of Whittle Communications. They provide the video equipment as well as the programs, as a free service. There is, however, one proviso, and that is that the school tweens watch the program as well as sit through the ads.

Channel One is not the only form of advertising that goes on in the US classroom. Marketing agencies promise its corporate clients that they can 'place samples of your brand into the hands of up to two million junior and senior high school students in a controlled classroom environment'. The marketing company then gathers product samples and coupons in a plastic bag and hands them out to tweens and teens in a Teenpack.

Edutainment

Agencies who specialize in promoting products directly to schools often couch their message in what can be called edutainment – educating and entertaining the tweens while at the same time achieving a commercial purpose. Lifetime Learning Systems is one such example of a company developing sponsored educational materials created with specific market-ing objectives in mind.

When US tweens go to school they participate in NutraSweet's Total Health program, where among other things they'll learn to control their weight with NutraSweet. From McDonald's magazine, *Wecology,* they'll learn about the economic advantages of Styrofoam packaging. The colourful posters that decorate the walls come courtesy of Reynolds wrap, Birds Eye frozen vegetables, Promise margarine and Bakers chocolate.

This form of advertising varies from country to country. Australian regulations allow sponsored classroom promotions, although Sweden doesn't. However, the United States allows the more commercial access to their schools than anywhere else.

Wherever you will find product placement, you will find a school system short of money. So teachers who lack adequate resources tend to join forces with advertisers in order to obtain equipment they couldn't otherwise afford. All the sponsored educational items blur the boundaries between the commercial message and the entertainment value of the product. Edutainment is a trend that's spreading despite local regulations in each country.

The edutainment excursion

It's 1.00pm, and Peter and Ann are heading for some real hands-on experience outside the classroom. They're going on a school excursion. They're heading for a car dealer who has invited the group to learn about some of the mechanics of cars, driving safety and new technological applications.

A growing number of businesses, including several large retail chains, have seen the value of blending the school excursion with a marketing activity. The Field Trip Factory based in Chicago is one of many compa-nies specializing in exposing school-children to company sites for real world lessons on everything from nutrition to health care. The Field Trip Factory's free program has appealed to the growing need to subtly market to tweens. In two short years, The Field Trip Factory has spread itself from 8 to 43 states.

Educators and tweens rate the field trips highly. They allow tweens to experience a hands-on environment and it extends the classroom into the local community. The trips cover a vast range of venues, for example at the Saturn Dealership tweens learn about car safety. They learn how to change a car's oil, and how to correctly buckle a seat-belt. The highlight of the visit is an unusual exercise. Tweens are asked to jump on the top of a car door to test the strength of steel.

Field trips open the doors for retailers and give them a chance to invest in education – but there is a pay-off. Today's school children are tomorrow's customers. And the field excursion to the Saturn Dealership reaches everyone – teachers, parents and tweens.

Celebrity endorsements

Celebrities are pitching to kids as never before. Fred Savage from *The Wonder Years* and Kirk Cameron from *Growing Pains* endorse Pepsi. Both shows enjoyed enormous popularity among tweens in the early 1990s. Paula Abdul endorsed Reeboks in a magazine ad that asked, 'Don't you wish you were in her shoes?' Later she joined forces with Michael Jackson to pitch LA Gear. Bo Jackson and Michael Jordan, two of the most popular sportsmen with tweens, endorse Nike.

Enter the celebrities

It's 3.00pm, and both tweens, home from school, are settling down to watch television on their local channel. Every seven minutes the afternoon movie breaks for obligatory commercial breaks. Among the dishwashing powder and toilet bowl cleaner there are celebrity testimonials endorsing products that appeal to tweens. Sporting heroes endorsing sneakers have been so successful that kids have literally killed to own a pair of the right brand shoes.

Celebrities have endorsed products for decades. However, the status products being pushed to tweens have never been so costly, and the celebrity commercials have never been so slick. But it seems that the powerful effects of celebrity endorsement are on the wane. The *BRANDchild* study reveals that tweens now have less respect for celebrities who promote products.

Commercials for US $120 Nike sneakers are regularly seen by tweens. During May 2000, for example, more Nike commercials appeared on

MTV than on sports shows. A new range of LA Gear shoes, which was introduced in August 2001, was timed 'to coincide with the back-to-school season'. LA Gear also sponsored an MTV Museum of Rock & Roll show that travelled to hundreds of malls, well-known teen hang-outs.

Ray-Ban sunglasses realized they were on to a winning thing when Tom Cruise wore them in the movie *Top Gun*. A representative of the company stated: 'We made our sunglasses into a hip, must-have item through celebrity emulation.' And true to their philosophy, celebrities have been endorsing their Ray-Bans ever since.

Meeting the cyber friends

Peter and Scott are cyber friends. They often catch up on AOL's ICQ, sharing gossip, sports news and music hits. Scott lives on the other side of the Atlantic, in the United Kingdom. This has not stopped the friends sharing even the most local news. Today's gossip is about Christina Aguilera. There's a rumour that she's launching a new CD with secret tracks.

At Electric Artists, music promoters work the Web on tweens' chat sites, talking up new artists, creating what they call a buzz. According to Electric Artists, Internet communities provide the most efficient way of spreading news and creating buzz. Electric Artists began stirring up the buzz months before the release date of her new CD. It had teenagers from Los Angeles to London, from Seattle to Sydney, talking about it. And this sort of news does not take long when, as our study shows, 25 per cent of wired urban tweens chat daily on the Internet. Within days of the CD being released, it had soared to Number One.

Spinning a web with Spider-Man

Movie ticket sales increased by 20 per cent in 2002 compared with 2001. According to almost every movie promotion company, the Internet was the main contributing factor in this rise. The film industry has found that using the power of the Web to drive marketing campaigns often results in box office successes like *Spider-Man*. According to AdRelevance, an online ad research company, *Spider-Man* is the most-promoted movie ever, with 483.9 million impressions during the period of 1 January to 19 May 2002. This strategy of online promotion could be what propelled *Spider-Man* to the lofty heights of fifth-highest grossing movie of all time.

When looking more closely at the other movies in the top ranks, a pattern emerges. *The Scorpion King* registered 402.8 million impressions, with the re-release of *ET* lagging behind with 259.5 million impressions. *Dragonfly*, presently in fourth place position, registered 120.9 million impressions, followed by the Oscar-winning film, *A Beautiful Mind*, with 119.1 million. Ranked sixth at 115.8 million is *Big Fat Liar*. It's clear that there is a strong correlation between the number of Internet ad impressions and box-office success.

Loyalty concepts

In just one year, six high-profile clubs were introduced by Nickelodeon, Fox, Burger King, Sassy, MTV and Disney. Most clubs required a membership fee, which ranged from US $5 to US $12.95 for Disney's Mickey Mouse Club. So far loyalty programs have only been associated with club membership. However, everything indicates that credit cards are poised to introduce reward programs for tweens similar to the programs that are in place for adults.

Belonging

> *Wednesday is always the highlight of the week, this is the day that the Nickelodeon magazine can be found in the letter box. It's even more special because Ann's Sassy Club membership card has arrived too.*

With competition in the tween and teen market constantly growing, the industry is seeing a trend in value-added marketing. Companies now have to work harder than ever for a share of the consumer dollar. Tween clubs, if organized well, are a great way to reach a tough market. And tweens like the idea of belonging. The club establishes an ongoing relationship with its members by sending them symbols that include them. There are membership cards and activities designed for their participation. The major form of this participation centres on purchasing items related to belonging.

This is the irony. Tweens and teens voluntarily join, and pay for, a club membership that's based almost entirely on advertainment. Take, for example, the Sassy Club. The membership costs US $5, and this does not include a subscription to the *Sassy* magazine. The magazine has pages devoted to the club's merchandise. When you sign up with the club, you receive a free gift, like a make-up brush, for joining. This gift changes each month. You also receive a membership card and a sheet of 12 Sassy dollars. These are money-off coupons you can use to buy club merchandise.

Membership to Fox Kids Club is free. Members receive a club membership card, Fox Kids Club stickers, a Simpson's puzzle, an official membership certificate, a welcome letter signed by DJ Kat, and a subscription to *Totally Kids*, the Fox Kids Club magazine. The magazine has ads for stamp collecting, a new movie, books, the Burger King Kids Club and a toy-store, all spread over its eight tabloid-size pages. The welcome letter urges new members to watch their favourite television shows on their Fox Kids station to find out about great discounts and ways to use their new Fox Kids Club membership card.

Burger King Kids Club, Nickelodeon Kids Club and the enduring Mickey Mouse Club all offer variations on a similar theme. And while the tweens are signing up for the privilege of belonging, the corporate owners of the brands – Nickelodeon, MTV, Sassy and so on – are building large databases of names which they can sell to direct-mail advertisers. For Toys 'R' Us Geoffrey's Fun Club it is a way to expand upon the toy chain's high holiday volume and boost its presence in homes throughout the other three-quarters of the year.

As advertising costs continue to rise, the club concept offers double the efficiency for their advertising dollar. On the one hand they are developing a valuable ongoing relationship with the customer, while at the same time the customer is paying for it. The only challenge is for the company to ensure that the consumer feels they are getting what they paid for.

One club, three purposes

1. To disguise commercial messages tweens are invited to join something that promises to be theirs – even if it turns out to be just another sales platform. Advertising messages come disguised as 'advice from your club', making them more difficult to resist. The reality is that the more a child's guard is down, the more effective an ad can be.

2. The club provides a platform for ads to regularly reach their target audience. They appear week after week, or month after month, and manage to attract tweens' full attention. No ad, commercial or branded education program can generate the same concentration.

3. Clubs also aim to build brand loyalty from a very young age. The earlier a brand starts creating loyalty, the stronger the ties it will build over times. However, a relationship established with a 10-year-old will not necessarily last forever. Loyalty has to be nurtured, particularly in the case of tweens, who are constantly seeking new trends. Brands that respect tweens' opinions, however, ensure that the brand grows alongside them, and so can establish a unique loyalty. Not many companies are able to fulfil these criteria.

Advertainment

Many brands specialize in a technique designed to ensure that tweens will read a magazine ad and actually spend time with it. They do this by turning the ad into a game, a puzzle, an advice column or a comic strip – anything but an ad. This technique is called advertainment.

Advertainment has proved to be one of the most effective tools in tween marketing and is increasingly common in children's magazines. *Kid City* (which used to be ad-free) and *3–2-1 Contact* both carry ads disguised as games for Hershey's Chocolate and Colgate Junior. Foot Locker ads in *Sports Illustrated for Kids* look like sports quizzes and hidden-object puzzles. *Seventeen* magazine's 'Ask Loren' column, which promises 'your personal answers to questions about make-up and fashion', is really an ad for Epilady products. A Popeye comic advertises Instant Quaker Oats.

Disguising promotions as games and comics makes it harder for tweens to be skeptical of advertising messages. This form of advertising prompts us to ask a number of questions about ethics, particularly how far can and should a brand go without losing credibility?

Classic product placement

Product placement picked up momentum when Reese's Pieces were portrayed as the favourite food of the beloved alien, ET. Fees charged by movie producers for placing brand-name products in movies range from US $10,000 to $1,000,000.

At the movies

It's early Friday evening, and Peter and Ann head out to the movie theatre. They're taking in a double feature. They see a Pepsi commercial before the movie starts. Will the kids have a three-hour respite from the commercial barrage of the day as they watch a double feature? Not with Domino's Pizza, Pepsi and Burger King as part of the action in the second feature, Teenage Mutant Ninja Turtles.

Both product placements in movies and advertorials in magazines create brand awareness and communicate promotional messages. Both are less-than-forthright ways of selling to adults. Yet these techniques also pervade the media tweens enjoy. For example, Disney's Buena Vista Distributing offered to place brand-name products in *Mr Destiny* for a fee ranging between US $20,000 and $60,000, depending on how the product was to be shown.

'*I like Micky clothes*', Hu Yu Hao, aged 11, China

In some cases, movie studios and producers accept merchandise or promotional support in exchange for placing a product. Burger King, shown in the *Teenage Mutant Ninja Turtles* movie, promoted that movie before it was released. Lexus, the on-screen sponsor of Steven Spielberg's futuristic *Minority Report*, planned a multi-million-dollar promotion based on the movie.

Product placement is much more than Tom Cruise shopping at GAP or driving a Lexus in *Minority Report*. Pepsi has a whole department dedicated to product placement – and the result is overwhelming. Pepsi products have been appearing in movies for years. To name a few, they've been placed in *Ferris Bueller's Day Off, Stand and Deliver, Teenage Mutant Ninja Turtles, Lean on Me, Cocoon: The Return, Flashdance, Back to the Future II* and *Big*.

Product placement in movies has become standard fare. Consider a short list of them:

▌ Domino's Pizza in *Teenage Mutant Ninja Turtles*;
▌ Nintendo Video Games and Mattel Inc.'s Power Glove in *The Wizard*;
▌ Chevrolet, Hardees, Coca-Cola and Exxon in *Days of Thunder*;
▌ GAP, Nokia and 28 other brands in *Minority Report*;
▌ Burger King and Coors Beer in *Gremlins*;
▌ McDonald's and Coca-Cola in *Mac and Me*;
▌ Toyota, Miller, Nike, AT&T, *USA Today* and Pizza Hut in *Back to the Future II*;
▌ Ray-Bans and Seagrams Champagne in *Top Gun*;
▌ Sanyo, Wheaties and Nike in *Rocky III*;
▌ Miller Lite in *Caddyshack II*.

Product placement is all about finding effective advertising methodologies. It creates brand familiarity, lends status appeal to products and subtly promotes them.

Bricks-and-mortar advertainment

The gaming market has become another effective tween channel. When ESM Marketing Group released It's Only Money, a new board game, 25 advertisers paid US $30,000 to be part of the game. The Pepsi logo appears on Nintendo's video game, Magic Johnson's Fast Break. Hobbico paid thousands of dollars in licensing fees for its remote-control car, Kyosho, to be part of the story in an Archie comic book. The *Wall Street*

Journal quoted the Hobbico director of corporate merchandizing as saying he hoped that young entry-level buyers would 'graduate into the more complicated products'.

Weekend time

Pete's school has arranged the party of the year. It's cooler than you can imagine, because Diesel is running it. There'll be just the best DJs and the latest in light equipment. There'll be free t-shirts, cheap drinks and loads of prizes.

The Nouveau Group, a Florida-based production company, specializes in delivering commercial message to tweens in non-school time. Their high school marketing program, Planet Gruv, takes state-of-the-art concert sound and lighting, video jockeys and video screens to local school dances. And these events are all sponsored by national advertisers who want to reach teens. *Teen People* renewed its sponsorship contract with Planet Gruv. The relationship allows the magazine to give its national advertisers an opportunity to sponsor the high school party tour and plug directly into the tween stream.

The result of this is that hundreds of high schools that were once closed to the idea of on-campus promotions are now opening their doors to advertisers and giving them direct access to their tween market.

Nintendo is another brand plugging into the event industry. In 2001, the company launched the largest promotion the video game industry has ever seen: the Nintendo World Championships. The travelling exhibition, seen in 30 cities, is co-sponsored by Pepsi, Reebok and General Foods.

THE FUTURE?

The first question you may ask is: where is all this going to end? Interestingly enough, similar questions were asked in the 1980s, 1970s and way back in the 1950s when direct marketing was first introduced. Each generation has adapted. But there is one major difference in this young generation. It is the first to take it thoroughly in their stride because they seem to have built-in filters allowing them to cope with a constant stream of branded messages. This commercial filter is happening at an ever-younger age.

Think about this. If you could go back in time to, say, the 1930s and pluck out a person at random, then place them in one of today's hypermarkets, I'm sure they would be totally flummoxed. It would take them days to find what they were looking for. In fact, the chances are that they would emerge with 10 times more than they were looking for, or alternatively would give up in exasperation after a few minutes.

This sort of shopping experience is something most of us now take in our stride. We have no difficulty navigating the world of hypermarkets, which carry close to 10,000 different brands on the shelves of a single store.

Nor does the term information overload exist in tweens' vocabulary. And it will be redefined as the tween generation reaches adulthood. Tweens have no trouble managing 100,000 brands at once. This is a generation that has been trained to recognize and be skeptical of brands from the cradle up. So the challenge will be for advertisers to adopt new strategies to woo a generation that's skilled at recognizing over-hyped messages that don't ring true.

Lifetime loyalty

It's likely that we will see greater movement to lifetime loyalty programs. In Denmark, many parents put their children's names down on waiting lists for attractive inner-city apartments in Copenhagen before their kids are born. As a part of the birth ceremony the kids receive a document showing their position on the waiting list – and 18 years down the track, when they're ready to leave home, they have an apartment waiting for them.

Since credit card companies are beginning to offer cards to kids as young as 13, loyalty is likely to be measured more on length of membership than points per purchase. Cards will be able to predict purchases based on years-long information. They will know what type of entertainment the cardholder prefers and will be able to supply information on music events and concerts happening before the standard notices announcing them are put out.

Retail business estimates that a cradle-to-grave relationship represents US $100,000 in revenue – and that's just retail business. What of banks, insurance companies, clothing and soft drink companies, movies or games? You name it. The interesting question to ask the American Expresses and the Visas is: what would they pay to recruit a young person for a lifetime? Many payment systems, similar to Visa's Buxx card, have gone broke. Small purchases, loads of transactions, high administration costs and limited interest being earned hardly encourages thriving business. Still, most card companies are keen to proceed with this young market because of its potential to last a lifetime.

The next generation of loyalty programs is likely to answer the needs of the next generation of tweens. A lifetime program that builds data will accumulate value for both the member and the company.

All loyalty programs for kids only go so far. They will cease when the young girl grows out of her Sassy Club, or when the tween is no longer interested in watching Nickelodeon, so that the Nickelodeon Club is no longer relevant. Very few programs manage to carry over to older generations. Almost no companies have been able to keep them over the age of 20. What is clear is that if the program, the brand and the tween manage to evolve over time and grow together, then the loyalty will mutually benefit both parties.

Is this good? If today's consumer was asked if they wanted to get rid of their reward membership cards for airlines, hotels and rent-a-car companies they would say no – probably because of the number of their points. But I'm also sure that if we could stop it all – go back 30 years in time before American Airlines invented the concept, no-one would be keen to accept the concept. We know the loyalty web we all are caught in – not necessarily with love or affection – for the brand we support daily is to gain points and status.

SUMMARY

▍ The spending power of tweens has grown to such an extent that the toy retail sector has been forced to re-evaluate their business platform.

▍ Age compression is now apparent in every move tweens make.

▍ The reality is that tweens are becoming more sophisticated at a younger age. Every statistic emanating from the *BRANDchild* study indicates that adult brands are substantially more admired among tweens than first anticipated. Tweens are attracted to lifestyle products, and they're going to go wherever they can find them.

▍ Research shows that children from as young as 18 months are able to recognize corporate labels. About a year later they are able to associate items in their world with specific brand names. For example, when they think about juice, they don't think just juice, they think company.

▌ Credit cards will most likely be a common phenomena among tweens in the next five years.

▌ The 24/7 brand has been born. Tweens expect to have access to brands 24 hours a day, 7 days a week.

▌ Infotainment (any program where the boundary between entertainment, information and advertising is blurred); edutainment (entertainment and education merged); and advertainment (entertaining advertising), will become increasingly commonplace.

▌ Celebrity endorsement is decreasing in popularity among tweens.

▌ Product placement is most likely to become the primary vehicle in tween marketing in the future.

▌ It's likely we will see a greater movement to lifetime loyalty programs. These gather data over a person's entire life and accumulate value for both member and company.

ACTION POINTS

▶ If you are a toy manufacturer, you are most likely feeling the heat. A merger with an adult world product is your best strategy for survival. No matter what category you belong to, your first step is to find out what it is that your audience admires in the adult world. What would they like to have access to?

▶ What's your 24/7 strategy? How do you intend to communicate the fact that your brand doesn't close down at 5pm? Through which channels do you intend to establish a 24/7 dialogue with your audience?

▶ Can you make learning engaging by satisfying a tweens psyche?

▶ What will you do to ensure that edutainment, advertainment and infotainment become integrated elements in your marketing strategy? Is your brand visible in the school-yard and in the late hours? Should it be?

► Product placement looks poised to become one of the most effective forms of advertising your brand. Will your brand be visible on television, in the movies, on computer games and in magazine editorials?

► What are your competitors' strategies? How visible are they?

► What is the age-span your product is aiming at? Is there any chance you can leverage the loyalty you already have established into an older age category? The answer might not be yes – but consider this well. At this stage you have invested substantial resources in creating loyalty with an audience which will leave you in two to three years. Is there anyone you could team up with to form a brand alliance ensuring your brand equity lasts longer than a few years?

14

Superchannels

The first thing I noticed as I slid into the back seat of a taxi in Tokyo was that along with the usual array of meters, there was a screen mounted next to the driver. This was not an ordinary screen but a large colour plasma one that, from the very minute I took up position in the back of the taxi, captured my attention for the full 45-minute drive.

Throughout the ride, the taxi driver consulted the screen, taking directions on the best way to the airport. What was surprising was that the whole trip, second by second, was replicated in a 3-D version on the screen. The display told us everything we needed to know and provided a running commentary on everything we passed. Consequently, well before we spotted the red and white stripes, we knew that we'd soon be passing a KFC. The screen advised on the closest gas station and communicated information about the design of the airport. It even explained where our plane would be waiting.

My attention was so taken by this screen's indefatigable supply of information that I completely neglected to notice the many brick-and-mortar billboards that we must have passed on the journey. Who knows? Maybe there weren't any. Maybe by some cataclysmic coincidence, they'd been dismantled. Hard to imagine, but it might as well have been the case, because the screen was full of every conceivable mini-billboard.

If you think my experience in Tokyo was mind-blowing then please take a seat, as this is just the beginning. Just imagine if the car was made aware of the people riding in it in order to tailor the message. So if children made up the majority of passengers, Toys 'R' Us could be featured in the commercials, or it could even send special happy birthday messages when a tween turned nine and happened to be passing by the store! What if the car were low on fuel? The Shell advertisement would perhaps make an appropriately timed appearance – and then it could take the opportunity to tell you of Shell's latest teddy bear promotion, offering all kids a free teddy. What if I was running early for my flight? Another airline might take the opportunity to offer me a special discount for flying with its earlier flight, rather than sticking with the carrier I'd booked. All this would happen in an intensive 45-minute one-on-one dialogue. I say intensive because a taxi's passengers form a captive audience and don't have much choice but to give their attention to the screen.

WELCOME TO THE BRAVE NEW WORLD OF MEDIA PLAYERS

Characteristic of the Japanese taxi scenario, the way information will be delivered in future will not only change the context of the message but will generate new media opportunities.

Think about this: what synergy could Toyota and KFC possibly generate? The products, the brand messages, the price level and even the frequency of purchase are totally in contrast. But what they do have in common is media synergy. As GPS (Global Positioning Systems) are installed as a standard feature in most cars, they are likely to become a mobile brand guide, allowing the car to sell valuable space to almost every type of brand. The car is the media.

It's rumoured that General Motors is considering how to leverage space in their cars to greater advantage. The space referred to is communication space rather than interior design. After all, on average we spend about an hour-and-a-half each day in our cars. Mostly we listen to the radio. General Motors currently has 250 million of their cars on the streets around the globe. So in fact, it is potentially one of the most attractive distribution channels in the world!

In the same way that the channel function on the Microsoft Explorer browser automatically links you to 15 or so brands, so it's possible for General Motors' car to do the same. The inbuilt GPS system is able to guide drivers or passengers to various brands targeting members of the family. It can also direct us to the radio, the music played in the car, television and to Internet capability accessible to passenger seats. In contrast with any other media except perhaps the cinema, passengers have nothing else to do but listen or watch whatever they can access when sitting in a car.

The profiles of the driver and passengers are already known, firstly by their choice of car. But when the personal profile of the driver and other family members is saved onto the car's hard disk, it will be of enormous benefit to companies like General Motors. They will then be able to further refine and customize their messages.

As we wait for General Motors to proceed with this media strategy, Microsoft is already implementing it. Microsoft is not only a software company but also a media giant with close to one billion people around the world in daily contact with its products and channels. It's entirely possible for Microsoft to log onto a computer and monitor behaviour by the second. This is not possible for traditional media companies who are dependent on monthly or bi-monthly research.

We are likely to see large organizations like General Motors, Nintendo, American Airlines, Starbucks and KFC establishing media sales and measurement functions like the one Microsoft already has. This will leverage their existing space for additional commercial use and develop complementary media channels outside their core expertise.

THE NEXT GENERATION OF MEDIA PLANNING

These new opportunities for media channels will alter the entire media landscape. They will allow multinational corporations to communicate with their consumer on a moment-by-moment basis in an integrated fashion. Companies like Sony will be able to offer cross-channel packages representing everything from movies to games and Web sites, and on to music, television and radio.

The real benefit of cross-channel strategies comes when the channels are interactive. Companies like AOL Time Warner or Microsoft have a clear competitive advantage over the more traditional media companies, since most of the channels they run are based on interactivity. This enables them to customize and integrate messages across multiple channels, all interlinked. So when a boy plays a game on Microsoft's Xbox, it's likely that he's already supplied his profile to the Xbox Web site. He's filled in details of age, player level and game preference, and can customize the communication he is exposed to when visiting the Internet via the Microsoft Explorer channels, Hotmail, MSN or CarPoint.

This integration across media allows the planner to purchase one media package with many components as product placements in a Microsoft game, exposure for ads on Microsoft's many Web sites, and even messages to cell phones. In order to survive, media companies will have to create alliances between offline and online media to a degree that's never been seen before.

Intelligent media planning, which will gradually integrate the many channels, will characterize all media plans targeting the tween generation. For a long time it's been recognized in the advertising and planning businesses that a comprehensive media plan will include the use of many media channels in order to be fully effective.

The future is all about brand alliances

Integral to the change in media planning direction is the formation of brand alliances. We've begun to see this shift happening, with companies teaming up in interesting alliances despite the fact that they share scarcely any product synergy. But what they do share is their audience.

Over the past 10 years, Microsoft has consistently based most of their distribution strategies on alliances. If you were to count all their alliances and partnerships you would be likely to reach several hundred thousand, representing everything from preferred Microsoft dealer partnerships to Microsoft certified programmers and content partners.

The brand alliance phenomenon has only just begun, and there are an unlimited number of potential allegiances still to be formed. Often the most unlikely allegiances can have very positive outcomes. Take, for example, Starbucks and Microsoft. Who would have imagined that a café and a software company could attain valuable synergy? But the exposure Microsoft gets by placing their games in the Starbucks cafés works well for both. The games attract more customers, and the Microsoft name is seen in this very popular chain.

In another example, the price of real estate is constantly increasing. So is the price of establishing a single brand store. Often the investment simply can't be justified. We are therefore seeing – in a trend that will no doubt continue – retail outlets and brands teaming up to share costs and audience. The Nike stores in India are now sharing their space and costs with other complementary brands.

It's essential that every marketer has a brand plan that includes developing a solid brand alliance strategy.

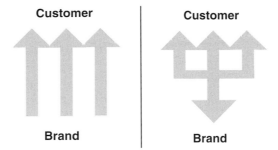

Figure 14.1 *Future brands need to play together. Successful marketing campaigns are all based on a domino-like media strategy.*

Back-door branding

A couple of years ago in Australia, Toyota ran a series of commercials using the cutest animals you can imagine as the leading characters. The animals had absolutely nothing to do with the car or the message. Despite the obvious incongruity, the commercials became the most effective car spots, streets ahead of all Toyota's competitors.

These were ads that appealed to tweens. The statistics from the *BRANDchild* survey show the direct influence urban tweens have on their parents' purchasing decisions, something substantially stronger than we first anticipated. The research reveals that the influence tweens have on the decision to purchase the family car is as high as 50 per cent. Nigel Hollis, the strategic planning and development director for the Millward Brown Group outlines this influence in his chapter in this book. These results are somewhat surprising knowing that tweens are too young to drive, cannot afford a car and so don't have too much experience with the product. But that aside, it's important to acknowledge that the emphasis on brand alliances that appeal to tweens should be a very high priority for planners.

Take, for example, Mattel's Matchbox cars. These have always been popular for the car manufacturers as well as for Mattel, not necessarily in terms of revenue from the sales of Matchbox cars, but in terms of real cars being sold due to tweens' influence. Similarly, Audi sponsors the whole LEGO car attraction in the German LEGOLAND Park. And in other categories like clothing, tween influence has proved to be just as important. So clothing companies such as the Gap kids range, or even the more luxurious brands like Gucci Kids and Prada Kids, build loyalty from an early age, and also affect the way tweens influence their parents.

Brand alliances should be built on strategies that take into account the factors that influence people surrounding the decision makers, but should also bear in mind future potential in terms of long-term relationship building.

Media planning as we know it is in the middle of a major change, as it's no longer limited to traditional media exposure. Now it needs to focus on how to integrate the media push at several different levels in order to create intelligent media synergy across all media. The days when media strategy typically involved seven key media elements is no longer adequate in an environment where everything that surrounds us is a potential media channel.

There are five important guidelines you need to consider before you create your future tween media and brand plan:

1. Turn your brand into a 24-hour worker

There's total integration of media in every tween's life, covering everything from home to school and playground. Brands need to be accessible 24 hours a day, because this generation has little understanding of the old-fashioned concept of 'opening hours'. In their world, every brand that's worthwhile is accessible on the Net 24 hours a day, 7 days a week. An answering machine that takes their call after five is strange: for this generation, it simply doesn't make sense. This 24-hour trend is set to become even stronger in future. Animal Crossing might help you to understand why.

A 'real' world, 24 hours a day... in fairyland

The latest trend among kids and tweens is a game called Animal Crossing, launched by Nintendo in 2002. Animal Crossing is a real time world for tweens, open 24 hours a day, 7 days a week. Players can unlock new levels, change the music and even put their own faces on their favourite characters. Animal Crossing allows players to interact with a virtual village of animals, which are each doing something different, every minute of every day. Animal crossing has a 24-hour clock which can be set so that the game's events can be in line with real time. As day turns to night in the real world, the sun will set in the game. Seasons change and special events occur in real time too. This dynamic setup will have players coming back every day to carry out their routines, build relationships with villagers, celebrate special days, collect furnishings for their homes and just live life in a place that's a world of their own. It's a perfect world –

Figure 14.2 *Animal Crossing, an online virtual world attracting girls from 5 to 12 years, has managed to capture its audience for several hours a day.*

where the kid's birthday never will be forgotten and everyone is always smiling.

Tweens expect everything in their world to be alive and interactive around the clock. Call centres and help lines should never close down. If your brand is not present, it will be forgotten.

2. Ensure 100 per cent connectivity

With connectivity as just another utility we would expect to have all television content available at any time, in exactly the same way we expect the Internet to be available. So instead of a dozen broadcast slots (which we call channels), we could tune into any number of myriad television productions available. We would also just as easily view our children's soccer match, even if we are travelling on another continent. We would be free to choose our viewing platform, be it a large low-resolution television set or a small very high-resolution reading surface.

Nintendo provides a good example of media connectivity. It is currently pumping millions of dollars into home links between its Game Cube console and its hand-held GameBoy Advance in order to ensure that tweens will have access to their games, their levels, their profile and their preferences at any time, no matter where they are. This strategy is likely to become standard among all major game players in the immediate future, enabling the brands to follow their audience 24 hours a day no matter where they are or what they are doing.

If companies know the position of their audience, and are familiar with their general playing patterns along with basic information such as age, gender and address, then games will become an extremely attractive media platform for advertisers. Tweens spend an average of six hours a day with media channels in one form or another. Of these six hours, three are dedicated to video games. But this is not the whole story. Remember the three hours are intensive and are approached with 100 per cent concentration and dedication. So if brands can expose themselves for a maximum of two minutes on television or for unlimited time on games, the places where brands will spend their advertising dollar become more and more obvious.

We're only just beginning to see a world of 100 per cent connectivity. It's entirely possible that branded messages placed in the games will be customized to the time of day, the level of play, the geographic location of the player, and even the local temperature. Based on only these data points, any marketer would be able to develop a sophisticated and highly targeted brand strategy with which no television or radio spot could adequately compete. If the game level is high and the temperature's running hot, then brands like Red Bull, Coca-Cola or Snickers would be perfectly placed in the computer game and appear as part of the advertainment. If it's close to dinner time, Pizza Hut will probably reap substantial benefits by exposing tweens to a branded message that appears at 7pm.

The connected world has much more than well-placed brand messages to offer. When Microsoft launched the Microsoft Passport, it enabled consumer access to pre-defined channels, as well as supplying the channels with personalized data they could adapt to the user's profile.

This trend is what communication experts Don Peppers and Martha Rogers call a Data Aggregation Agent (DAA). As the increasing demands of marketers and service providers for tween information begin to clash with privacy concerns, the DAA will become a central point in our lives.

DAAs will consolidate and control outside access to tweens' personal information, a key element to protecting privacy and fostering the trust that's vital to building profitable tween relationships.

DAAs will also help businesses read the customer's mind, providing constant data about their purchasing patterns, media habits and geographic location. The technology for DAAs is available but just how ready consumers are for this innovation is questionable. There is, however, no doubt that this technology will be of dramatic benefit to both consumers and marketers. It will open up a whole range of variables that branding experts have until now barely considered.

At the moment, marketing plans are primarily based on age, income bracket and areas of interest. In future, they will need to include hundreds of pre-defined actions over varying periods of time. They will have to consider what messages and which channel to use when the tween is moving from home to school, when the tween has a lunch break, when the tween plays football or other games, has dinner, watches a movie, surfs the Internet and even talks on the phone. The challenge is not only to find and combine the most appropriate channels – which are likely to be much more concentrated on game consoles, the Internet and mobile phones – but to target the message, ensuring the best possible conversion rate.

3. Ensure your brand thinks mobile

More than one-third (37 per cent) of all Americans who own consoles or computers report that they also play games on mobile devices like hand-held systems, personal digital assistants (PDA), like Palms, and mobile phones. Close to 20 per cent of all urban tweens worldwide currently have their own mobile phone, compared with 55 per cent who use the Internet (not necessarily with their own connection).

Contrary to what you may think, the *BRANDchild* study indicates that only 13.5 per cent of tweens in the United States own their own mobile phones. By contrast, 51.5 per cent of tweens in Germany own theirs. What's interesting is that if they had to choose between either a mobile phone or access to the Internet, 47.6 per cent would choose the Web. However, that means 44.9 per cent would choose the phone. Tweens in India clearly prefer the idea of a phone, and 57 per cent choose this option.

Marketers will realize that they can no longer focus on messages that have a fixed position. There's already 20 per cent mobile phone penetration in the global tween segment – and it won't be long before these mobile phones also have Internet access. The term outdoor advertising is poised to take on a whole new meaning. Small hand-held digital displays with colour screens are going to take over from static outdoor billboards, presenting yet another opportunity for intimate one-to-one communication.

Teachers around the world are beginning to notice that PDAs are rapidly replacing the paper diary. Tweens think mobile – and expect brands to be visible via these channels. Fisher-Price was taken by surprise only days after it launched the Pixter. The Pixter is a cross between a Palm hand-held and an electronic Magna-Doodle. It doesn't store phone numbers or receive e-mail, but it does have a touch-sensitive LCD screen that lets children draw pictures and play games. It is very likely to be one of Fisher-Price's most successful products. Incidentally, the average age of the Pixter consumer is five!

Surprisingly few brands are visible in the radio mobile environment. One reason is that there simply isn't any established media as yet offering this opportunity. But this shouldn't hold you back from expanding into this arena. Quite simply, you should be where your audience is – and if this requires inventing new ways to get there, it shouldn't hold you back.

4. Contextualize

Every future media channel will be integrated in a line that traces the effects of the customer's ongoing purchasing behaviour. Already Telstra, the Australian telecommunications company, has introduced mobile phone controlled parking meters. You pay for the meter using your phone, which will add the parking fee to your bill. Ten minutes before the meter expires, a SMS message is automatically sent to the mobile phone owner reminding them that more money is required.

Several airline companies are introducing digital ticketing systems recognizing your m-ticket which is stored in your mobile phone. Naturally, your digital ticket will inform you about any delays. There's enormous scope for this. Imagine buying an m-ticket to see your favourite band in a concert. The show's fabulous. And then on your way home you receive an SMS offering you a special price on the band's latest CD.

Brands will need to transmit relevant messages at relevant moments, and consumers will need to be in the mood to receive unsolicited information on their mobiles. For instance, they're more likely to be receptive to the CD offer within half an hour of exiting the concert than when they're running late for work the next day. You might be quite happy to be reminded about the latest *Star Wars* movie on DVD just as you're passing the video store on the way home. And you'd be pleased to receive a Red Bull offer as you enter a nightclub – just show the message to the bartender for your free drink.

This channel-to-channel effect will extend beyond the mobile world. Integration across media has begun to take place. In 2002 Coca-Cola ran a campaign that asked the consumer to send instant feedback via their mobile phone, and follow the progress of competitions on the Internet.

Payment systems integrated into games are also likely to create invincible integration between all the different channels. Xbox Live introduced the first digital wallet in August 2002. This allows players to purchase support while playing a computer game – *in* the computer game!

Project Entropia, one of the first online games, requires players to buy online money with real cash. One US dollar equals 10 PED (Project Entropia Dollars). A laser sword costs about US $3, but can be bought online at one of the many online auctions for as much as US $1000. A first-aid kit costs around US $1.50, and the going rate for a shovel is about 20 cents. There's many a business niche to be found in Project Entropia: taxi drivers and safari guides, miners and blacksmiths, bartenders and barkers, healers and assassins. There's even a guy named Jared who's establishing a virtual church to spread the gospel on calypso.

What's common to all these channels is that sooner or later they're going to integrate with others. Tweens will be able to order a pizza in a game at the virtual Pizza Hut and purchase new 'weapons' on their mobile phones. Contextual branding will be more and more relevant as digital communication becomes a major part of every tweens' life.

A café chain in Japan recently introduced a match-a-friend promotion. Everyone within a radius of 500 meters who owned a Do-Co-Mo phone was sent a message inviting them to join the cell phone owner over a cup of coffee – the invitation comes with a coffee voucher. Johnson & Johnson's Tylenol headache tablets are another example of strong contextual branding. The Tylenol banner ad appears on e-broker Web sites whenever the stock market falls by more than 100 points! Then there's Unilever's mobile recipe book. It's based on the digital mobile phone system in Europe and is intended to be used as you're shopping. It suggests recipes and breaks them down into their required ingredients, identifying Unilever products wherever possible.

According to Digitas, less than 1 per cent of larger sites compile meaningful customer profiles. As a result of this lack of consumer behaviour data, even fewer marketers manage to situate their messages within appropriate and compelling contexts.

Where does all this leave a brand? It can no longer be isolated in just one place, but needs to be part of a highly integrated strategy across all digital channels. By integrated I mean connected in such a way that if the

Figure 14.2 *Logging on to church. On the Internet, 36 million pages cover the topic 'God'. Religion has turned into a digital product. The Virtual Church, which is connected to one of the major computer games, fulfils a need for online prayers amongst tweens – a phenomenon never seen before.*

tween decides to interact with the brand via one of the channels, the others immediately pick up on it and reinforce the decision.

5. Team up with a top brand before your competitor does

Everyone can successfully team up in brand alliances, regardless of the size of your brand equity. There's only limited research in the field of brand alliances, but a study by Judith Washburn, Brian D Till and Randi Priluck at MCB University, published in the *Journal of Consumer Marketing* (2000), has reported some very interesting findings.

▌ 2 + 2 = 5. A successful brand alliance creates a positive synergy that is so substantial that hardly any other marketing tool can compete.

▌ Size doesn't matter. Big brands can team up with small brands and still exercise leverage from the alliance. In terms of brand equity, the value will always be more rewarding for the small brand.

▌ Brand platform loyalty is required. The study also shows that if a brand's line extension departs too far from the brand platform, the equity of the master brand will become diluted. However, the most important element in establishing a brand alliance strategy is to have a solid platform allowing space for extensions.

Turn the consumer's problems to your advantage

Experience shows that consumers can't help companies develop new products if they simply can't imagine the potential. No consumer could have invented the airbag or ABS brakes. What they can do is to help you detect the problems that arise during driving. And this is exactly what you need to keep in mind when developing your brand alliance strategy. It's how you can turn consumer concerns into brand alliance opportunities.

It's now or never

As the world becomes more and more integrated, and as tweens become more and more wired, things are bound to speed up. Remember this generation was born into a world where they expect a new gadget to be launched every day. But this is also a group that comes complete with the thickest brand filter ever seen by any generation anywhere.

Wisdom in Denmark tells us that to follow your competitor's tracks in the snow will never get you ahead. Listening to what tweens have to say will mean you stand a good chance of leading where they are going. In all probability this will place you in front of your competitors.

SUMMARY

▌ We are likely to see large organizations like General Motors, Nintendo, American Airlines, Starbucks and KFC establishing media sales and measurement functions like Microsoft's.

▌ Multinational corporations are likely to communicate with their consumer on a moment-by-moment basis in an integrated fashion. Companies like Sony will be able to offer cross-channel packages.

▌ A new term is likely to be introduced. Intelligent Media Planning will gradually integrate many channels, a technique enabling us to customize messages instantly according to type of audience.

▌ The future will be all about brand alliances. Companies will be teaming up in interesting alliances despite the fact that they share hardly any product synergy.

▌ Back-door branding. Kids are affecting parents' brand choice to a much stronger degree than anticipated.

▌ We are about to see a Data Aggregation Agent (DAA). The DAA will become a central point in tweens' lives, consolidating and controlling outside access to their personal information.

▌ There are four important guidelines you need to consider:

1. Turn your brand into a 24-hour, 7-day brand. Brands need to be constantly accessible.

2. Ensure 100 per cent connectivity. With connectivity as just another utility we would expect to have all television content available at any time – in exactly the same way we expect the Internet to be available.

3. Ensure your brand thinks mobile. Close to 20 per cent of all urban tweens, worldwide, currently have their own mobile phone. Your brand has to be mobile too.

4. Contextualize. Every future media channel will be integrated in a line that traces the effects of the customer's ongoing purchasing behaviour.

ACTION POINTS

▶ Is your brand prepared for an Intelligent Media Planning strategy? How are you going to ensure synergy across media message, channel and audience? Based on the audience description you've developed so far, and the media consumption profile developed, you will need to develop a strategy that will create a domino effect between the differ ent channels.

▶ To secure optimal access to channels and audience, you need to team up with other brands. Identify five brand alliances that your competitor might enter, which you would fear most. Using this information, identify in order of priority 10 companies with whom you would like to establish a brand alliance.

▶ Now select each of the potential alliance partners on the basis of a brand values match. Second, list them in terms of potential synergy of product portfolio offerings, channel access and audience overlap. Then narrow this down to three companies and develop a plan for each brand, outlining how the potential partnership could be structured.

▶ When one or several of the brand alliances has been established, the goal should be to create a contextual branding strategy. How can you ensure that the right message will be sent at the right time to the right audience? Your new partnerships will hopefully give you access to new channels, new content and a new audience, enabling you to develop a true contextual brand strategy.

15

Kidzbiz

Barbie's just turned 40. McDonald's has 70 years or so in the bag, and since its introduction in 1887, Coca-Cola has remained one of the world's most successful brands. These brands can hardly be considered hot trends, and yet they still maintain the loyalty of the tween audience. Then there are the others who were equally well known in their time, but seemed to disappear as quickly as they came. Tamagotchis lasted not much more than a couple of years, Cabbage Patch dolls made it through a decade, and now very little is heard of the Pokèmon phenomenon that swept through the globe at end turn of the 20th century.

In the last few chapters, I have mentioned a lot of up-and-coming brands. These are brands which, due to their innovative nature, and their ability to target new groups and address new behaviours have managed to appeal to a tween audience to an unprecedented degree. However, this is far from the full picture. According to statistical data from a TRU Teenage Marketing and Lifestyle study, close to 90 of the 100 most popular tween brands can be characterized as classics. Classics are defined as those with more than 20 years of brand success. In fact, if you were to examine the longevity of the 10 coolest tween and teen brands, the youngest – Tommy Hilfiger – is 18 years old and Coke, the oldest, is 120 years old. Table 15.1 lists the brands that US tweens and teens regard as cool. Common to all these brands is that they have created a formula that consistently appeals to the tween audience.

Table 15.1 *Top 50 coolest brands according to tweens and teens*

Brand	Percentage
Nike	38
Adidas	19
Tommy Hilfiger	18
Sony	11
Gap	10
Pepsi	9
Coca-Cola	8
Levi's	7
Ralph Lauren	7
Nintendo	6
Old Navy	5
JNCO	5
Abercrombie & Fitch	4
Cover Girl	4
Calvin Klein	4
Dr. Pepper	3
Nautica	3
Mountain Dew	3
Ford	3
Reebok	3
Sprite	3
Fila	3

Source: TRU Teenage Marketing and Lifestyle Study 1999

WHY TWEENS?

Before discussing how these very successful brands have managed to appeal to an ever-demanding tween and teen audience, we should revisit the relevance of this young market segment. According to Teenager Research USA, the average spending power of tweens and teens has risen dramatically. In 1998, US tweens and teens had a combined income of US $121 billion – up from US $86 billion in 1993.

Although one imagines that tweens are insulated from natural economic trends, their income does rise and fall with the economy. Many parents say that if they're suffering financially, their children will be the last to feel it. But when the economy dips, tweens income also drops, because much of it comes from parents. The trend follows a similar pattern during economic upturns.

It should come as no surprise that tweens have a direct bearing on products like breakfast cereal, candy and clothes. Parents have less time and so it often falls to tweens to do a little food shopping each week. In fact, many are now responsible for keeping the home larder stocked. Parents may indicate 'cornflakes' on their list, but it's at this point where tweens' influence kicks in. They will determine if the cornflakes are to be Kellogg's or another competing brand.

One of the largest categories of influence in the purchase of all FMCG (fast-moving consumer goods) brands is impulse. When shopping with a parent, or especially when doing it alone, tweens are tending to make brand selections, often overruling the parent. Tweens have their tactics. They'll slip it into the shopping cart or hand the item directly to the cashier or even throw a mini-tantrum causing the parent to capitulate rather than be embarrassed.

If we were to compare this purchasing behaviour to that of 10 years ago, we would observe a dramatic change – some may say for the worse. But it's interesting to note that tweens' perception of their own power is in fact underestimated. When asked to think of their direct influence purchases, they tend to recount how often they have to ask, how much they have to nag, or how much they have to plead for a certain item. But our *BRANDchild* study shows that their influence extends way beyond the day-to-day shopping situation. Even when they're not present, purchasing decisions are made at their request. Parents have a basic desire to please their children. So if they know that their child favours X over Y, they'll purchase X. This is a relatively new trend. But then tweens are more brand savvy than their contemporaries of 10 years ago.

So what kind of influence do they have over the purchase of cars, computers and other electronic goods? Tweens are also influencing their parents over purchases of technology-driven brands, or brands that tend to be more fashionable. Often parents take along their tween or teen to the store to have their advice on tap. According to *BRANDchild* research data, urban tweens influence an astounding 60 per cent of all car purchases made by their parents, and 45 per cent of their mobile phone purchases. And since production life cycles increase every year, and more and more brands contain ever-newer technological innovations, there's every indication that the influence of tweens will increase over the next few years.

The interesting question then becomes which brands tweens influence most and which brands are purchased without the mediation of a tween or teen.

Growing big and staying big

It is clear that almost all categories of brand need to secure a dual appeal as an essential element in their future marketing strategies. The days where one brand appealed to a single audience are over. Securing youth appeal not only establishes brand loyalty at an early age, but has a dramatic influence on parents' purchasing patterns. The important thing to remember here is that even if tweens cannot afford to enter the market, they still exert power over the purchase.

Talk about a challenge! Until very recently, most brands built and maintained their position based on a consistent appeal to one market segment, typically the adult one. However, brands that now ignore the young market are doing so at their peril. Brand decisions are no longer an isolated phenomenon taking place between adults. Rather, the entire purchasing process is hugely influenced by tweens. So for a brand to ensure a future, it will need to appeal to two often contradictory segments of the market – the young and the old. This raises further challenges to the communication strategies that need to be developed in order to satisfy both audiences.

Take, for example, Colgate. Over the years the company has diversified its classic toothpaste and toothbrush range to incorporate the tastes and fashions of children, tweens and teens. There's a Colgate Barbie toothbrush with a matching anti-cavity toothpaste. The range extends to Barney, Monsters, Bugs Bunny, Pokèmon and every Disney character that you can think of. There's also a comprehensive non-licensed product line which appeals directly to the adult market. This strategy has helped Colgate reach several market segments with one basic item. Only the packaging changes.

Strong awareness of brands such as Disney, Colgate, Nike and Coke places them, however, in an awkward Catch-22 situation. Levi's used to be the one and only brand in jeans. But as brand choices have increased, tweens can now select smaller brands which make a bigger statement about their personal style. This has been crunch time for Levi's. How to appeal to their lifelong loyal consumers while at the same time entering the personal statement fashion market? The jury is still out on this one.

On the one hand, constant visibility has for years generated high awareness. Naturally the more popular a brand becomes, the more visible it tends to be. And this is where the dilemma begins. Because tweens are attracted to newness and like the idea of discovering brands, it's difficult for a brand the size of Levi's or even Nike to maintain high and broad

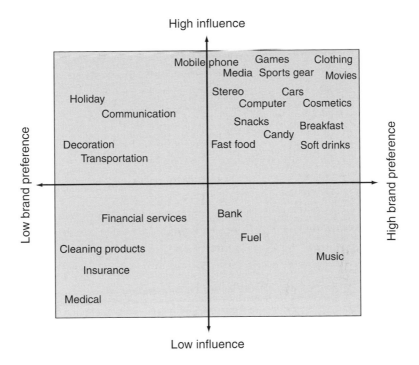

High influence

Mobile phone   Games   Clothing
Media   Sports gear   Movies

Holiday   Stereo   Cars
Communication   Computer   Cosmetics

Snacks   Breakfast
Candy

Decoration   Fast food   Soft drinks
Transportation

Financial services   Bank

Fuel

Cleaning products   Music

Insurance

Medical

Low influence

Low brand preference

High brand preference

Figure 15.1 *Brand purchases influenced by tweens. The* BRANDchild *study shows that parents are much more influenced by their children than first anticipated. The kids in the family influence more than 60 per cent of all car purchases.*

profile without scaring away tweens. To avoid just such a conflict, Nike has chosen to use celebrity endorsement and new product development as two key ingredients in their market strategy. These two ingredients have now almost become one. The constant product development is sufficient to maintain tweens' interest and thus their support. Nike keeps it up by releasing more sub-brands like Nike Goddess, Nike Jumpman, Nike ACG and Nike Presto. Nike Presto is a sub-brand which, similar to Jones Soda, builds on emerging artists. They each support the Presto brand within their area of interest.

By using currently 'cool' artists and talents, Nike builds on potential tween idols, which potentially adds value to their new product launches, and ultimately keeps Nike in the tween loop. In the process, cool artists have the potential to turn into superstars. Tiger Woods was picked up by Nike in 1991 when he was a young pro on the golfing circuit. Now he is a megastar, attracting millions of fans to the Nike brand.

According to a TRU teenage Marketing and Lifestyle study conducted in 1999, 42 per cent of all boys think it's really cool to see a sports star in a commercial. This pronouncement of 'cool' fails to apply to commercials for the same brand which do not feature a sports star. Sports stars far outstripped the second-ranking preference – 22 per cent preferred seeing supermodels in their advertising. However, as we've already noted, our *BRANDchild* study shows that things have changed since 1999. There's now less admiration for testimonials by stars. It seems that tweens have simply been over-exposed to these types of commercials.

Attracting a young audience can sound easier than it is. Attracting a tween audience can possibly scare off the adult one. This is exactly what Calvin Klein learned when he mounted a controversial campaign using teenage models in overtly sensual poses to sell his jeans. Tweens and teens loved it. Adults didn't go near it.

Categorizing brand trends

To what extent can we predict the destiny of brands? How are brands likely to progress when appealing to both a youth and adult market? Using the global research company Millward Brown's extensive database, which contains information on 20,000 brands spread across 53 countries, it's possible to determine the likelihood of a brand's performance. Their methodology of data gathering places brands into eight broad categories.

Olympic brands

Olympic brands are universally known and loved. These are brands like Coca-Cola, McDonald's and Disney, which have permeated popular culture and are known and used by millions around the world. The strongest performing brands are called Olympic.

To maintain one's Olympic status is, in many ways, a fight for survival. A couple of years ago Disney conducted a survey to determine the health of their brand across the globe. The results proved shocking for the executives. They learned that their brand was not in good shape. Over the years, Disney's licensing business had become such a large portion of the corporation's revenues that control over the core brand value had become diluted. Disney could be found everywhere – from traditional merchandizing through to food and extending its reach into financial services. Quality control had been compromised and the Disney logo was

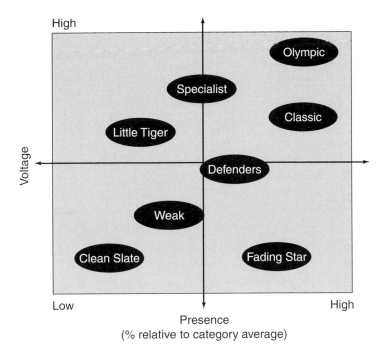

Figure 15.2 *Eight brand categories. Today brands can be split into eight different categories indicating the performance of the brands. The* BRANDchild *study shows that the movement between each of the eight categories with tween brands is substantially stronger than with adult brands.* Source: Millward Brown

prominently displayed on low-quality and down-market products. This widespread dilution brought the integrity of Disney into question. It was also leading to confusion among consumers, who could no longer distinguish the brand's core philosophy.

Over a two-year period, all Disney brand activities were aligned. Licensing deals not aligning with the core philosophy were terminated and brand guidelines optimized. The result is that Disney now has a multi-brand policy. All Disney films come under the Buena Vista and Touchstone banners, empowering them to produce films of every type without endangering the revered Disney name.

Similarly, when the success of an innovation is uncertain, it would be foolish to risk associating it with a successful brand. Using just such logic, Nintendo launched Pokèmon as a separate stand-alone brand. At its peak, it almost outgrew the size of its mother company.

As a result of this restructure, Disney enjoys the five main benefits of being an Olympic brand. These are:

1. **A substantial, dominant and sustained market share.** Disney predominates in animated features, theme parks and as a leading film producer. They're doing what their vision states – making people happy!
2. **Premium prices.** Disney theme parks, hotels, and merchandise command significantly higher prices than competitors' offerings. Often Disney is able to charge two to three times more for their products than a generic version.
3. **A track record of extending the brand to new products.** The Disney brand was launched in 1923 with the first Mickey Mouse cartoon. It has since been extended to films, network and cable television programs, studios, theme parks, hotels, merchandise and even a National Hockey League team, the Mighty Ducks.
4. **Covers the full market.** From Disney's original focus on children, the brand has been extended to the full range of demographic groups, covering ages 8 to 80.
5. **Extends to new geographic areas.** Disney's films and products are distributed worldwide. Theme parks are open or planned in the United States, Europe and Asia.

Note that three of these five benefits represent not what the brand can do for the company today, but the options it can create for tomorrow. This may ultimately be the true power of an Olympic brand.

Classic

Second in the brand hierarchy is the Classic brand. These are almost as strong as Olympic brands. Weaknesses include that they may not be globally strong.

Sony is a good example of a Classic brand. It has an overwhelming strength in some markets, such as its home market, Japan. It's also very strong in the United Kingdom and the United States, but is weaker in a market like Germany.

Specialist

Brands that appeal to particular groups rather than a mass audience belong to the Specialist category.

This classification exists more often for brands with an adult target. The reason for this is that tweens are quick adopters and usually act in groups, so tween brands are able to move directly from Little Tiger to Classic or Olympic status. Specialist brands are relatively expensive, but for those to whom the brand is relevant, it will be a passion. They will be strongly committed to it.

Prada and Gucci are examples of brands that can be considered Specialist. They're high-priced and exclusive. It's unlikely that these will ever move on to become Classic or even Olympic, since this is simply not in the manufacturers' interests. However, it's interesting to note that there seem to be fewer and fewer price barriers preventing tweens from participating at this level.

Little Tiger

Increasingly, brands are being positioned as Little Tigers. These are brands which are less well known but attract a strong following among those who've discovered them. Brands like FUBU, Billabong and Jones Soda all entered the global marketplace with a Little Tiger strategy. This was to appeal to a small but clearly-defined segment, using peer-to-peer networks to spread the word of their brand. Examples of brands which for a shorter period belonged to this category are Red Bull, Nokia mobile phones and Palm Pilots.

Defenders

Defenders are survivors. They're neither strong nor weak. They occupy the middle ground in the market. Although they lack a leading edge, they're also accepted by many. Brands like Hasbro and LEGO are typical of this category. The interesting feature of this category is its ability to change. With the introduction of Fisher-Price's Pixer or the LEGO Group's Bionicle, the whole situation looks different.

Clean Slate

Clean Slates have usually just got started. They command only low levels of awareness. Typically, two types of brands tend to be represented in this Clean Slate category. First are the totally new brands with a fresh image.

Second are established brands which are being introduced to new markets. For example, Do-Co-Mo's I-mode phone was launched under licence by the Dutch Telco Giant KPN in markets such as Holland, Belgium and Germany. In Japan tweens took to the I-mode phone with such enthusiasm that it's clearly an Olympic brand over there. However, in Europe it represents a more focused product with fewer options and value.

Fading Star

Fading Stars are brands in trouble. They are still well known and often still relevant to many, but have been overtaken by a competitor. They clearly lack advantages or differentiation in their field.

It is likely that this segment will continue to grow as a casualty of ever-changing trends and new offerings. A good example of a Fading Star that has turned around its fortunes is Adidas. Nine years ago it was a very popular brand. But over the last three years or so, it failed to meet consumer demands and suffered major losses.

It was Robert Louis Dreyfus and his associates who were given the task of reversing the trend when they bought the brand from Bernard Tapie in 1993. Up until then, Adidas had done everything by the book. They had a top-quality product, consistency in their brand, and excellent distribution. But despite all this, sales were down. In 1992 they reported a loss of 500 million francs.

It took Robert Louis Dreyfus two years to steer Adidas out of the Fading Star category. Eventually he turned the corner, reporting a 515 million franc profit. The Adidas brand had succeeded in moving into the Defenders category – heading for the Classic – a move more and more brands today are able to make.

What's fascinating about this story is that brands do have the ability to step out of the Fading Star category. In Adidas's case they adopted three dramatic changes to the core ingredients of the total Adidas proposition. One of the most prominent factors was that the brand was technically good, but the design held no appeal for tween and teen consumers. So almost all the existing designs were replaced bearing this crucial market in mind.

Furthermore, the advertising and marketing budgets were multiplied by five, while many sponsoring activities were cut to almost zero. Finally, the development and marketing departments were reorganized according to sectors where one sport prevails: basketball in the United States, and soccer and jogging in Europe. They steered clear of yuppies at Yale and stayed true to their roots by targeting young African-American kids in the urban ghettoes of the United States.

The strategy excited interest by sponsoring youth and rap group competitors. Adidas cut out all discount offerings, and distribution channels were optimized, placing them alongside Nike and Reebok on the sports shoe stands. Adidas's market share in the United States went up 1.9 per cent, to 3.8 per cent in 1994. Six years later it had climbed to 15.1 per cent. According to Interbrand, by 1999 Adidas was ranked as the world's 68th most valuable brand, compared to Nike's 35th position.

Weak

The last category of all is the Weak category. Several tween brands like the Cabbage Patch dolls and Meccano have found themselves here. Not surprisingly, more brands targeting tweens die faster and more dramatically than those brands appealing to other age segments.

The brand trend

You will have noticed that the brand picture among the adult population is significantly different from the way brands are positioned in a tween and teen market. But besides the fact that tween brands are characterized by an ever-changing profile within the eight categories, the speed with which they move from category to category is unlike any other age segment. In a survey conducted for WPP by Millward Brown, it was found that about half of today's top 1,600 brands change categories every two years. It seems likely that tween brands change more often than this.

But even more interesting is how brands change their equity. In classic marketing we are familiar with the life cycle of a brand. This takes them through distinct phases, from introduction to growth, on to success and eventually into decline. One of the most respected models still studied at universities across the globe is the Boston Matrix. This model introduced the terms Problem Child, Star, Cash Cow and Dog. In it, a tween brand would move from Clean Slate to Little Tiger to Olympic, and then down to Classic, ending with Fading Star. What's emerging is that that no such pattern exists any longer. In fact, studies conducted by Millward Brown from 1998, show that only half of today's brands travel along this path. The rest demonstrate very unpredictable patterns.

Take, for example, Clean Slates. From 1998, only 8 per cent moved to become Little Tigers. However, 9 per cent became Defenders, 5 per cent changed classification to Weak, and 2 per cent to Specialist. The remaining 76 per cent maintained their Clean Slate classification. An even more dramatic trend is found in the Little Tiger classification. Over the same period, 33 per cent of these moved to a Defender classification, while 10 per cent moved to the Specialist category, and 7 per cent became Weak. Less than half, at 41 per cent, maintained their Little Tiger status.

A quick look at the Fading Stars will show a trend rarely seen 20 years ago. Only 9 per cent moved to the Weak category while 58 per cent maintained their position. But what's most interesting is that 31 per cent strengthened their position and moved to the Defender category, indicating just why the Boston Matrix life cycle model is no longer valid when applied to a tween or adult audience.

So how can we determine who's going to sink, who's going to tread water, and who's going to swim in this volatile market? Like any other specific market segment, we can apply the 80:20 rule. This suggests that 80 per cent of online brand building comes from traditional building, while 20 per cent can be attributed to interactivity. In the same way, 80 per cent of what is known of classic marketing still holds true when communicating with a sophisticated tween audience. However, 20 per cent is different. This 20 per cent variable can be attributed to what this audience is being exposed to on a daily basis. Different because this generation, like no other before, is truly interactive. They expect brands to act and communicate in a dialogue as opposed to classic monologue-based messages. This generation also sees things from a multi-dimensional, multi-media perspective, presenting new angles, new dimensions and offering new attributes to whatever context the brand uses.

There are 10 factors which make the tween audience unique. In order to succeed in appealing to this most critical audience, all these need to be taken into account.

1. Emotions are driving tweens – and so are brands

'My puppy still has bad breath even after I gave her a Tic Tac'

When NutraSweet launched its product in 1983, both Coca-Cola and Pepsi agreed to display the NutraSweet logo on their cans and bottles. This made history. Not only was it the first time Coke had showed another commercial brand name on its logo, but it did it in unison with Pepsi, its major competitor. The fact was that NutraSweet was in a unique position.

It owned the patent for the sweetener. However, in 1992 the patent ran out. You would have expected the NutraSweet relationship with Coke and Pepsi to run out with the patent, but both chose to remain with the artificial sweetener product – even if they could have gotten a cheaper generic brand.

It's fascinating that in just nine years, NutraSweet managed to establish a strong customer loyalty base, forcing two of the world's largest purchasers of artificial sweetener to pay top dollar for their product. They in fact forced both Coke and Pepsi to increase the price of their soft drinks. Coke and Pepsi had done their own research, which highlighted the fact that NutraSweet was a major factor in customer loyalty. It was a done deal.

Walter Landor, one of the 20th century's foremost design pioneers, once said 'Products are made in the factory, but brands are created in the mind.' This emphasizes the importance of building the product on emotions rather than facts. NutraSweet survived because of emotional ties. Interestingly, the success NutraSweet enjoyed in the US market never translated to Europe, where the brand was not incorporated on the bottles and cans of Pepsi and Coke. This lack of visibility kept NutraSweet from creating the necessary connection with the consumer.

The *BRANDchild* study shows that, more than ever, values-driven brands appeal to the tween segment. A brand without values is doomed. It means no personality, and therefore there's no way tweens can identify with the product. It's quite extraordinary that 72 per cent of all tweens talk about commercials with their peers at school. And when asked to trade cards representing various brands, they instantly know how to prioritize – even though there can be as many as 100 cards in a total selection.

Another vital aspect in the emotional aspect of a brand is its authenticity. There's an ever-increasing demand among tweens for brands that are deemed authentic. They will travel miles and miles for the right brand of sports shoe – even if a similar brand is locally available at half the price.

When Rollerblades were first released the product sold out within minutes. Competing brands offering the same functionality were rejected. Tweens searched every possible outlet for the 'real' Rollerblade. On the other hand, Rollerblades did whatever they could to control distribution, ensuring that they maintained the perception of a high-value product.

Some of the most successful brand strategies targeting tweens have one thing in common – authenticity. The blockbuster movie, *Titanic*, was an authentic story with a romantic twist. And it passed on its stamp of authenticity to its star, Leonardo Di Caprio.

Then there are the 11 authentic spices and herbs that go into making KFC the desirable take-away chicken that it is. It's these 11 secret ingredients that differentiate it from its competitors. This perception has been part of sophisticated promotional activities. In January 2001 it was rumoured that the original recipe of Colonel Harland Sanders from Shelbyville, Kentucky was in danger of being sold at public auction by a couple who supposedly had found the list. The story made headlines worldwide.

Although KFC believed it was improbable that the couple had obtained the secret recipe, the company took the claim seriously and asked a court to prevent them from selling or disclosing the list of ingredients. KFC investigated the couple's claim thoroughly and compared their list to the Colonel's secret recipe. According to KFC, the recipe found by the couple was nowhere close. KFC dismissed the lawsuit. And the secret list of the Colonel's 11 herbs and spices still remain safely locked in the KFC vault in Louisville, Kentucky. Coincidence? Public relations stunt? Whatever – it managed to build the brand and maintain the mystery around the KFC image.

It's important to establish a brand around pre-defined brand values, and then it's possible to push the brand a step further, turning its identity towards a position where the product is seen as truly authentic. More and more, brands are instantly copied. But the brand with an authentic foundation will still survive. There are games like Pokèmon, DragonBallZ and Digimon which make extensive use of secret recipes, authentication of numbers, holograms or secret symbols placed on the products, adding another authentic image enabling tweens to select what's real and what's fake.

2. Brand consistency: in search of solid connections

As the touch points in tweens' lives become increasingly unreliable, consistency gains greater currency. In a world where relationships seem often to break and employment is increasingly insecure, it's not surprising that a survey conducted by Roper Starch Worldwide shows that 55 per cent of American's believe the 'good old days' were better than today. This is markedly different from a similar study conducted in 1974, when 54 per cent of those surveyed believed there was no time better than the present.

In times where everything is in a state of flux, solid focal points are enormously attractive. Tweens simply want to surround themselves with things that they can rely on and trust. Brand consistency is therefore an essential ingredient of success. If brands are able to include historical signals in their marketing, all the better. The effort to manufacture nostalgia has over recent years created a trend among tween brands. Pepsi's 2002 advertising campaign was based on five decades of history tied together by Britney Spears. In 1994, Coca-Cola brought in a plastic version of its famous contour bottle and watched sales grow. Over the past few years, Coke has enjoyed a comeback of sorts and have seen sales soar by 25 per cent. This could be attributed to a packaging redesign that harks back to its roots.

The nostalgic mood recalling the past has encouraged several advertisers to jump on the bandwagon – even when they don't have archives to pillage. Ford Motor Co., hoping to equate longevity with quality, has put to air commercials commemorating the fact that Henry Ford put America on wheels. The spot includes what appears to be grainy historic footage of a Model-T puttering down Main Street. But the sepia-toned scene was actually shot on a Hollywood back lot, and was given its vintage look by using a 1920s hand-cranked camera, old emulsion film and special editing.

KFC learned that forgetting authentic elements in their brand's history was a mistake. A few years ago, they decided the brand needed some advertising help from founder Colonel Sanders. After all, research had shown that consumers still trusted him. However, there was a slight problem. Sanders had died in 1980 and the company was unable to find old film clips that would work in a modern context. So they dressed up an actor in the Colonel's starched white suit, and filmed the commercials in black and white.

It didn't work. KFC was roundly criticized for defaming the dead. After less than a year, the ads were pulled. Sales had plummeted and tweens had seriously questioned the authenticity of the KFC brand. Still, KFC hasn't given up on using the Colonel. Instead, the company decided the best – and safest – way to evoke his memory was to enlarge his image on the red and white buckets of chicken.

It's one thing to hope consumers will equate longevity with quality, but it's another to be consistent in every element of the communication strategy. Consistency is all about ensuring that the same values, the same graphics and the same tone of voice is used. This goes a long way to reassure the consumer about the solidity of the brand. Brand consistency is everything. It's the uniforms, the name badges, the ads, the site navigation, the call centre, the service – even the signage on the toilets. In short it's the link which ties together all the communication elements and goes towards one brand image.

Levi's has banned all third-party use of its brand on the Internet, in order to retain ownership of its concept and prevent potential misrepresentation. Being consistent can be an expensive affair. In the autumn of 1991, continental Europeans were exposed to a massive advertising campaign which informed them that the chocolate bar they knew as Raider was to now be called Twix. Twix is the name used everywhere else in the world from New York to Tokyo to Sydney.

This was different from Mars Incorporated's previous brand transfer. When they changed Treets to M&M's, everything altered – including the product. This time, great care was taken not to disturb the customers. The only thing that changed was the name. It was successful and necessary, because in order to secure brand consistency and leverage on the advertising materials produced all around the world this had to happen. Only five years before it would have been possible to run totally separate campaigns for the same product and no-one would have noticed. But urban tweens are a global generation and 45 per cent of them research products on the Net before making an offline purchase. There's no difference to a tween between a site based in the United Kingdom, Australia or the United States. What's important is that the representation is authentic. Different messages, values and propositions in different markets are increasingly difficult to justify – and should be carefully considered before being undertaken – simply because it could very well damage the brand.

Brands with different audiences present the most challenges in maintaining consistency. As a result, many brands run several parallel campaigns appealing to different audiences at the same time. Gap is also Banana Republic and Old Navy – each brand appealing to different age and income segments, and each with their own brand clarity. Likewise Niketown and NIKE iD are two brands representing different types of audiences, and Levi's SILVERTAB, Corduroys, and Levi's Engineered are all attempts to build ties between different audiences. The only thing these three umbrella brands have in common with their sub-brands is the brand, its attributes and values. They succeed because every message they send is in harmony with the core image of the mother brand. The products might be very different, but they are all still based on core values. The brand embodies consistency across each sub-brand, ensuring that audiences won't question the integrity and consistency of the brand.

This level of consistency has a lot of weight with tweens. They love brands created for them, and adore concepts carefully crafted around a sound story. When participating in one of our many *BRANDchild* group sessions, it quickly became clear that this audience – more than any other – expects to be treated in a unique way. They demand respect and expect brands to keep their promises.

3. Product innovation: justifying the brand value to tweens

Attributes associated with being a new brand, and attributes associated with being an established one are equally important in the mind of a tween. According to a TRU study, nearly 10 per cent of tweens associate newness with coolness. This underlines the fact that the tween market is fertile ground for new products. Innovation promotes a sense of leadership and that places the brand ahead of the game. Innovation is also an opportunity for renewal, a space for brands to reinforce what they stand for and demonstrate what they can deliver. Some of the most successful and long-lasting brands do exactly this – re-inventing the product to stay in touch with consumer tastes, but ensuring that they continue to express the values that the brand embodies.

This might very well be the reason why some of the world's most respected brands like P&G, L'Oreal and Gillette allocate income from 3.2 per cent of their sales to research and development. Not surprisingly, the R&D budget for tween-related brands is even higher at Sony, Mattel and LEGO, which tend to dedicate about 5.2 per cent of their income to new products.

Consider this. In 1993 Gillette allocated 37 per cent of their sales to launching five new products. In bringing their innovations so quickly to the market, Gillette managed to stay ahead of the pack. But product innovation doesn't necessarily mean that totally new products have to reach the market ever year, before the brand's future is secured. People mistakenly believe that Coke succeeds without innovation. Even though they have marketed the same product for over 100 years, they've never stopped segmenting their brand to address the demands of new markets. Diet Coke, sugar-free Coke and caffeine-free Coke are just some aspects of the segmentation. Then there's the packaging, which comes in all sizes, shapes and forms. Cans to fit vending machines, large bottles for parties, PVC and PET. Each new shape is considered a new product launch, and each new size has its own impact on consumers. Each change sends out a message of modernity.

4. Price management: tweens are prepared to pay the price

Coca-Cola's philosophy is based on what's called the 3-A principle: Availability, Affordability and Awareness. Coke must be within reach everywhere, be cheap and on everyone's mind. R Goizette, the former CEO of Coca-Cola said Coke must be the same price as tea in China. Price management is probably one of the toughest disciplines to handle, since it clearly has to be in harmony with the consumer perception of the brand. Customers do not buy solely on low price.

Every indication from the *BRANDchild* study is that price has less and less relevance in the tween market. They buy according to customer value – that is, the difference between the benefits a company gives tweens and the price it charges. More precisely, customer value equals customer-perceived benefits minus customer-perceived price. So the higher the perceived benefit and/or the lower the price of a product, the higher the customer value and the greater the likelihood that tweens will choose that product.

Children from the very young age of six are aware of the value of money and the value of what they purchase. By eight years of age, they're able to determine if the product they buy is giving them adequate value for money. By 12, almost 100 per cent are able to comparison-shop.

PlayStation 2 was first released at a price of US $599. Four months later the official price was halved. The price strategy managed to ensure that a premium was charged as long as possible, and when this audience segment was fully secured, a lower price would gain purchases among a new target audience with less money. The fascinating part of this story is that PlayStation 2 managed to change its price without necessarily diluting its quality perception among tweens.

But more often than not, discounting dilutes the value of the brand. Throughout the 1990s, KFC in Australia diluted their brand by incessantly promoting discounted meals. Almost every television commercial and print ad was based on price. They never used an emotional connection in their campaign strategy. In the end, consumers were 'educated' by KFC to only visit their outlets if there was a special deal. Price became the focal point of the interaction rather than the value of the KFC brand. So many brands – including Coke, Disney and Nike – have very strict pricing policies, with rigid guidelines for discounting the product. Coke only offers discounts on bulk purchases.

Most Olympic and Classic brands are continuously involved in price evaluation and re-evaluation. They do not get involved in estimating this, but stay in touch with their target markets, balancing feedback with the perceived position they desire for their brand. More than anything else, price positions the brand's image in the minds of tweens. Be careful before setting any price strategy in stone.

5. Portfolio management: tweens don't buy products, they buy brand solutions

Everyone recognizes brands like Walkman, PlayStation, Trinitron, Vaio and HandyCam. Next to their logos we always see the well-spaced capital letters SONY. Sony is obviously the endorsing brand. Under its umbrella there is a wide diversity of product brands, line brands and range brands.

Very few companies have managed to establish a brand portfolio that achieves the highly desirable cradle-to-grave brand strategy. Sony is probably one of the very few companies that come close to achieving this. From Walkmans, designed to be used by three-year-olds, they follow life cycles through games, movies, digital cameras and video cameras, televisions and hi-fi equipment. So a brand loyalty created at age three, is well worth the effort.

When Nestlé puts its name on the Crunch and Kit Kat bars, on coffee or on Nesquick drinking chocolate, like Sony, it's endorsing the quality of the merchandise, and the Nestlé name becomes the guarantor. Just using the name dispels uncertainty. In principle, the Nestlé brand takes a back seat, leaving the product itself as hero. On the other hand, when consumers sees Mattels' Barbie, the name is more than a simple endorsement. Here Barbie is the brand name which holds sway and which accords Mattel the seal of approval and distinction which it would not otherwise enjoy. Barbie is the key to the door of the Mattel emotional universe.

The problem with many brands is that they were converted from source brands to endorsing ones. Within the source-brand concept, the family spirit dominates, even if the offspring all have their own individual names. With the endorsing brand, however, the product is autonomous and has only the brand in common. The benefit from a source-brand strategy is the ability to separate different messages and even appeal to different segments. It also enables brand-builders to establish an in-depth emotional experience based on a particular strategic direction.

A wide range of sub-brands, however, is no sure-fire guarantee of success. It may make good economic sense when launching a new product, but maintaining a large portfolio of brands is a costly affair. Despite the fact that this strategy is possibly the cheapest of them all when launching new products, it is clear that it can still be a very costly affair for any company to maintain a large portfolio of brands. Mars, for example, constantly evaluate their full brand portfolio to determine which brands to keep and which to sell off. Their philosophy clearly favours supporting only Classic brands, or mega-brands worth more than one billion US dollars. Their strategy for sub-brands is constantly focused on five points:

1. The brand must be a leader in its market segment;
2. The brand must have a high level of public confidence;
3. It must have a presence that is physically and financially viable, throughout the world;
4. The brand must represent the highest level of quality;
5. It is able to meet important durability requirements on a global scale.

Since the 1980s, Mars Incorporated has terminated dozens of brands, ensuring an absolute focus on its global brand portfolio.

Ferrero, a leader in the European chocolate market, has managed to maintain market dominance in each candy segment by exercising an extensive product portfolio strategy. In some countries the Kinder Surprise has no competitors. Likewise Nutella dominates its segment just as Roche d'Or does. But the fascinating element in the Ferrero story is that all these products are direct results of vigilant monitoring of economics of scale in the manufacturing process. For instance, there is Nutella in Ferrero Rocher, while Kinder Bueno is Nutella without the chocolate. The company constantly evaluates how a new product, positioned differently, can be manufactured on the same assembly line already in use for an existing product.

Extending the brand into merchandizing is what Coca-Cola, Disney, LEGO, Mattel, Fisher-Price, Kellogg's, Sony, Colgate, Nintendo, Microsoft and Pepsi have in common. Over the past 10 years they have all changed their marketing strategy to form merchandizing partnerships with brands that are stronger than they are in certain segments.

They have realized that not every brand can be invented by their own marketing and R&D departments, no matter how much funding they allocate. There was a time when – let's call it pride – got in the way of their even considering joining with a brand they had not invented. So if it were 'not invented here' it could not even be considered. Over the past few years this attitude has undergone radical change. In order to fulfil the tween demand for merchandise, adopting other brands has become a necessary marketing strategy for everyone. In order to maintain a top position in the tween segment of the market, merchandizing partnerships are the way to go.

The risk of building a solid brand merchandizing relationship with an outside brand is, in theory, extremely high. However, more and more companies are succeeding at building almost their entire marketing strategy on merchandizing partners. And tweens love it.

6. Channel optimization: at any time, tweens are using any channel

Channel optimization is everything. The important thing is to ensure the right message is sent at the right time to the right audience via the right channel. And it is this distribution and communication that work together to create positive brand synergy.

Distribution is more important than ever before. It's the way McDonald's locates its stores close to high-flow traffic points. It's the way 7-Eleven and Starbucks secure real estate on prime city corners. It's the way Pepsi is available in all bars – particularly when there's a new advertising campaign running. Consumers don't have the patience, nor the time, to wait for a brand to become available.

Mass distribution brands ensure their own brand appears on every shelf, thus excluding other manufacturers' brands. The ice-cream maker Haagen Dazs tends to control the market of upmarket ice-creams. They provide a high-quality ice-cream through a well-managed word-of-mouth marketing campaign, but primarily they maintain a presence through displaying their product in its own refrigerator in supermarkets and hypermarkets.

It's one thing to secure visibility in a store, but it's quite another to control the quality of that visibility. In 1996, Levi's launched the first e-commerce jeans site that allowed the consumer to custom-design their jeans online. To this day, people in the industry are still debating whether this design-your-own jeans site was a success. The general opinion seems to be that most thought it was a success, but three years after it was launched, the site was closed down because of a change in strategy.

Now all major retailers selling the Levi's product can be found on their homepage. It's a good example of how a brand has established a detailed distribution and selection program over the years. Levi's expects retailers to respect five criteria:

1. Only to offer recognizable jeans brands – no price leaders or generic lines;
2. The sales environment must be as upmarket as the product;

3. Product ranges that could affect the image of Levi's must not be found close by;
4. The service must be in tune with the brand;
5. The store must be a fixed construction (not a market stall) with adequate space reserved for jeans, and capable of attracting young people.

Levi's fought tooth and nail to stop Tesco from selling its jeans in their UK supermarket chain. They argued that the brand would be devalued, since a grocery supermarket was not able to supply a 'Levi's experience', and that Tesco's staff were not trained to add value. All this demonstrates that a solid branding strategy is not restricted to creating an image through advertising, but that a distribution strategy is just as important.

Promotion is the other side of the story. Today, on average, two-thirds of marketing budgets spent worldwide are dedicated to promotional activities. There is no doubt that tween-focused brands live and die by the quality of their promotional campaigns. These promulgate the right hype at the right time, and are vital in helping the brand push the peer-talk button. The closer you can get to the consumer at the particular moment of decision, the greater the chance you have in affecting their choice of brand.

The Häagen-Dazs strategy is admirable but difficult for any distributor to build. As a result more brands concentrate their efforts on in-store and sales promotions, events, competitions, happenings – you name it – to secure the necessary attention. Electronic media have added a new venue for promotions. Securing a channel-to-channel synergy will become increasingly important. If you happen to shop online you do not want to repeat the whole purchasing procedure if you choose to pick up the product at the nearest store. Each channel needs to work together and this will show tweens that the system is intelligent – learning more about them in the process and taking less of the customer's time.

Tweens don't like to be talked *at*, and they expect this respect – and even love – to be reflected in the brand's history. Harry Potter was at first a book, then a movie, a game, cards and merchandizing. It was all tied together around the Harry Potter brand, pushing the traffic from channel to channel. Brands like Harry Potter, Disney and DragonBallZ are all based on brand channel synergy, educating tweens to expect a similar flow for all other brands.

7. Perception management: reading the tween mind

Intel's Andy Grove once said, 'There is at least one point in the history of any company when you have to change dramatically to rise to the next performance level. Miss that moment and you start to decline.'

Almost every brand has, over the years, witnessed brand dilution. Often the dilution happens when the brand's image is out of tune with the consumer's expectation. In some cases this can have catastrophic results, seriously affecting the brand's future. In most cases senior management only become aware of the dilution when it's almost too late to repair – or at least when it's become a costly and time-consuming exercise to turn around.

In a nutshell, a solid brand-perception management strategy starts with a rigorous assessment of the brand audience and of the brand positioning in the minds of tweens. What beliefs pop up in their minds when they think about the brand and its category? What are the good memories? What are the bad memories? How do they justify their support for the brand? What is the product worth? Is the brand attractive? Basically, what does the brand-association network look like?

The Levi's experience is telling. Kurt Barnard, president of Barnard's Retail Trend Support said: 'Levi's is basically a troubled company. Although their name is hallowed in American history, few people these days wear Levi's jeans.' It was comments such as this that Levi's was hoping to avoid when the company put together a comprehensive brand equity measurement system in the mid-1990s. From this system Levi's realized that their brand image was slipping badly.

In fairness, Levi's was always going to be vulnerable in a sustained period of market recession, because of its intransigent stance on premium pricing and its historical position in the denim industry. Although it has since weathered this storm, the company has lost substantial market share over recent years. This is due in large part to an influx of competition. There's a host of recognized brands who have been in the denim jean market for quite some time. Companies such as Calvin Klein, Tommy Hilfiger, Gap and Armani have all strengthened as brands, but only Gap has strengthened markedly. The major issue was the rise of Vertically Integrated chains like Gap and H&M as well as the decline of denim and rise of cargos and combats in the late 1990s. The tween market has been attracted to a much baggier look, and competitors have rushed in to provide it.

Managers of strong brands appreciate the totality of their brand's image. They have an understanding of all the different perceptions, beliefs, attitudes and behaviours tweens associate with their brand, whether created intentionally by the company or not. As a result managers are able to make decisions regarding the brand with confidence. If it's clear what tweens like and don't like about a brand, and what core associations are linked to it, then the brand should also be clear whether any given action will dovetail nicely with the brand or create friction.

The BIC brand illustrates the kind of problems that can arise when managers don't fully understand their brand's purpose.

Over the years, BIC has produced everything from ballpoint pens in the 1950s to disposable cigarette lighters in the 1970s and disposable razors in the 1980s. It seems this is where the logic stopped. The company then went on to develop a perfume product for men called Big Sport, and for women called Nuit and Jour. Both sold for US $5 and were displayed on racks near the check-out counters of 100,000 drugstores. This was supported by a US $20 million advertising campaign.

But somehow sales fell way below expectations. Although based on the philosophy of high quality at affordable prices, BIC customers somehow never associated their brand with a perfume. There was virtually no interest in a discount disposable perfume, even though the price was extremely affordable.

Smart brands are more concerned with brand relevancy and brand resonance. Strong brands generally make good use of frequent in-depth brand audits and ongoing brand-tracking studies. Brand audits are designed to assess the health of a given brand. Typically they consist of a detailed internal description of exactly how the brand has been marketed (also called a brand inventory) and thorough external investigation through focus groups and general consumer research. Brand audits are particularly useful when they are repeated consistently year after year, enabling brand managers to track the progress of brands and detect any possible threats. Tweens might not be your core audience – but remember, if you start tracking their perception of your brand, you will know exactly what problems it is about to face or whether they are ready to consume and adore it. Historical data cannot be re-created, but only earned over time. This explains why it is so important for companies to include tweens in the brand research.

8. Brand flexibility: no-one can predict what tweens will be like in two years

Over a period of seven years, the LEGO Group's product development time has been reduced from five years to one. Disney, Mattel and Fisher-Price have witnessed similar R&D reductions. No one can predict the future, not even five years ahead – particularly when the audience your product caters for falls into the tween segment. Brand flexibility is the key, the ability to act at the very last moment in order to secure the very best approach to the market's trends and needs.

Let's look at Benetton. The essence of Benetton's brand identity is colour. Colour is not just an advertising theme. It is both the symbolic and actual basis of the brand. It's helped Benetton stay ahead of its competitors through its capacity to meet the latest fashion requirements at any given moment. They can produce an entire range of the 'it' colour almost instantly, because unlike their competitors Benetton dyes clothes after they're made, which can help save crucial fashion time. But most importantly, this gives them the flexibility to decide on which colours they will finally present in their collection. Benetton's a brand that constantly innovates.

Not many are able to manage to innovate in the way Bill Gates did in 1997. When he realized the Internet was here to stay, Gates turned the entire Microsoft organization around to accommodate this, within a short two-year period. He secured a future for the Microsoft brand that, according to Interbrand, is the second most valuable brand in the world. Microsoft owns the Number One browser, handling close to 70 per cent of the world's entire Internet traffic, not to mention the multitude of Microsoft sites which are among the best performers around the globe.

Microsoft achieved what Sony was – until the mid-1980s – leading: an ability to re-invent itself to suit the needs of the market. Just think of Walkman, the compact disc, PlayStation or the Trinitron system. They're all invented and owned by Sony. However, over the past few years, Sony's ability to maintain its innovation flexibility seems to be flagging. Increasingly investors are demanding proof that Sony is able to meet its current business challenges. Its stylish Vaios, which command more than 30 per cent of the consumer market for PCs in Japan are hardly an innovation leap. Sony followed in Nintendo's tracks in the games market. And while robot pets like Aibo are novel and cute, Sony has sold only 110,000 of the pups since they went on the market in June 1999.

So what can Sony hope for in the short term? For the past 10 years Sony's talked of the networked home, but still there's no evidence of its existence. And flexibility, which was once Sony's great attribute, seems to have dwindled, leaving the company in a situation where the hi-tech industry is able to take it by surprise.

Brand flexibility is all about reading the signals in the market and reacting to them instantly. The larger you get the more difficult this is – Sony, Levi's and LEGO can all testify to this. That's the reason why flexibility is one of the key phrases a brand needs to build on, to survive with the tween generation.

9. Brand interaction: monologue is out, brand dialogue is in

When the computer-controlled Furby was launched in 1998, many people were surprised that a soft toy could sell more than a million units in five weeks. For parents it was perhaps not so surprising – they had already witnessed the invasion of dialogue-based brands.

These brands have come alive. LEGO bricks are no longer passive. They can 'talk' to you. The latest version, LEGO Mindstorm, can even listen and feel, based on small sensors built into the classic plastic bricks. Furbies can talk, listen and react. And Barbie can dress up for you and walk the catwalk. The days when brands based all communications on a one-way communication are long gone. A brand without a Web and e-mail address is seen as old-fashioned. There is now a communication channel established for the tweens to 'talk back' to the brand.

Coke faced a major crisis in Belgium in 1998. Some tweens were poisoned due to a mishap at one of Coca-Cola's manufacturing plants. Despite being the world's leading brand, the importance for dialogue became transparently clear. It so happened that the CEO of Coca-Cola at the time was visiting Belgium. But he chose to let the local office handle the issue. This decision led to uproar in the community. It took several days before Coke even acknowledged the crisis on their local Web site, and then it was hidden in the Q&A section on the local Belgium site.

The problem was not so much that the accident had happened, but that the ongoing silence from Coca-Cola was interpreted as a sign of arrogance. What the tweens and their parents expected was an open and frank dialogue. What they got increased their anger and anxiety. Within weeks Coke was banned not only in Belgium but in several European countries, affecting the brand to an unprecedented degree.

Figure 15.3 *Dealing with the Coke crisis in Belgium. Coke was banned after more than 200 people in France and Belgium were suffering from stomach upsets, nausea and headaches after drinking Coke produced at bottling plants in Antwerp and Dunkirk in June 1999.*

There is no doubt that the Coke story serves as a precautionary lesson in building future brand strategies. We need only to look back a few decades or so to see truly passive consumer behaviour. This is no longer the case. Tweens, and to some degree their parents, form an active, demanding, critical and aware consumer body, and they expect nothing less than total transparency from any given brand. The huge corporate collapses in the first years of the 21st century are pushing this demand for transparency to unprecedented levels.

Brands which are going to be the market leaders of the future will need to be based on the sound principles of Talking, Listening, Learning and Reacting.

Brands that are able to listen to consumer information, learn from the data, and react with the consumer intelligently will be winners. In short, brands need to do more than talk. They need to listen, to ask the right

Figure 15.4 *Talk, listen, learn and react. The future brand can no longer survive just by 'talking' to its tween audience. It also has to 'listen, learn and react'. Peer-to-peer is one of the strongest techniques to secure a true audience-interactive brand.*

questions and to establish the right dialogue that enables them to learn. This is not traditional research, but information gleaned from simple exercises like asking for feedback on a Web site – and then taking notice of it!

Most importantly, the brand needs to be able to react, to show the consumer that their word has weight. When M&M's ran a worldwide colour competition in 2002 it wanted to know what new colours they should include in their range. There was an overwhelming demand for pink. And within days pink became a standard M&M's colour. Such a process creates a connection to the brand, which in turn is rewarded with comments like, 'We like it because it's a part of our community' or 'It understands our needs'. And so the consumer comes to claim ownership of the brand.

When consumers claim ownership they tend to support the brand, even in hard times. Some years ago the iconic Australian biscuit brand, Arnott's, was faced with an extortion threat by a criminal who claimed to have poisoned the company's product. Experts advised Arnott's that such a threat was indeed capable of being carried out swiftly. The extortionist had given the company just three days to respond to the demands. So Arnott's recalled all its biscuits, destroyed them, and produced a totally different package design. Within days it was ready to relaunch the brand Australians had known for generations.

In the meantime, the PR department spun a story designed to appeal to the Australian consumer's sense of loyalty. This had distinct patriotic overtones. It emphasized the danger of Australian companies being lost to overseas interests and stressed the loss of such a loved Australian brand to international competition. The strategy worked well. It garnered plenty of community sympathy and support. The brand was no longer just a brand, but had become 'our' brand.

10. Leadership: tweens deal only with the leader of the pack

Once a humdrum manufacturer of commodity electronics, largely sold under other names, Samsung Electronics more than doubled its profits to reach an astounding US $1.6 billion in 2002. What it did was move aggressively into the higher-end products that carried fatter profit margins. Placing a huge emphasis on cutting-edge design, the South Korean-based Samsung is producing everything from flat-panel television monitors to wafer-thin DVD players. In short, Samsung has managed to do an 180-degree turn from being a market follower to becoming a leader, building its brand on the DigitAll experience.

Brands, particularly in the tween segment, need to reflect just this sort of leadership attitude. In the same way that tweens like to be seen as the leader of the pack at school, they simply do not purchase brands that do not lead in their field. Being a leading brand within a category is therefore essential if you want to succeed within the tween segment. Remember, leadership doesn't necessarily mean being the biggest or most well known. In fact being an unknown 'secret' leader is almost more attractive among this audience, which loves to discover the news on their own and spread it among their peers.

The human brand

Relevance, simplicity and humanity – rather than technology – will distinguish brands in the future. The future is all about a brand's ability to see itself through tween eyes.

The importance of wearing the right brand – even at eight years old – has become essential for more and more tweens as they intertwine their sense of self with their particular brand choices. This tells others how they wish to be perceived. In the world of tweens, brands need to reflect more than just a commercial message. They need to announce an attitude towards life, an attitude towards their surroundings and an attitude about the world. For this reason cause-related brands are positioned to do extremely well.

The *BRANDchild* study shows that more than any other generation, tweens prefer to support and pay more for brands which stand for a cause or reflect an opinion. The more distinct the cause, the more effective the brand is likely to be with this generation. Even though tweens are prepared to pay more for the cause-related brand, they're not prepared to pay *much* more. They will support the brand – even if there's an alternative choice.

Human brands are more than just cause-related. They're brands that are not afraid to show feelings or admit mistakes. They can be funny, ironic, serious or direct. Future brands are far more likely to reflect different moods – depending on the context. If a message from Pepsi happens to appear on a cell phone, it should be short – and fun! If it's in the local school paper, it should be casual but relevant. If it appears on the Net, it should be informative and light-hearted.

Each channel, each location and each tween personality type will expect the brand to be able to adapt to various situations, and have the flexibility to change the message according to the context. Tweens have no problem giving brands human characteristics. They shun megabrands with no personality and therefore no soul. The days of global brands living in impersonal 40-storey headquarters protected by steel doors are long gone. Brands that are present in the school playground, the living room or in a tent are relevant and trustworthy, and most importantly are owned by the consumer and not the corporation.

When tween brands fail, it often has little to do with quality problems or distribution challenges – more often than not, the failure is a direct result of not involving the tweens. As the wheels of product development and launches keep spinning ever-faster, a direct line of knowledge between tweens and brand is essential. If this cannot be maintained, it will probably result in the death of the brand. Brand suicide!

Brand-building is the same as nurturing a human being. It changes interest, preferences, language, skills and desire – all the time. For a generation of tweens it just so happens at double the speed with half the attention span. That's the reason why it is even more important to tick the 10 branding criteria.

SUMMARY

▌ Close to 90 out of 100 most popular tween brands can be character-ized as Classics. Classics are defined as those brands with more than 20 years on the board.

▌ According to *BRANDchild* research data, urban tweens influence over 50 per cent of all purchases.

▌ Securing youth appeal not only establishes brand loyalty at an early age, but has a dramatic influence on parents' purchasing patterns.

▌ Everything we have found out so far indicates that brands which ignore the young market are doing so at their peril.

▌ There are 10 factors characterizing the tween audience:

1. Emotions are driving tweens – and so are brands.

2. They're in search of solid connections and so are looking for brand consistency.

3. Justifying the brand value to tweens means keeping product innovation alive.

4. Tweens are prepared to pay the price for what they want.

5. Tweens don't buy products, they buy brand solutions.

6. At any given time, tweens are using any given channel so make sure that your message is sent at the right time, through the right channel.

7. Reading the tween mind helps you manage perceptions in a more relevant way.

8. No-one can predict what tweens will be like in two years, so it's essential that your brand has flexibility.

9. Monologue is out, brand dialogue is in. Interaction is vital. Brands will need to be able to talk, listen, learn and react.

10. Tweens only deal with the leader of the pack, so it's important to focus on leadership.

ACTION POINTS

▶ If you happen to be a brand appealing to an adult market, you will probably be noticing that your brand needs to appeal to tweens as well.

▶ Conduct some field research and evaluate how influential the tween segment is in your category.

▶ If you discover that tweens have a major impact on their parents' brand choice, you will need to develop a dual strategy which enables you to appeal to both audiences.

▶ Depending on the degree of tweens' influence, you will need to develop three types of marketing activities: the first that appeals to tweens, the second that appeals to both tweens and their parents, and the third that focuses on adults.

▶ Integrate this exercise into your overall marketing plan.

16

Tweens take to hats

Patricia B Seybold

In the US, as in many other countries, tweens still flock to shopping malls to buy 'cool' stuff. What's cool? 'Music and clothing that expresses my personality.' 'Apparel that older kids wear that looks cool.' For many tweens, especially guys, that means cool hats – hats with teams' logos on them, hats that fit really well, hats that tell the world I'm cool.

But selling hats to tweens is not an easy task. It's a science – one that has been perfected by two now-merged specialty retailers in the US – Lids and HatWorld. Note that this science includes understanding what kids care about the most, focusing fanatically on the in-store experience, blending the offline and online experience, and taking to the streets with guerilla marketing.

WHERE DID YOU GET YOUR LID?

In 1991, Ben Fischman and Doug Karp sat in the lecture hall at Boston University waiting for class to start. They watched their classmates pour into the hall for one of the university's most popular classes. Ben elbowed Doug. 'Look at all those hats!' he exclaimed, 'everyone's wearing them. Where do they get them?' Ben knew how hard it was to find the 'right' baseball hat to make the correct fashion statement. He had his own hard-won collection. You got hats at sporting events; you found them at sporting goods stores. But the bulk of the apparel retailers that sold clothes for the tween, teen, and early-twenties-markets had a very limited assortment. And the few fashion retailers that did sell the kinds of headwear these kids were wearing typically put hats on a hard-to-reach shelf in a corner of the store. Moreover, the sales people in these stores didn't appreciate it when you tried on several hats to find the one with the perfect fit, and then bent the brim to get the right look. 'Don't do that,' they'd exclaim, 'you'll ruin the merchandise!'

'We should be selling hats!' Ben and Doug told each other as they looked at the heads of the hundreds of young adults that had now filled the lecture hall. Once the idea occurred to them, they started their market research. They began asking around: 'Cool hat, where'd you get it?' was the opening line. What they discovered astonished them. Kids their age were spending a lot of time and effort finding stores that sold hats. And even when they found a retailer that carried them, it was hard to find hats with the right fit, and even harder to find hats that looked good and carried the logo of the sports teams they really cared about.

This was crazy! High school and college kids were all wearing hats – they had become a core part of the hip look. They realized that soon the fashion statement that older teens were making would hit the younger tween set – yet there was no easy place that any kid could go to buy hats! That was when the entrepreneurial bug hit. Ben and Doug decided it was time to get into the retail business. They came up with the concept, and began shopping the idea around among their parents' friends. It wasn't long before they had the financial backing and the mentoring they needed to launch the first Lids store.

Ben and Doug conceived of Lids as a specialty retailer. The stores would sell only one thing: hats, in a large variety of styles and sizes. They'd place their stores in shopping malls where teens and tweens could easily find them. The hats would be displayed so that customers could grab them and try them on. Customers would be encouraged to try on hats, get the perfect fit, reshape the brims, mangle the merchandise! In other words, customers would be in control of their shopping experience. The stores would be staffed by young people who loved hats and knew a lot about fit and style. Lids would license the official sports and college logos for every sports team in the country, so no matter which teams you loved, you'd be able to find a hat with that team's logo on it, in the style and colours that you preferred to wear. Ben knew that authenticity, style, and fit were what mattered to their target customers.

THE LIDS CUSTOMER EXPERIENCE

For eight years, Lids kept its original, customer experience intact, as it grew from 1 to 500 stores and from 0 to $180 million in revenues. Lids'

stores are small (500–600 square feet) and are staffed by young sales associates (18 to 25 years old) who identify with their customers and make
them feel at home. The majority of the stores are in shopping malls.

Lids' typical customers are 8 to 18-year-old guys. (While the baseball
cap fad began on college campuses, it quickly spread to the younger tween
market.) The teens and tweens hang out at shopping malls after school and
on weekends, often with their buddies and their girlfriends. These young
men typically visit malls six to eight times per month. They often have
$25 in their pockets. They usually spend that money on CDs or hats.
These customers usually buy 12 hats per year, typically half of them at the
Lids store in their local mall.

As soon as a group of prospective customers walks into the store, the
sales associate engages them in conversation and gets them trying on hats,
leading them to the mirror. These customers quickly gravitate to the size
and style hat that suits them the best. Then they select the colour and logo
they prefer. In addition to shopping malls, Lids has stores and kiosks in
selected airports; these cater to the travelling businessmen who also like
the youthful look and the assortment of styles and sizes Lids carries.

The fit and style of the hats they wear matters a lot to these young
buyers. So does the authenticity of the hats. Lids offers official team logos
from every major pro baseball, football, and basketball team as well as
every major college and university team in the United States. And if the
customer isn't a sports fan, Lids has a wide selection of non-sports-related
hat designs from which to choose. Another important part of the Lids
experience is a constant influx of hot new merchandise and styles.

Lids' advertising and marketing mix includes guerilla-style marketing
events – Lids' distinctive logo mysteriously appears in the public places
most commonly frequented by its tween and teen customer base. All of a
sudden, you'll see the Lids logo appear on posters, in sidewalk art, on
trucks and t-shirts. This kind of 'hit and run' marketing campaign is a
popular way to get tweens' attention.

ENCOURAGING REPEAT BUYING BEHAVIOUR

By 1998 the Lids team realized that they had something few retailers even
dream of: loyal customers with repeat buying behaviour. The 200 plus
stores were meeting their numbers in terms of sales per square foot. But it
was time to start focusing on customer loyalty as the real engine of

growth. So Ben developed and spearheaded a customer loyalty program that was launched in early 1999. Called HeadFirst®, it was a simple rewards-and-recognition program: buy seven hats and get the eighth hat free. The stores also featured special 'happy hours', inviting HeadFirst customers to the stores for special events on Friday evenings and offering them a 20 per cent discount during the happy hour.

Within six months Lids had 500,000 HeadFirst customers, and membership was growing quickly. By the end of the first year of its HeadFirst program, Lids had 800,000 HeadFirst customers. By the end of the second year of the program, there were 1.5 million active HeadFirst customers. The average sales for each of these customers had increased from 1.5 hats per year, to 7.5 hats per year. Lids' HeadFirst customers were bringing in close to US $33.5 million per year in profits!

EARLY PIONEER OF THE INTEGRATED CLICKS-AND-BRICKS EXPERIENCE

Like many retailers, Lids put a basic Web site up in 1998 that had a small assortment of hats. But it was in December 1998 that the Lids team decided to go full tilt for a clicks-and-bricks strategy. Tweens were flocking to the Internet. They expected and demanded 'cool' Web sites. Nancy Babine-Kacinski, Lids' then President, was the first retail executive who told us, 'I want to use the Web to drive traffic to my stores.' She was absolutely convinced that the Web would complement, not cannibalize, Lids' retail store sales. Also, Nancy and Ben understood right away that they could attract and serve loyal customers by extending the Lids experience to the Web. And, they felt they had no choice: Lids' demographic demanded that Lids pioneer a great Web experience as an extension of the Lids experience.

Lids has evolved its Web site as an integral part of its in-store retailing mix rather than as an alternative channel. All in-store promotions are mirrored on the Web site. The site is viewed as a virtual, 24-hour extension of the in-store experience.

There was only one problem the executives foresaw as they added online retailing: the majority of Lids' core customers were too young to have credit cards. In fact, 85 per cent of in-store sales were cash transactions. Would they be able to make it easy for these non-credit card-carrying customers to shop online?

® HeadFirst is a trademark of Lids, Inc.

Supporting non-credit card buyers

In the fall of 1999, Lids introduced the first retailer-branded stored-value card in the United States that worked both online and offline. A customer or a customer's parent could purchase a Lids cash card (either with cash or by using a credit card). The anonymous cash card could then be used to make purchases in the store or on the Web site. Each cash card had a unique ID. Once the stored value on the card was used up, it could be refilled online or in the store. As Lids evolved its Web site, it made it easy for parents to purchase Lids cards for their kids online as well as in the stores, and to make it easy for tweens to redeem those cards both online and in the store.

Lids' cash card transactions quickly accounted for 15 per cent of Lids' Internet business.

The melon meter: getting a good fit on the Web

Lids offers both fitted and adjustable size hats. Because fit is so important to tweens, the Lids.com team wanted to be sure that customers could figure out their hat size if they didn't already know it. Realizing that few of the customers in their target audience would be likely to know where to find their mother's tape measure, the Web site designers included a 'melon meter' – a tape measure you could print out, tape together, and use to measure your head. You might expect online customers to order adjustable-size hats, instead of fitted hats. Yet Lids' customers know what they like and need; 80 per cent of Lids' online sales are for fitted hats. Once you know your size, you can easily browse through a selection of hats that are currently available in inventory for your exact head size.

Make the entire inventory available online

The Lids.com team's first priority was to get every hat online so that customers could order any size, style, colour, and team logo they wanted. When tweens shop in the store, they usually go in flocks – for the younger set, it's usually all boys, as they get older, the girls join in the fun, helping with fit and style choices and often buying their own hats. Kids typically try on hats for style and size, then, when they've found the style and size they like, they refine their selection to hat colour and team logo. For a small footprint store, stocking the amount of inventory required to support tweens' esoteric choices of sports teams, colours, and styles is a challenge.

It's very common for a store in the Boston area to have lots of requests for a team in Denver or Seattle, or even Kalamazoo. That's where the Web site and the in-store Web kiosks come in.

Delivering a seamless clicks-and-bricks experience

The Lids.com team knew that customers wanted to be able to order online and return hats to a store, or order online and pick a hat up at a store, or order online while *in* the store. They should also be able to call Lids' 800-number to check on the status of an order or to place an order.

The Lids management team knew that its sales associates needed to be incented to promote the Web site. Store associates were given credit for any sales from local customers that came in from the Web. However, it wasn't until Lids began placing Web kiosks in the stores themselves that the high-turnover, in-store sales staff began to 'take' to the Web site. But once they had the Web site live in their stores and were trained to give demos to customers, they began enthusiastically encouraging customers to shop online, both in the store and from home.

Scott Hastings, Lids' then CTO, tried a number of different approaches to give Lids' retail stores online access. He tried in-store Web kiosks and added browser capabilities to the in-store point-of-sale terminals. After piloting a few different approaches, by mid-2000 Scott hit upon the combination that really worked. He arranged a satellite feed into the stores by partnering with Pixel Systems, a company that provides background music for stores in shopping malls. This satellite feed gave Lids the cost-effective bandwidth it needed to roll out Web kiosks in many of Lids' shopping mall stores. Now customers could use the Lids Web site in the store to participate in interactive polls and quizzes; shop online for styles, sizes, and colours that weren't in stock; or send an e-mail wish list to a relative. Lids became one of the first US retailers with a successful implementation of in-store Web kiosks.

OVERZEALOUS RETAIL EXPANSION LED TO A MERGER WITH HATWORLD

Lids grew its retail empire aggressively. By the end of 2000, the privately-held Lids had close to 500 stores. But it was strapped for cash. Since it takes two to three years for each Lids' store to become profitable. Enter HatWorld.

Although Lids was the number one specialty retailer, there was a number two. HatWorld had been founded by Glenn Campbell and Scott Molander in 1995. Campbell and Molander got their start as successful managers with a national athletic retailer and decided it was time to go into business for themselves. They piloted their concept with a single hat shop in a mall and sold more than 6,000 hats in just eight weeks. HatWorld grew from a single store to five stores the first year, and by 2001, it had grown to 157 stores in five years. The merger of HatWorld with Lids in the Spring of 2001 resulted in a specialty retail chain with 400 stores in 44 states and an online business, which you can reach from both hatworld.com and lids.com. The Lids stores retain the original Lids branding. The Web sites have been merged into one co-branded site, but the hatworld.com/lids.com site retains the Lids.com look and feel, since that was what younger customers had grown up with.

The HeadFirst loyalty program and HatWorld's Passport loyalty program were merged. Customers who want to join, pay $3 to become a member and get a Lids/HatWorld Passport, but they gain that back on the 20 per cent off discounts they receive on their first few hats.

Giving customers the ability to design their own hats

It wasn't until after the merger that the new management team was able to fulfill one of the needs that customers had been requesting for years: 'Let us design our own hats!' Now, at the Lids/hatworld.com Web site, customers can design their own hats using a variety of colourful logos and/or by creating and emailing their own. The hats are shipped out within 48 hours. This is the ultimate in cool! A hat I create with the personal branding I choose!

SUMMARY

What can marketers and retailers learn from the Lids/HatWorld story?

1. Fit, authenticity, and a broad selection of brands will appeal most to discerning tweens.

2. If yours is a product that tweens will buy often, make sure to reward them for their loyalty and for identifying themselves to you by

offering them a loyalty program that gives them real tangible benefits – a free product, discounts, etc.

3. Use the Web to augment your physical retail experience: offer
   access to all of your inventory, the ability to order online and pick
   up at the store, the ability to custom-design products.

4. Give customers access to your Web site *in* the store.

5. Offer products that customers can brand with their own personalities and aspirations.

6. Offer a fun, hands on, in-store experience.

7. Reward your sales associates when your customers shop on-line.

8. When you merge two brands – if one has a strong tween following,
   don't bury it, flaunt it! HatWorld has preserved the Lids brand on
   both the stores and in the online world.

17

Calling kids

'Market research is when people in suits ask funny questions'

It's perhaps a bit to harsh to say that there's a mid-life crisis brewing in the marketing departments of the world. Rules honed over decades that succeeded in making everything from cereals to credit cards irresistible to baby boomers have turned out to be a major turnoff for tweens. You could say that these new consumers are turning the marketing canon on its head. Take their attitude towards ads. While boomers mistrust advertising, their kids love it – if it's witty and not condescending. Ads are another form of entertainment. The trick is to hit the right note. Ads aimed at this group can't be too obvious, and they do have to be honest about their intent.

So what are the rules of engagement when it comes to tweens?

Don't talk down

This rule has always applied – but it's become stronger and more emphasized over the past years. Just think about it. Tweens are likely to spend more time on their own than with their parents – and this includes the number of sleeping hours in the family home. It's a scary fact that even the television set has spent more active time with the tweens than their parents. So it's hardly surprising that we now have a generation that's created its own identity, its own life and its own opinions at an earlier age than has ever been seen before.

The *BRANDchild* study shows that 41.1 per cent of all kids worldwide believe they know more about computers than their parents. And this applies across the global board: 42 per cent in Denmark, 49.4 per cent in the United States, 52 per cent in Brazil and 56.7 per cent in Spain. This is a generation with the master key to the interactive world. But it doesn't stop there. Their endless choices continue to impact on this trend. There are an unlimited number of products targeting tweens through a vast array of channels – the endless radio and television stations, the billions of pages on the Internet, music CDs, videos and computer games. Each one is a potential carrier for commercial messages and taking their brand expectations to previously unheard-of heights.

Forget the authoritative 'experts' who persuaded the tweens' parents. This group won't believe a word they say. In short, tweens insist on drawing their own conclusions, whether about brands, music, film, games or social choice. Bear in mind the many anti-smoking and anti-alcohol campaigns waged across the globe that get the thumbs-down because they merely dictate a particular opinion. They fail because they do not leave room for tweens to reach their own conclusions. Rather, they tell them what opinion to have – an approach to which tweens simply don't respond.

KGOY

Tweens consider themselves grown-up consumers with their own minds and opinions. This is the true KGOY (Kids Grow Old Younger) generation – and they demand to be treated with respect and enough freedom to make up their own minds. So if you happen to be a brand marketer, talk up. Respect the tweens, create a dialogue with them, listen to their needs and understand that in all likelihood they are more savvy that you will ever be at understanding brands, using a computer and handling the ever-increasing media pressure.

Watch your brand radar carefully

If there's one important lesson to be learned, it's to always stay true to your brand's DNA. Because if you don't, tweens will instantly pick it up on their well-honed brand radar. Remember, this is a generation that was born exposed to at least 30,000 brands. They have spent 20,000 hours in front of television commercials and have personal experience of nearly 1,000 brands themselves. They know brands better than any other consumer group, and can detect a marketing spin from miles away.

The risk is not to produce a product, but to produce one that fails to match the brand's history, its promise or its philosophy.

Interestingly brands like *NSync, Britney Spears and the Backstreet Boys survived as long as they did because they never claimed to be anything other than manufactured. They didn't pretend to have a history, an interesting story or some philosophical message – and so the tweens took them at face value and bought them hook, line and sinker. The identity of the brand was utterly loyal to the communication. But it goes further. If a brand's image, its values and core identity try to skew themselves towards tweens by simply overloading with tween icons such as skateboards and rap music and computer games, this simply will not work.

1-800-PROVEIT

This is a no-bullshit generation. Tweens put a premium on straight talk and are drawn to brands that display utter confidence and offer full-on accountability. Given the many recent corporate collapses, the adult world has hardly proved to be a role model of honesty and transparency. But the emerging trend clearly leans towards straight talk.

Procter & Gamble is a huge company which has launched several campaigns based precisely on this straight talk philosophy. Their Old Spice High Endurance deodorant has put its reputation on the line with a money-back guarantee and an invitation to phone 1-800-PROVEIT. The tweens love it – and they've embraced the brand and the product.

Irony

Any brand that even so much as hints at feelings of self-importance will secure itself a permanent space in the tween product graveyard. However, the opposite attitude could provide just the ticket to brand stardom. More than ever, a sense of irony is the way to this generation's heart. Tweens hate brands that take themselves too seriously, but embrace those that are able to have a laugh at themselves.

The Yoo-hoo Beverage Company is not afraid to make fun of itself by sending a garbage truck painted in the brand's signature yellow and blue to hand out samples of their chocolate milk. The man behind the drink, the top flavour guru, is Dr Yoo-hoo, who's introduced as 'The Tsar of Tastiness! The Sultan of Scrumptiousness! The Maharaja of Mmmmm'.

On the Yoo-hoo site you can download wallpaper of Dr Yoo-hoo's picture and it's of a quality that can hardly be called professional. You can also sneak a peek of the secret formula that goes to create the Yoo-hoo drink... but be warned, the sneaked peek is of a picture of Dr Yahoo standing in front of a safe!

When Yoo-hoo mounted a Stinkin' Summer Tour tweens flocked to hear groups like Blink-182 and listen to 'the gospel of Hoo'. So the whole tour managed to integrate the message and the brand, and needless to say the tweens were drinking the Yoo-hoo drink in 'every town, parish and raging metropolis' across the United States.

Irony permeates every element of Yoo-hoo's in-store promotion. It's part of the label design, and a true reflection of the way it has infiltrated its brand strategy can be found on Yoo-hoo's official site, under its FAQ section. In contrast to most other brands, it boldly mentions other brands.

What exactly is that 'Yahoo Stuff'? Can I get some Yahoo?
Yoo-hoo is not a search engine. The syllable 'Yoo' is pronounced 'you' as in the pronoun, not in any way to be construed with the sound 'Yah'. So, no, we cannot get you on the net, we cannot check your email, and no, we do not have DSL.

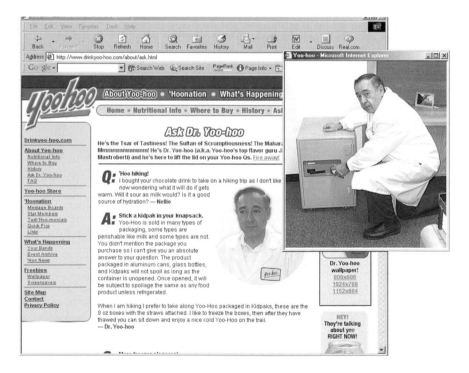

Figure 17.1 *Yoo-hoo has secured its market share by being ironic – and the tweens love it!*

Despite being a corporation, Yoo-hoo's ironic style has no doubt played its part in making it the Number One chocolate drink in the United States.

The invisible brand

It's important to bear in mind that irony is also about underplaying a brand's role. The days of the biggest type ensuring the greatest visibility are long gone. Diesel, the popular clothing brand which always carries a provocative message, decided to change its name for a season. So part of the company's autumn 2002 campaign involved changing its name to Action! – the brand that never stays still. So instead of the Diesel label wrapping itself around their usual provocative message, they used the Action! label instead.

This strategy takes its inspiration from underground messages which carry an air of secrecy and exclusivity. But most importantly it allows tweens to discover (or re-discover) the brand themselves. It's not surprising that the Diesel name is found plastered all over at rock concerts and

Majara Regina F Rodriguez, aged 14, Brazil

other tween events that it sponsors. There is a risk. Not everyone will be aware of the temporary naming strategy. However, it still sparks enough curiosity among tweens to draw them to the product, and gives them a fresh opportunity to re-affirm their loyalty to the brand.

So is such risk-taking effective? The *BRANDchild* study shows that 45.6 per cent of all tweens globally consider Diesel to be a 'cool' brand. One-third – 37.6 per cent – think it's 'fun', but a fair 14.1 per cent think it's 'weird'. The numbers speak for themselves.

Figure 17.2 *Diesel replaces its brand name with another as part of its Autumn 2002 campaign.*

To use irony to its fullest means that you do not only manage to look at yourself with a sense of humour. To a certain extent it also involves downplaying the brand's name. In some cases it's useful to help the audience discover the brand on its own and then allow them to spread the message. This can result in the greatest success. If it sounds viral, you know you're on the right track!

Find your niche

One way to understate your brand is to become a niche channel. Mainstream media like television and newspapers will play a substantially smaller role in the media strategies of the future – perhaps not today, but a couple of years from now. This trend has already begun, because mainstream media is too broad for tweens' specific tastes. As we've discussed, tweens don't like messages that tell them what opinions they should hold. Equally, they dislike the notion of sameness. They don't want to be like everyone else and certainly aren't attracted by any message that tells them with whom they share their tastes. Television will remain a constant feature and will often drive broad awareness. However, real brand equity will increasingly be driven by sources that are formed underground.

The fact that tweens move in groups imitating one another is a whole different issue. It would probably be safe to say, however, that the use of mainstream media to convey a message to tweens would be a bad idea. It would be far more prudent to begin any campaign with niche media and then only when you've established a loyal following should you move it on to more mainstream channels.

A good marketer will be able to identify new and interesting messages and establish future directions for a brand, like undertaking the temporary Diesel name change. This is where the good will be separated from the average. A good marketer will be familiar with many channels and be able to match the message with exactly the right channel to deliver it in the quickest possible way to its target audience.

Invent your own sub-channel

Forget everything about the classic list of media choices – there's potential advertising space where you least expect it. Baby carriages in Copenhagen provide advertising space for savvy marketers – providing the parents first give their approval. Mobile phone screens, ring tones and headsets are all spaces currently available to carry ads in Australia. You might have already recognized the Always Coca-Cola tune as a ring tone at your local café. If not, you probably would have noticed that mobile phone covers are now coming in recognizable shapes – the Absolut vodka bottles, Pepsi drink or Fubu brands. Even navigation buttons on the Yahoo search engine sites are said to be for sale – with M&M's as a likely buyer, changing all buttons into M&M's for a week.

But these examples aside, true niche media channels are even less obvious. They would be visible only at the local playground, and appeal to a very specific targeted audience, a small community sharing interests concentrated in the same location. Taking this as our ultimate niche channel definition, a media plan would in reality reflect the use of hundreds if not thousands of different channel possibilities. These could be combined in clever ways, all supporting the message and values of the brand. But most importantly of all, this strategy is designed to achieve synergy between channels that will complement and highlight one another, thereby giving the campaign a life of its own.

Reviewing product placement

Our *BRANDchild* study has confirmed what we have long suspected about ongoing questions relating to product placement. Based on the qualitative segment of our research, we learned that rather than looking to traditional media, tweens take their brand cues from how the brand actually performs in various communities. Interestingly, we learned that product placement is the largest and most influential form of endorsement influencing tween brands. In almost all our group studies we learned that a substantial part of tween brand perception is either built on a general opinion within the tween community, or is the result of product placement seen on television programs like MTV's *Cribs*, where several products seem to grow their brand equity.

Advertainment

Entertainment has become the major ingredient in most tween brand success stories. As David Ogilvy said in his book *Ogilvy On Advertising*, if you don't have anything to say, sing it. The days of an ad consisting merely of an arresting image are long gone. Previous generations may

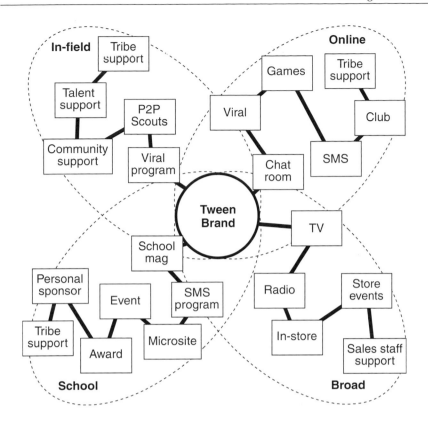

Figure 17.3 *Peer-to-peer support grid. Successful tween campaigns represent a complex and well-planned grid of media activities all leading to peer-to-peer support.*

dislike the blending of ads with content, but tweens love discovering brands in unexpected places. DVC, a game manufacturer, weaves brand names like McDonald's and General Mills into the content of the games. The California Milk Processor Board allows youngsters to create their own television ads. Sounds like product placement? You're right! Advertainment is getting stronger and stronger every day.

From a parent's point of view, the good news is that tweens have no trouble separating the commercial from the editorial content. The bad news is that we will probably be seeing an increasing blend of ad and content. When the movie *Blade Runner*, adapted from a Philip K Dick novel, was released, it featured huge neon ads for numerous big corporations. Twenty years later, *Minority Report*, another movie adaptation from a Philip K Dick story, included 30 brands. According to *Io*, an online magazine, these paying brands added a substantial US $25 million to the movie's budget.

Carlsberg beer stepped into the advertainment waters in the 1990s. They created a commercial that looked like a forthcoming release of another type of *Top Gun* movie. Movie-going audiences loved it.

The merger between entertainment and advertising is likely to grow even stronger as industries touch all bases in their attempts to reach tweens. Product placement will soon become as commonplace on computer games and mobile phones as it already is in most Hollywood movies. For a generation used to total separation between these two worlds, it sounds horrifying. But as long as brands stick to the truth and fully acknowledge a commercial payment is part of the deal, they will succeed.

I'll go further and venture to say that hardly a tween brand will survive in future unless they include elements of product placement in their strategy. It will never be the driving marketing vehicle, but there's no doubt that product placement and establishing an online presence will become a vital element in launching a brand aimed at a tween market.

Pandora's branded box

The structure of marketing brands in future will closely resemble Pandora's box. If you ask an 11-year-old boy about the story of Digimon digital monsters, you will most likely receive a 20-minute spiel about each of the characters, their pasts, their skills and their powers. Tweens are familiar with all the different aspects which make each one unique.

This is not a new phenomenon. Hans Christian Andersen introduced characters with magic skills in his stories written almost 200 years ago. What is new is that a brand can no longer survive without having many layers of history. This historical element is not necessarily restricted to brands like Coke which date back to the 19th century, but applies to brands that have new layers of news, multiple-angle or information adding another dimension to the product. The link between each of these layers need only be the curiosity of the tween, who wants to explore every dimension of the brand and will actively seek it out.

Bearing this in mind, it hardly comes as a surprise that a brand like Yoo-hoo has achieved such notoriety and success. The brand is so much more than a chocolate milk product with a secret recipe and a few other flavours. It embraces a whole philosophy. And to quote their Web site, 'the breathing nerve center of drinkyoo-hoo.com', everyone knows that 'Yoo-hoo fans are the coolest people on earth'!

Many other concept variations have been launched successfully around this Pandora's box model. A recent campaign from Nokia was based on a plot similar to the movie, *The Game*. By signing up, the user would constantly receive new hints, new directions and clues to help them win the game. Often a response to the clue was required within hours – demanding the consumer to be on permanent standby with their mobile phone in hand.

A reported 600,000 people are estimated to have participated. At every stage of the game tweens were required to explore and discover new and existing dimensions of the brand. By inviting this involvement, Nokia managed to satisfy the curiosity of its younger audience.

Back to the future

There is another dimension to the Pandora's box philosophy. Brands based on historical information are also gaining large chunks of market share. From our study it is clear that old values are perceived to be substantially more solid than new ones. Some of the biggest commercial successes – *Titanic, Lord of the Rings, Harry Potter* and *Spider-Man* – all hark back to an historical past and deliver multiple-story lines, enabling tweens to understand the characters from different angles and gain more information about them over time. These combined factors succeed in engaging their young audience, and in the end create loyalty.

The renaissance is not restricted to the movie industry, but applies to almost all product categories. For example, a surprisingly high number – 54.6 per cent – of all kids worldwide considered Volkswagen's new Beetle 'cool'. And even more – 66 per cent – gave the new Mini the thumbs-up.

Today's tween hero: the brand!

We've always had heroes. From Davy Crocket to Robin Hood. From Bond to Superman to Spider-Man. And let's not forget new sporting heroes who emerge with every season.

From our *BRANDchild* study we can clearly conclude that the most dominant values tween boys exhibit when playing sport is that they play to win. They strive to be the best, and they set out to conquer all opposition. It is interesting to note that the devastation of September 11 has pushed this phenomenon to a level never seen before, and these behaviours are substantially stronger than ever seen before in our history.

Such attitudes have also contributed to the changing role of brands. These boys consider brands a tool to be used in helping them win the fight. Brands help them validate their efforts and are also part of recognizing their genuine accomplishments. They want equipment that will help them deliver and demonstrate that they are more accomplished than those who use lesser equipment.

There was a time when heroes were heroes and brands were brands. But these have now merged. Sporting heroes become their own brands with their names on merchandise ranging from baseball caps to after-shave. Cartoon heroes like Superman and Spider-Man come with extensive merchandizing programs. Computer games have pushed the merger between heroes and brands even further, introducing real heroes who are in a position to enhance anyone's skills – all you need is a few extra dollars to purchase the services. A magic sword in the online game EverQuest can be bought on eBay for a whopping US $2,400.

The role of brands has changed. They were once a stamp of quality. Now they're an emotional tool vital for tweens to secure acceptance among their peers.

Our survey shows tween friendships are no longer built on individual chemistry, but tend to be structured around sport or hobby activities like skateboarding, rollerblading or surfing. As brands within these communities succeed in establishing a much more visible presence, they tend to become a membership card to various groups.

Change the operating hours

The major difference between today's tweens and yesterday's is that today's tweens no longer expect to be informed by traditional media. The purpose of television commercials is no longer to communicate product details to them. Today they simply aim to inspire. Once the inspiration has kicked in, then ideally the brand will become interactive, since there will be other channels that will do the informing. Tweens will investigate the brand on the channels available to them day and night. Forget the days where a brand closed down at five in the evening and opened at nine. If your brand truly wants to survive today's tweens it will need to focus its operations around their lives, not traditional business routines. This audience might very well be most affected by communication from 2pm to 11pm Monday to Friday – and then at any given hour on weekends.

Tween hours tend to peak at the same time as the peak hours for television commercials. At the same time, chat room dialogues are running hot, and events are happening. It's very important for companies to be operating simultaneously, because this is the instant generation, and if they hear of something new and exciting then they want it to be accessible.

If the most important brand dialogue time can be considered to be Sunday – then the head office marketing department should be there to monitor the action. And so operating hours need to change. This is an audience that expects its brands to be available 24/7.

A transparent brand

According to our *BRANDchild* survey, branding goes much deeper than stunning graphics, great commercials and a product that fulfils all promises. Tweens are a very environmentally-focused generation. In fact, 83.9 per cent of all kids across such diverse markets as the United States, Germany, Spain, Brazil, China, Japan and India believe that products that are bad for the environment should be totally banned. A mere 5.5 per cent disagree with this. Interestingly, when you break down these numbers, 70.5 per cent of tweens in the United States believe environmentally harmful products should be banned. The most environmentally focused tweens are to be found in Brazil and China, with 91 per cent supporting a total ban.

An interesting fact that emerged from this aspect of our survey indicates that tweens expect a lot more from their environment, and therefore from brands. Brands need to show an attitude, not only to the user group but also to their surroundings. There's every indication that this trend will become stronger as tweens become teens and will no doubt incorporate other political aspects of their thinking.

Brands need to stand alone, have many dimensions and be open to rigorous scrutiny. It would be naïve to assume that company policy will be sufficient to carry a brand. Nike calls this Global Citizenship and it covers four categories: Community, Diversity, Environment and, probably the most discussed topic of them all, Manufacturing Practices. It wasn't so long ago that Nike was involved in a media furore which criticized questionable manufacturing processes that appeared to ignore basic human rights during the production of Nike shoes. This placed the whole Nike brand in jeopardy. Quite a few years later, Nike is still repairing the damage.

Nike learned from this, but many companies and brands have very weak philosophies around their local or global citizenship, leaving them extremely vulnerable. They may not even survive the next generation.

Brand equity has changed, and now includes another layer. Tweens like their brands to be transparent. They want them to incorporate a world

Figure 17.4 *Nike's cross-band strategy. Due to Nike's global manufacturing crisis in 2000, the company has now established a philosophy across all its brand categories. More companies are expected to follow Nike's example.*

view that represents a responsible corporate attitude to society. Our research confirms that brands need to do more than talk the talk. And if their walk contradicts their talk, they will be instantly rejected by the tween generation.

Previous generations might have bought brand promises that were never delivered. This generation will not. A brand has to deliver on every promise it makes. There are no acceptable excuses. It's almost as if advertising has become self-regulating. The audience will control and evaluate the quality of the message in relation to what is actually delivered. This form of regulation achieves results that no formal rules of censure would obtain.

The brand is now a citizen and has to live up to all its civic responsibilities.

Privacy

'I'd rather be sick than have a virus on my computer'

Let me be honest. When Millward Brown and I were formulating the *BRANDchild* questionnaires, one of my hypotheses was that today's tweens were more concerned with computer viruses than they were with privacy issues. I was wrong! Our study revealed that 44.5 per cent of tweens were more concerned with privacy.

Our qualitative *BRANDchild* group sessions revealed that their privacy concerns related to the handling of personal data, monitoring of their behaviour and the use of their data for commercial purposes. This also indicates that the emphasis a company places on privacy is much more valuable than anyone would have thought. Perhaps this is because, more than any other generation, tweens know the true nature of the Net and the interactive world.

It also means that a brand can no longer just survive by putting up a standard privacy policy on their site or their company brochures. Privacy has to be a well-communicated document that reflects the brand's core values.

Despite this, it was surprising to learn from our study conducted by Millward Brown that 28 per cent of all wired urban tweens were quite willing to let the government check all their e-mails – to protect them from terrorism. Tweens in the United States were among the lowest-ranking of those willing to allow it (26 per cent), with Brazilian tweens ranking the highest (51 per cent). Close to half explained that this would generate more national safety.

Involve them in your plans

Ten years ago, most companies would work in product development cycles that lasted five to six years. But with the advent of the Internet, product development cycles have had to become considerably shorter.

Now it's not uncommon for such a cycle to be as short as six months. Even big and to some extent traditional corporations like Mattel, Disney, Sony or LEGO now involve hundreds of external people when developing new products, simply to secure a constant flow of inspiration.

This trend is likely to become more entrenched in future, as brands become more interactive, more in-your-face, more one-to-one and more present around the clock. It is increasingly clear that a brand has to involve its core audience even to survive. And if they don't, they run the risk of being perceived as arrogant. Involvement will require more than consultation in a research study. These studies will still be there, but research as we know it will become more visible and will focus on showing tweens that the brand actually cares about their opinions. This trend takes its cue from software companies, who included thousands of test players and brainstormers long before they released any new software. By including the consumer they not only used their feedback to enhance their product but also had the added benefit of creating a pre-release viral buzz around the product.

In short, the brand has moved and will continue to move even closer to its audience. Asking and involving them is one of the most effective tools you can use. There are many benefits to be had from this closer relationship. Although there's a shorter period in the development stage, there's greater certainty that the product will match the needs of the market. Additionally, there's an element of pre-selling the concept to a market that will feel as if they've had an active role in developing the product.

The term brand citizenship has therefore changed. It is no longer a matter of putting out well-written communiqués. It's about being visible at a grassroots level in order to tap into the passions of tween communities.

Show empathy

'When teachers get old, like over 55, they're always in a bad mood'

It's surprising to learn that close to half of today's tweens across the globe look forward to being grown up. A huge 80.3 per cent of Indian tweens have a positive view of the future. It's significantly lower in countries like China (34 per cent) and Japan (34.3 per cent).

It has never been easy to be a tween, and these figures show that not much has changed. Increasingly tweens are adopting brands as important symbols in their lives. Brands are well placed to offer hope and convey the fact that they understand the tweens' situation.

A number of brands have succeeded in doing just this. The Hershey Food Corporation aligns their minty Ice Breakers with the stress a young man feels when approaching a girl at a club. Tweens identify with this age-old theme of courting angst and identify with the character in the commercial who tells himself not to trip, not to drool and to relax – while questioning the quality of his breath. And then, just like the character in the ad, tweens are predisposed to pop an Ice Breaker under their tongue when making their nervous approach.

THE DRAMATIC SHIFT IN MARKETING PLANNING

Firstly I must stress that many of the classic tools and models from the old school of advertising still apply. However, with the introduction of interactive communication we would be naïve to assume that it's advertising business as usual. It can't be, because interactivity introduces a completely new way of seeing and being.

At the most basic level, e-mail has reduced the average written reply from 15 days to one. More data are transferred via telecommunication cables than traditional phone conversations. Interactivity has had a dramatic affect on the world of broadcasting, and in 10 years close to 100 per cent of information will be via narrowcasting. All kinds of information are now available, 24 hours a day, 7 days a week, no matter where you are. The world has become smaller, faster and more demanding.

Once a typical marketing strategy would take close to two years from first outline to execution. The long lead times in product development have increased the length of the process, but also allowed the company to think through the many dimensions of their campaign. The luxury of time is gone. In fact, by the time you launch your campaign, you should expect that the tween audience has changed its opinion quite a few times since you first conducted your research.

Interactive marketing planning

Any tween-focused campaign has to include interactive components. The planning and execution must be totally and absolutely up-to-date. The computer industry calls this an iterative process. In practice, there is no longer a single marketing plan, but a work-in-progress that has to be constantly revised and adjusted to the market before, during and after the launch.

In other words, a marketing campaign needs to be milestone-based. You will only be in trouble if you attempt to plan every campaign element in step-by-step detail. It will fail before execution. What you need is flexibility and space for unexpected feedback. The tween audience picks up on trends very quickly, introducing unexpected elements and making it impossible to plan.

Take the case of the Adidas boxer shorts inspired by Mohammed Ali. They seemed to come from nowhere but in a very short time proved to be huge. Adidas's flexibility allowed them to accommodate the unexpected demand, which was never predicted in the original marketing plan. You cannot pre-plan these events in a marketing strategy.

The way marketing planning will be handled in the future therefore needs to be dramatically different. Your brand values, the main elements in your campaign still need to be planned well ahead. You naturally also need to determine the outcome of the campaign, the success factors, and prepare the majority of distribution channels. But this is probably as far as you can go in your pre-planning.

The brand war room

For many marketers and product developers, their job is a constant battle for market share. They need to develop and launch their product before it's too late – and as we have now established, on the day the launch takes place nothing is predictable. It is, however, likely that campaigns in the future will have to run live, forcing companies to build in the necessary flexibility to change direction, media, tools and message. You would be quite close to the mark if you thought about marketing departments as brand war rooms – teams of people who constantly monitor market reactions, achievements of the brand and develop new strategies.

The purpose of the brand war room is to detect any new audience behaviour and to be vigilant about identifying new and interesting ways for users to adopt the brand. The room's role is akin to operating in a real battlefield. Participants need to monitor, identify trouble spots, re-plan and react, with new strategic moves securing a constant brand leader position.

The future of marketing planning is therefore most likely to change in relation to both new product launches and general brand maintenance campaigns. There will be a substantially reduced planning period. Much more flexibility will need to be built into any marketing plan, allowing the company to respond to unpredictable market reaction. A future marketing plan will be milestone-based, but will leave some space open for use of new media channels and even new alternative campaign messages, according to how the market reacts.

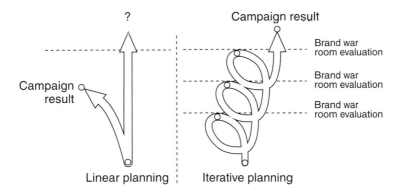

Figure 17.5 *Long-term planning cycle vs interactive planning cycle. Long term marketing planing is no longer possible. The only way to secure optimal effect is to use a iterative marketing planning technique which is based on several milestones that can constantly evaluate the performances of the campaign.*

We are witnessing a dramatic change in the role of brands. The tween segment is the first generation responding to interactivity, putting any company and brand appealing to this segment to the test. Over the next couple of years we will see any serious brand available all day every day and through the night-time hours as well. The key word to survival will be flexibility.

SUMMARY

▋ Don't talk down. Forget the authoritative experts who once persuaded tweens' parents. This group won't believe a word they say.

▋ If there's one important lesson to be learned, it's always to stay true to your brand's DNA. Because if you don't, tweens will instantly pick it up on their well-honed brand radar.

▋ This is a no-bullshit generation. Tweens put a premium on straight talk and are drawn to brands which display utter confidence and offer full-on accountability.

▌ Any brand that even so much as hints at feelings of self-importance will secure itself a permanent space in the tween product graveyard.

▌ The days of the biggest type ensuring the greatest visibility are long gone. Find your niche. One way to understate your brand is to become a niche channel.

▌ Invent your own sub-channel. Forget everything about the classic list of media choices – there's potential advertising space where you least expect it.

▌ Product placement is the largest and most influential form of endorsement influencing tween brands.

▌ Brands based on historical information are getting large chunks of the market share.

▌ Change the operating hours. Tweens will investigate the brand on the channels that are available to them, day and night.

▌ Tweens are a very environmentally-focused generation.

▌ Tweens are substantially more concerned about privacy than ever before.

▌ Involve them in your plans. Their feedback is one of your most effective tools.

▌ Marketing campaigns should be milestone-based, allowing lots of room for flexibility.

ACTION POINTS

▶ You now have a solid framework for a tween marketing strategy. Read all the guidelines outlined in this chapter's Summary and check your activities against the rules of engagement.

▶ How does your brand fare when measured against these three trends? Involving tweens in research and development; communicating with the no bullshit generation; and your brand's environmental focus will pay off.

▶ This is an ever-changing world. Team up with a permanent base of tweens who can advise your brand and your strategic direction on a daily basis.

▶ Many of the principles outlined in this book should still be valid 10 years from now. However, since this is an ever-changing audience, you should stay in touch with me by checking out your membership number in the back of this book. Then visit DualBook.com which will offer you a constantly updated library of tween-related articles. You can also visit MartinLindstrom.com for more detailed reports on 360-degree branding.

Appendix 1

The *BRANDchild* research: the world's most extensive study of tween attitudes and brand relationships

Objective

We wanted to talk to the kids likely to represent the future global consumer population, those that the marketing world would consider desirable targets for new products and services, and the ones likely to have the ability to buy those products and services now, or in the future.

Representation

We chose seven countries representing a cross-section of economies and Western and non-Western cultures. We limited our research to urban kids. In doing this, we were taking account of the fact that in his book *The Kids Market: Myths and Realities,* James U McNeal estimates the global urban kids market at US $1.88 trillion in total. He says that the significant growth in population over the next 25 years will happen in urban areas outside the developed nations.

Sample

So who did we talk to? Tweens aged between 9 and 14 years old, split equally between male and female, younger (9 to 11) and older (12 to 14), and living in major urban areas. All the kids had a socio-economic status which put them in a home with a television, the opportunity to be online, and in contact with upscale brands. We interviewed kids face-to-face in malls or other venues, so that the comparison between countries would be unaffected by methodology, even though this affected representation within a particular country.

Research overview

This table gives some basic context to our data, with some statistics drawn from the CIA *World Factbook* 2001.

Country	% world population of kids (rank)	Population growth rate	GDP per capita $PPP	Notes from our research data
India	18.7 (1)	1.55%	$2,200	82 per cent of mothers did not work. Only 17 per cent of kids claimed to have their own television. Only 23 per cent use the Internet. Only 4 per cent have their own mobile phone. 31 per cent of households had a car.
China	17.6 (2)	0.88%	$3,200	Over 90 per cent of kids were only-children or 'little emperors'. Highest level of working mothers at 77 per cent. 1 in 5 kids claim to have their own TV. 31 per cent use the Internet. Only 3 per cent have their own mobile phone. 84 per cent of households did not have a car.
US	3.2 (4)	0.90%	$36,200	Over 40 per cent of kids were African–American or Hispanic, reflecting the ethnic shift taking place within society. Second highest level of working mothers at 74 per cent. 65 per cent of kids had their own TV. 73 per cent use the Internet. Only 14 per cent had their own mobile phone. Only 5 per cent of households did not have a car, 30 per cent had 3 or more.

Brazil	2.8 (7)	0.90%	$6,500	Sample was more upscale than might be expected, resulting in a higher household income than the urban average and more college educated parents.
Japan	1.0 (18)	0.17%	$24,900	Only 1 in 5 kids claimed to have their own TV.
Germany	0.7 (23)	0.27%	$23,400	52 per cent of kids have their own mobile phone.
Spain	0.3 (40)	0.10%	$18,000	Only 32 per cent of kids use the Internet. 33 per cent have their own mobile phone.
Denmark	0.05	0.29%	$28,000	

Other research sources

The *BRANDchild* study was supplemented by the following information sources:

▌ BMRB's UK Youth TGI, an annual study of brand purchasing, attitudes and media use among 6,000 British 7 to 19-year-olds.

▌ WPP's BRANDZ study conducted by Millward Brown in over 30 countries and covering over 20,000 brands.

▌ Qualitative research conducted in the United States for the *BRANDchild* book by Greenfield Consulting, a Millward Brown Group company.

▌ Millward Brown's Kidspeak team and research conducted for clients around the world.

Appendix 2

Code of ethics

Dealing with tweens is like dealing with the future. By affecting them we affect the shape of our future world. Tweens have a greater capacity than adults to trust, and to use products in innovative ways. Because of this, they are a very special audience. Many marketers could easily be tempted to use cheap tricks to secure next year's sales, forgetting that there are ethical practices that need to be followed when marketing to young audiences.

Some would prefer that marketers were not allowed to structure advertising campaigns targeting tweens. They'd prefer a zero tolerance approach, one which did not entice children with special offers or targeted promotions. They perceive marketing to children as exploitation. This is one extreme. But the role of marketing is to create and maintain brands filling a whole variety of needs. In the case of tweens, these include safety, comfort and let's not forget fun, in all its dimensions.

I was once told that if sugar were a new invention it would not pass the safety tests because of the numbers who suffer from sugar-related disease. But the fact is that our world won't go back in time and ban sugar. Sugar will not disappear.

An easy solution would be to exclude kids from any commercial message until they reached an appropriate age – 15 or 18 years old, say. Despite the fact that the logistics of this would be virtually impossible, I also think we would be doing the next generation a disservice, because if the big gates of advertising swung open only on Peter's 18th birthday, he would be completely unable to cope with the onslaught of new information.

Be that as it may, it still cannot justify giving the advertising industry *carte blanche* to market to a young audience exactly as they choose. A code of ethics must be vigorously followed.

In partnership with the Australian Federation of Advertising, I've developed four guidelines which I think are simple enough for everyone to honour. It is essential for us not to forget these in everything we do when communicating with tweens:

Produce quality products that are safe

A brand that is consistently successful has also over that time produced quality products. It is no coincidence that brand names like Disney, LEGO and Mattel keep appearing in *BRANDchild*. They come up because they've delivered high quality products for years. Their products are safe ones.

Keep your word

Kids are not as thick skinned as we are. They trust – often to a point where it's too late. No-one in branding has ever failed by keeping their word. In fact that's what branding is all about: quality stamping a product that always keeps its word.

Be honest

The kids will find out if anything is wrong with your product. They never forget a bad experience.

Don't abuse your freedom

If you happen to be marketing to kids, you are one of the luckiest people in the world. There is no more exciting audience to work with. They're fun, inspiring and always changing. But marketing to kids also places a huge responsibility on you. You're being closely watched by parents, who will not hesitate to criticize anything that they consider wrong. So if you fail to maintain an ethical approach, it will soon come to light. And that will undermine the freedom of access that is granted in most countries across the globe. We need to earn and maintain this trust from both tweens and their parents.

Index

	DATE DUE		